1. The first "work plan" for the years 1977 and 1978 included forty-three articles, which expanded in the following years. East German negotiators described the 1979/80 Cultural Work Plan as "one of the most extensive and comprehensive cultural agreements with developing countries." The Political Archive of the Federal Foreign Office, PA AA M 60/294681.

LEA MARIE NIENHOFF AND AMBRE AL[I]

FOREWOR[D]

"The freedom of the people depends on the us people, a relationship of equality and cooperation only can make freedom possible."

Mankew V. Mahumana, in a letter to the East German Academy of Arts, 1984

This research edition is set in the 1980s, a few years after Mozambique's independence in 1975. The protagonists are two Mozambican artists: the painter Mankew Valente Mahumana and the theater director David Abílio Mondlane. Through their practice, they sought an active role in the decolonization and construction of their country, fostering people's confidence in the revolutionary transition. We follow them as they navigate the fragmented space of cultural exchange between the People's Republic of Mozambique (PRM) and the German Democratic Republic (GDR), where both traveled as visiting artists. Through Mankew's and David Abílio's journeys, we explore how cross-cultural relations were established between these two socialist countries, highlighting the possibilities and shortcomings of the interrupted project of socialist internationalism and its early attempts to decolonize the international art world.

The PRM and the GDR became close partners in the 1980s. In a state-mandated "work plan," the two countries agreed to cultural and scientific cooperation, specifying the number of consultants, trainees, and artists to participate in workshops and exhibitions.[1] However, Mankew and David Abílio disrupted the official exchange program with their own vision of artistic collaboration and quest for recognition on equal terms. Mankew, written as "Mankeu" in East German publications, was received as an acclaimed artist, and his paintings were shown at the Berlin Television Tower and the East German Academy of Arts. David Abílio, head of the Theater Department in the National Directorate of Culture in Mozambique, was allocated an internship at the local theater in the town

LEA MARIE NIENHOFF UND AMBRE ALFREDO

VORWORT

„Die Freiheit des Volkes ist abhängig von den neuen Beziehungen unter uns Menschen, eine Beziehung von Gleichberechtigung und Kooperation erst kann die Freiheit möglich machen."

Mankew V. Mahumana in einem Brief an die Akademie der Künste der DDR, 1984

Diese Forschungsedition behandelt die 1980er Jahre, also die Zeit kurz nach der Unabhängigkeit Mosambiks im Jahr 1975. Die Protagonisten sind zwei mosambikanische Künstler: der Maler Mankew Valente Mahumana und der Theaterregisseur David Abílio Mondlane. Mit ihrer Kunstpraxis nahmen sie eine aktive Rolle bei der Dekolonisierung und dem Aufbau ihres Landes ein, um das Vertrauen der Bevölkerung in die revolutionäre Umwälzung zu stärken. Wir begleiten sie auf ihrem Weg durch den Kosmos des kulturellen Austauschs zwischen der Volksrepublik Mosambik (VRM) und der Deutschen Demokratischen Republik (DDR), die beide als Gastkünstler besucht haben. Anhand der Reisen von Mankew und David Abílio untersuchen wir, wie interkulturelle Beziehungen zwischen diesen beiden sozialistischen Ländern aufgebaut wurden, und beleuchten die Möglichkeiten und Hindernisse des unvollendeten Projekts des sozialistischen Internationalismus sowie der frühen Versuche, die internationale Kunstwelt zu dekolonisieren.

In den 1980er Jahren gingen die VRM und die DDR eine enge Partnerschaft ein. In einer gemeinsamen Verordnung, dem „Arbeitsplan", vereinbarten die beiden Länder eine kulturelle und wissenschaftliche Zusammenarbeit und legten die Anzahl der Berater·innen, Praktikant·innen und Künstler·innen fest, die an Workshops und Ausstellungen teilnehmen sollten.[1] Mankew und David Abílio unterliefen das offizielle Austauschprogramm jedoch, setzten diesem ihre eigene Vision von künstlerischer Zusammenarbeit entgegen und strebten nach Anerkennung auf Augenhöhe. Mankew, in ostdeutschen Publikationen als „Mankeu" bezeichnet, wurde als anerkannter Künstler empfangen, seine Bilder wurden im Berliner Fernsehturm und in der Akademie der Künste der DDR ausgestellt.

1. Der erste „Arbeitsplan" für die Jahre 1977 und 1978 umfasste 43 Artikel, die in den Folgejahren erweitert wurden. Die ostdeutschen Verhandlungsführer bezeichneten den Kulturarbeitsplan 1979/80 als „eines der umfangreichsten und umfassendsten Kulturabkommen mit Entwicklungsländern". Das Politische Archiv des Auswärtigen Amts, PA AA M 60/294681.

of Schwerin. Their experience of the East German art sphere was starkly different. David Abílio, who criticized East German theater as "reactionary," was sanctioned by GDR officials and forced to return to Mozambique earlier than planned. In contrast, Mankew was celebrated and honored as a distinguished artist during his visits to East Germany and collaborated with several East German institutions. The difference in opportunities and treatment reflects the ambiguities of Mozambique and the GDR's "comradeship."

Lived and staged moments of solidarity existed side by side. While on the one hand, it created avenues for artists like Mankew and David Abílio to link their work to the broader political project of building a postcolonial future, this "comradeship" was overshadowed by Cold War dynamics, economic inequality, and persistent structural racism. In calling it a "troubled comradeship," the title of this research edition reflects the challenges inherent in fostering solidarity. Nonetheless, we specifically chose the word "comradeship" to honor those individuals from both countries who genuinely embraced the principles of friendship and built a common ground for collaborations in the arts.

Our research edition aims to unearth the perspectives of those who have been pushed out of history and to ground the myth of "International Solidarity" in the experiences and memories of historical actors. It is the result of many conversations we had with artists, researchers, and diplomats—those historical actors who shaped and materialized the bonds between Mozambique and East Germany in the 1980s. It also builds up around photographs, artworks, personal letters, and official reports from (mainly German) national cultural institutions. To compensate for the lack of archival documents from Mozambican institutions, we also sought to exchange and collaborate with colleagues from Mozambique on this shared history. Thanks to the research of art historian Alda Costa and her invaluable contribution to this book, the publication includes a contemporary Mozambican perspective that recognizes the lasting influence of the journeys and collaborations pursued by Mozambican artists after independence.

Mankew Valente Mahumana passed away on 13 September 2021, at the age of eighty-seven, shortly before we began to learn about his life and paintings.

David Abílio, Leiter der Theaterabteilung in der Nationalen Kulturdirektion Mosambiks, wurde ein Praktikum am Stadttheater Schwerin zugewiesen. Ihre Erfahrungen mit dem ostdeutschen Kunstbetrieb waren sehr unterschiedlich. David Abílio, der das ostdeutsche Theater als „reaktionär" kritisierte, wurde von DDR-Funktionären sanktioniert und musste früher als geplant nach Mosambik zurückkehren. Im Gegensatz dazu wurde Mankew auch bei seinen folgenden Besuchen in der DDR als Künstler gefeiert und geehrt und arbeitete mit mehreren ostdeutschen Institutionen zusammen. Die unterschiedlichen Möglichkeiten und die unterschiedliche Behandlung spiegeln den ambivalenten Charakter der „Kameradschaft" zwischen Mosambik und der DDR wider.

Gelebte und inszenierte Momente der Solidarität existierten nebeneinander. Während sie einerseits Wege für Künstler wie Mankew und David Abílio eröffnete, ihre Kunstpraxis mit einem breiteren politischen Projekt zum Aufbau einer postkolonialen Zukunft zu verbinden, wurde die „Kameradschaft" zugleich von der Dynamik des Kalten Krieges, wirtschaftlicher Ungleichheit und anhaltendem strukturellem Rassismus überschattet. Mit der Bezeichnung „Troubled Comradeship" spiegelt der englische Titel dieses Forschungsbands die Herausforderungen wider, die mit dem Herstellen von Solidarität verbunden sind. Wir haben das Wort „Kameradschaft" dennoch bewusst gewählt, um jene Menschen aus beiden Ländern zu würdigen, die sich die Prinzipien der Freundschaft zu eigen machten und eine gemeinsame Basis für die Zusammenarbeit in den Künsten schufen.

Unsere Forschungsedition zielt darauf ab, die Perspektiven derjenigen zu ergründen, die aus der Geschichte verdrängt wurden. Anhand der Erfahrungen und Erinnerungen der historischen Akteure wird der Mythos der „Internationalen Solidarität" beleuchtet. Das Buch beruht auf zahlreichen Gesprächen, die wir mit Künstler·innen, Wissenschaftler·innen und Diplomat·innen geführt haben – jenen historischen Protagonist·innen, die die Verbindungen zwischen Mosambik und Ostdeutschland in den 1980er Jahren gestaltet und mit Leben gefüllt haben. Das Buch stützt sich auch auf Fotos, Kunstwerke, persönliche Briefe und offizielle Berichte von (hauptsächlich deutschen) staatlichen Kultureinrichtungen. Um das Fehlen von Archivdokumenten mosambikanischer Institutionen zu kompensieren, haben wir auch den Austausch und die Zusammenarbeit mit Kolleg·innen aus Mosambik zur Erforschung dieser gemeinsamen Geschichte gesucht. Dank

EDITORIAL NOTE

The *Entangled Internationalisms* research edition includes case studies from India and pan-African geographical regions such as Ghana or Mozambique, while providing a documentary record of the anti-colonial voices that crossed, resonated, and left traces in the German Democratic Republic (GDR). Entanglement here implies a weave of different threads or different directions: at the point where two threads cross over and overlap, one strand always covers the other, concealing it from view depending on which side you look at the fabric from. Yet without interweaving, there would be no surface, no support, no ability to create shapes and forms.

Each edition consists of documents drawn from private, nongovernmental, or national archives, commentaries in the form of essays and oral history interviews, and artistic reflections. The starting point in each case is a historical context in one of the entangled geographies that relates to the GDR and looks beyond it. Here, a film, a photograph, a building, a painting, or a document becomes an archive of its own, out of which images and languages become apparent that can be used to talk about the entanglements inherent in the ambiguities they contain.

The aim of the research edition is to compile an incomplete archive that brings together concepts, names, places, materials, and techniques with the help of which we can reflect on a *geopolitics of memory* celebrating global forms of political friendship. These are located in the structures of state socialism, cultural diplomacy, delegation programs, and communist organizations, while at the same time existing as expanded forms of artistic practice, extending all the way to architecture, that eluded state cooptation and the rhetoric of the Cold War or took advantage of other kinds of independence. They can still be found today as undercurrents in collections, archives, and architecture as well as in families, friendships, and out on the street. The afterlife of these internationalisms affects the archives not only of the global East in Europe but also of global geographies—on the African continent or in Southeast Asia—where the manifestations and traces of this modernity persist. What binds them together are forms of knowledge and practice reflecting an equivocal engagement with modernity in the conflictual zone between decolonization and neocolonialism and between emergent states and community in the global fabric post 1945.

Rather than reconstructing specific forms of cooperation in the context of the global Cold War, the research edition looks at the past in terms of how it has mutated into the present. The idea is to make research visible as a transhistorical process: any time archival material is viewed—no matter how much historiographical rigor is applied—it is invariably actualized and de- and recontextualized. This is caused by the interaction of disparate forms of knowledge and different ways of thinking in academic, museological, institutional, artistic, and curatorial settings.

EDITORISCHE NOTIZ

Die Forschungsedition *Verflochtene Internationalismen* umfasst Fallstudien aus Indien und panafrikanischen Regionen wie Ghana oder Mosambik und sie dokumentiert antikoloniale Stimmen, welche in der Deutschen Demokratischen Republik (DDR) hörbar wurden, Widerhall fanden und dabei ihre Spuren hinterließen. Verflechtung meint hierbei ein Gewebe verschiedener Fäden oder Richtungen: An dem Punkt, an dem sich zwei Fäden kreuzen und verknüpfen, verdeckt – je nachdem, von welcher Seite man auf das Gewebe blickt – immer ein Strang den anderen. Jedoch erst die Verflechtung ergibt Fläche, Halt und Formbarkeit.

Jede Edition besteht aus Dokumenten aus privaten, nichtstaatlichen oder nationalen Archiven, Kommentaren in Form von Essays und Oral-History-Interviews sowie in einigen Fällen künstlerischen Reflexionen. Ausgangspunkt ist jeweils ein historischer Kontext in einer der verflochtenen Geografien – mit Blick auf die DDR und über diese hinaus. Ein Film, eine Fotografie, ein Gebäude, ein Gemälde oder ein Dokument werden dabei jeweils selbst zu einem Archiv, aus dem heraus Bilder und Sprachen offenkundig werden, mit denen sich über die Verflechtungen in ihren Ambiguitäten sprechen lässt.

Das Ziel der Forschungsedition ist die Erarbeitung eines unvollständigen Archives, welches Konzepte, Namen, Orte, Materialien und Techniken zusammenbringt, anhand deren wir über eine *Geopolitik des Erinnerns* an weltumspannende Formen politischer Freundschaft nachdenken können. Diese verorten sich einerseits in Strukturen von Staatssozialismus, Kulturdiplomatie, Delegationsprogrammen und kommunistischen Organisationen. Andererseits existieren sie als Praxisformen der erweiterten Künste bis hin zur Architektur, welche sich einer staatlichen Vereinnahmung und den Rhetoriken des Kalten Kriegs entzogen oder andere Formen der Unabhängigkeit in Anspruch nahmen. Bis heute finden sie sich als archivarische Unterströme in Sammlungen, Archiven und Architektur, aber auch in Familien, Freundschaften oder auf der Straße wieder. Das Nachleben dieser Internationalismen betrifft dabei nicht nur die Archive des globalen Ostens in Europa, sondern insbesondere auch jene in Regionen – auf dem afrikanischen Kontinent, in Südostasien –, welche bis heute die Manifestationen und Spuren dieser Moderne tragen. Was sie verbindet, sind Wissens- und Praxisformen einer ambivalenten Moderne im Spannungsfeld von Dekolonisierung und Neokolonialismus, zwischen Staatswerdung und Gemeinschaft im globalen Gefüge nach 1945.

Anstatt einer historischen Rekonstruktion konkreter Formen der Zusammenarbeit im Kontext des globalen Kalten Krieges betrachtet die Forschungsedition das Historische in seinen Mutationen in der Gegenwart. Dabei geht es darum, Forschung als transhistorischen Prozess sichtbar zu machen: Jede Aufrufung archivarischer Materialien bedeutet – bei aller historiografischen Präzision – ihre Aktualisierung und Dekontextualisierung. Sie ist das Resultat des Zusammenwirkens verschiedener Wissens- und Denkformen in akademischen, musealen, institutionellen, künstlerischen und kuratorischen Umgebungen.

Während ein Teil der wissenschaftlichen Befunde im Kontext des Projektes *Decolonizing Socialism. Entangled Internationalism* (2019–2024) erarbeitet wurde, ist die kuratorische sowie künstlerische

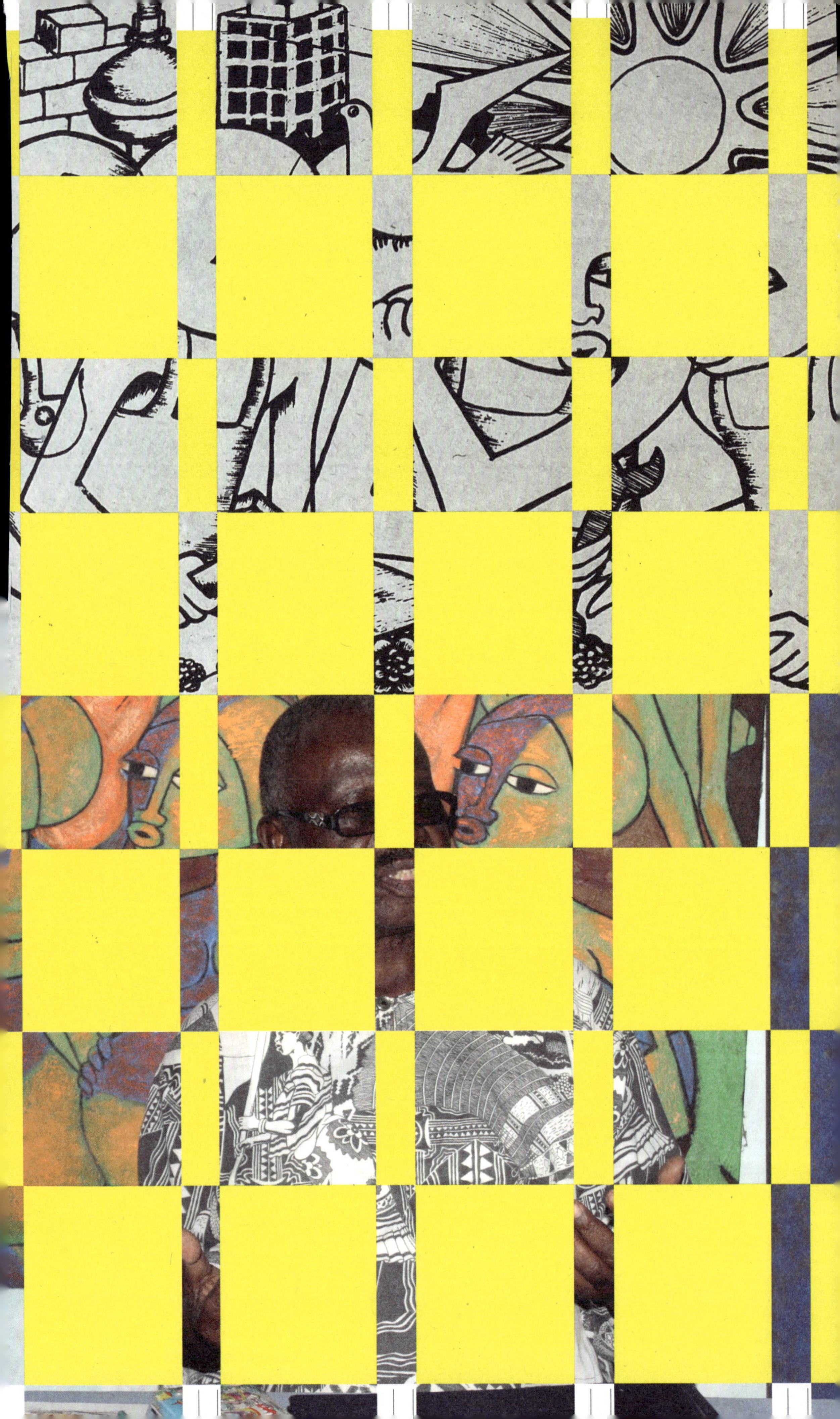

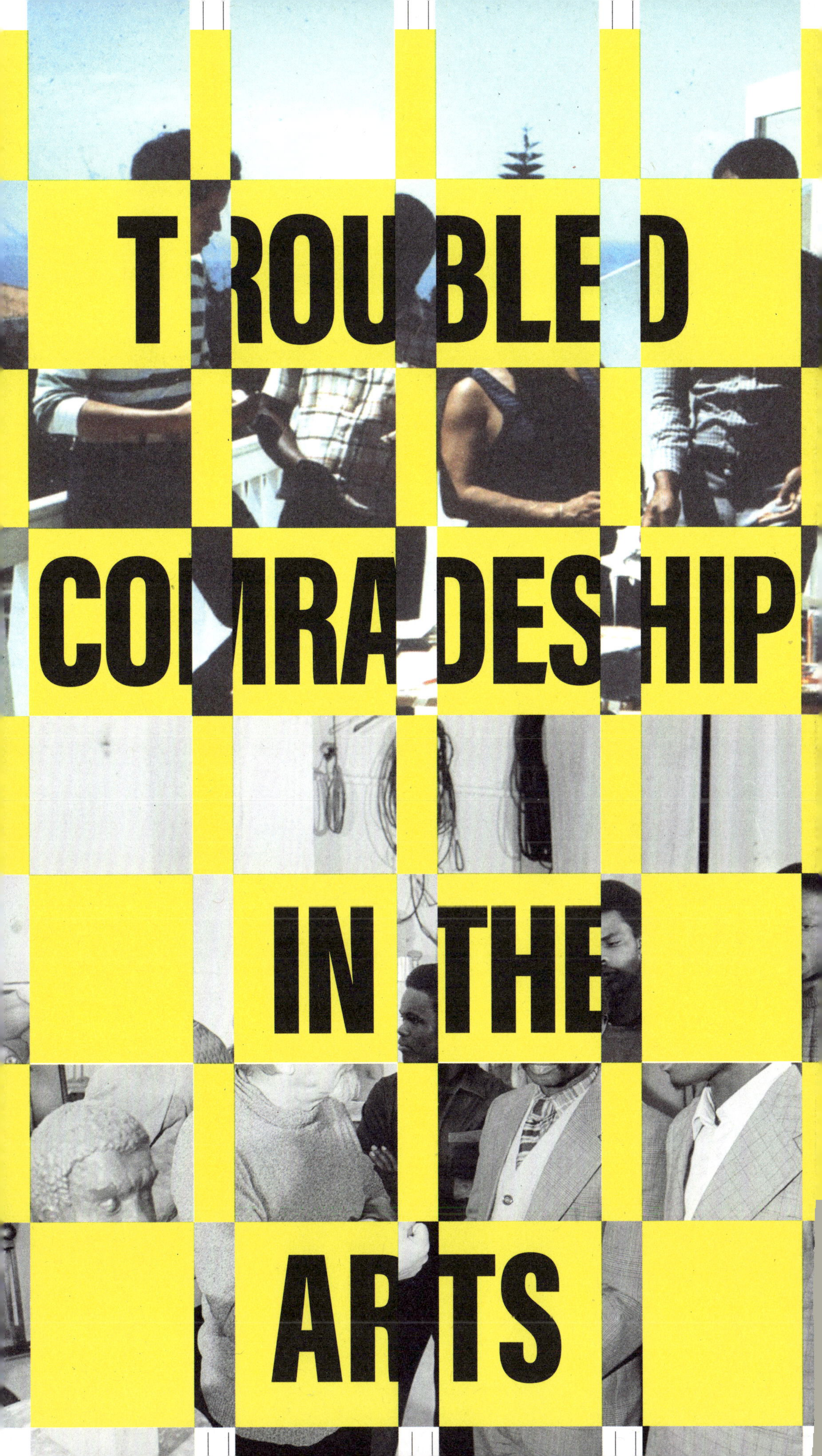
TROUBLED
COMRADESHIP
IN THE
ARTS

While some of the scholarly findings emerged in the context of the project *Decolonizing Socialism: Entangled Internationalism* (2019–2024), the curatorial and artistic work of processing them has been carried out in partnership with institutions such as Van Abbemuseum Eindhoven (*Deviant Practice*) and Haus der Kulturen der Welt (HKW) in Berlin (*The Whole Life*) and with collectives like blaxTARLINES in Kumasi, Ghana, and the Oralities Research Lab in Jaipur, India.

It was significant that the object-based portion of the research was conducted at the Dresden State Art Collections (Staatliche Kunstsammlungen Dresden, SKD), as this not only fed into the cooperation with the HKW but also helped build correspondences with the exhibition and research project *Revolutionary Romances: Transcultural Art Histories in the GDR*, which ran concurrently at the Albertinum. While *Revolutionary Romances*, with its focus on art history, constitutes a radical reappraisal of a transcultural collection history conducted by the institution itself, *Entangled Internationalisms* engages with the holdings of the SKD, looked at from the perspective of researchers from India, Ghana, Mozambique, and the pan-African movements.

Aufarbeitung in Partnerschaft mit Institutionen wie dem Van Abbemuseum Eindhoven (*Deviant Practice*), dem Haus der Kulturen der Welt (HKW) in Berlin (*The Whole Life*) und mit Kollektiven wie blaxTARLINES in Kumasi (Ghana) oder dem Oralities Research Lab in Jaipur (Indien) entstanden.

Maßgeblich für den objektbasierten Teil der Forschung war die Verortung an den Staatlichen Kunstsammlungen Dresden, die nicht nur die Kooperation mit dem HKW ermöglichte, sondern auch Korrespondenzen mit dem zeitgleich realisierten Ausstellungs- und Forschungsvorhaben *Revolutionary Romances. Transkulturelle Kunstgeschichten in der DDR* im Albertinum. Während *Revolutionary Romances* eine grundlegende kunsthistorische Aufarbeitung einer transkulturellen Sammlungsgeschichte durch die Institution selbst vollzieht, tritt *Verflochtene Internationalismen* aus der Perspektive der Forschenden aus Indien, Ghana, Mosambik und der panafrikanischen Bewegungen in einen Dialog mit den Beständen der Staatlichen Kunstsammlungen Dresden.

TROUBLED COMRADESHIP IN THE ARTS

KAMERADSCHAFT IN DEN KÜNSTEN

2

Albino Mahumana, who followed in his father's footsteps as a painter and photographer, shared with us his memories of his father, the stories he told about East Germany, and the friendships that connected him to Germany throughout his life. Fortunately, we had the chance to interview David Abílio Mondlane in person. The choreographer and cultural manager remains a prominent figure in Mozambique's cultural scene. Our conversation ranged from the legacy of Bertolt Brecht's work in East Germany to the transformative role of theater in postcolonial Mozambique. In addition to highlighting Mozambican perspectives, the publication includes viewpoints from East German actors involved in the collaboration. Ginga Eichler, Peter Stobinski, and Harald Heinke with his personal archive were crucial in allowing us to construct an East German perspective on the collaboration and the manifold memories thereof.

The multitude of pictures, commentary, historical newspaper articles, and memories, invite the reader to reflect on history on their own terms and spin relations into the present. As the editors and authors of this research edition, Ambre Alfredo and I began to relink and relate to each other's home country in a new way. Recognizing the intertwined nature of both countries' histories and studying their past relations, we asked ourselves: When will there finally be a more equitable relationship and reconnection? And what images and visual culture would this engender?

This research edition was made possible thanks to the unwavering commitment of Doreen Mende and the fruitful collaboration with the Dresden State Art Collections (Staatliche Kunstsammlungen Dresden, SKD). Our research was deeply enriched by earlier exhibitions and projects that broadened the perspective on the East German art sphere by shedding light on its transnational dimension and the largely unexplored works of international artists in the museums' collections. The exhibitions *Revolutionary Romances? Global Art Histories in the GDR*, presented at the Albertinum (SKD, 2024), and *Re-Connect: Art and Conflict in Brotherland* at the Leipzig museum of fine arts, Museum der bildenden Künste (MdbK, 2023), along with their respective catalogs, laid an important foundation for further investigation. *The Missed Seminar* by Doreen Mende (Albertinum,

der Recherchen der Kunsthistorikerin Alda Costa und ihres unschätzbaren Beitrags zu diesem Buch enthält die Publikation eine zeitgenössische mosambikanische Perspektive, die den bleibenden Einfluss der Reisen und der Kollaborationen von mosambikanischen Künstler·innen nach der Unabhängigkeit aufzeigt.

Mankew Valente Mahumana ist am 13. September 2021 im Alter von 87 Jahren verstorben, kurz bevor wir begannen, mehr über sein Leben und seine Bilder zu erfahren. Albino Mahumana, der als Maler und Fotograf in die Fußstapfen seines Vaters getreten ist, hat seine Erinnerungen an seinen Vater mit uns geteilt und erzählt, was dieser über die DDR berichtete und wie dessen Freundschaften ihn ein Leben lang mit Deutschland verbanden. Glücklicherweise hatten wir Gelegenheit, David Abílio Mondlane persönlich zu interviewen. Der Choreograf und Kulturmanager ist nach wie vor eine prominente Figur in der mosambikanischen Kulturszene. Unser Gespräch reichte vom Erbe Bertolt Brechts in Ostdeutschland bis zur transformativen Rolle des Theaters im postkolonialen Mosambik. Neben den mosambikanischen Perspektiven kommen in der Publikation auch Akteure aus der DDR zu Wort, die an der Zusammenarbeit beteiligt waren. Ginga Eichler, Peter Stobinski und Harald Heinke mit seinem persönlichen Archiv haben entscheidend dazu beigetragen, dass wir eine ostdeutsche Perspektive auf die Zusammenarbeit und die Bandbreite der Erinnerungen darstellen konnten.

Die Vielzahl an Bildern, Kommentaren, historischen Zeitungsartikeln und Erinnerungen lädt die Leser·innen ein, die Geschichte auf ihre eigene Weise zu reflektieren und die Verbindungen bis in die Gegenwart weiterzuknüpfen. Als Herausgeberinnen und Autorinnen dieses Forschungsbands begannen wir beide, eine neue Beziehung zum Heimatland der jeweils anderen aufzubauen. Als uns die Verflechtung der Geschichte beider Länder deutlich wurde und wir ihre früheren diplomatischen Beziehungen untersuchten, kam unweigerlich die Frage auf: Wann wird es endlich gerechtere Verhältnisse geben und eine erneute Verbindung, die tatsächlich auf Augenhöhe stattfindet? Und was für Bilder und was für eine visuelle Kultur würde daraus hervorgehen?

Der vorliegende Band wurde durch das unermüdliche Engagement von Doreen Mende und die fruchtbare Zusammenarbeit mit den Staatlichen Kunstsammlungen Dresden (SKD) ermöglicht. Unsere Forschungen wurden durch frühere Ausstellungen und Projekte sehr bereichert, die den Blick auf die ostdeutsche

2. Lea Marie Nienhoff, "Mankew Valente Mahumana," in *Revolutionary Romances? Globale Kunstgeschichten in der DDR*, eds. Staatliche Kunstsammlung Dresden; Mathias Wagner, Hilke Wagner, Kerstin Schankweiler, Kathleen Reinhardt (Spector Books, 2024); Lea Marie Nienhoff, Ambre Alfredo. "Der mosambikanische Maler Mankew V. Mahumana und die DDR: Künstlerfreundschaften und Kulturpolitik" (part 1 & part 2).

2023) and *Till the Sun Rises: Sequence 1* by vinit agarwal (Albertinum, 2024) have provided further inspiration in making palpable the shared horizon of "international socialism." We would also like to give a special mention to the project "Art in Networks—The GDR and Its Global Relations" (TU Dresden), which assembled an oral history platform to document personal memories connected to international exchanges in the arts. The support and trust of Kerstin Schankweiler, Pauline Hohn, and Nora Kaschuba, as well as Mathias Wagner and Hilke Wagner, have made it possible for the first iterations of the research on Mankew V. Mahumana to be published.[2]

We would also like to express our profound gratitude to our many interlocutors for their faith in this project. We extend heartfelt thanks to our contributing authors, who generously shared their knowledge and collected further sources to enrich this research edition. Furthermore, we would like to thank Gabriele Baumgarten-Heinke, who not only granted us access to her husband's rich archive of pictures and documents but also supported our research with her encouraging kindness and extensive network. A huge thank you also goes to our colleagues at the Department of Urban Studies at the University Basel, in particular to Patricia Noormahomed for her valuable feedback. We also extend our gratitude to Nikolai Brandes, Carlos Fernandes, Heike Pander, Su-Ran Sichling, and Eva Wiegert. We are deeply grateful for their generous insights and the time they dedicated to enriching our work.

Kunstsphäre erweitert haben, indem sie ihre transnationale Dimension und die weitgehend unerforschten Werke internationaler Künstler·innen in den Sammlungen der Museen beleuchteten. Die Ausstellungen *Revolutionary Romances? Globale Kunstgeschichten in der DDR* im Albertinum (SKD, 2024) und *Re-Connect. Kunst und Kampf im Bruderland* im Museum der bildenden Künste in Leipzig (2023) sowie die dazugehörigen Kataloge schufen eine wichtige Grundlage für weiterführende Forschung. *The Missed Seminar* von Doreen Mende (Albertinum, 2023) und *Till the Sun Rises. Sequence 1* von Vinit Agarwal (Albertinum, 2024) lieferten weitere Inspiration, den gemeinsamen Horizont des „internationalen Sozialismus" zu veranschaulichen. Eine besondere Erwähnung verdient auch das Projekt „Art in Networks – The GDR and its Global Relations" (TU Dresden), das eine Oral-History-Plattform zur Dokumentation persönlicher Erinnerungen im Zusammenhang mit dem internationalen Austausch in der Kunst geschaffen hat. Dank der Unterstützung und des Vertrauens von Kerstin Schankweiler, Pauline Hohn und Nora Kaschuba sowie Mathias Wagner und Hilke Wagner konnten die ersten Ergebnisse der Recherchen zu Mankew V. Mahumana veröffentlicht werden.[2]

Für ihr Vertrauen in dieses Projekt möchten wir auch unseren zahlreichen Gesprächspartner·innen unseren tief empfundenen Dank aussprechen. Unser herzlicher Dank gilt den Autor·innen, die ihr Wissen zur Verfügung gestellt und weitere Quellen aufgetan haben, die diesen Forschungsband bereichern. Darüber hinaus danken wir Gabriele Baumgarten-Heinke, die uns nicht nur Zugang zum reichen Bild- und Dokumentenarchiv ihres Mannes gewährte, sondern unsere Recherchen auch mit ihrer ermutigenden Freundlichkeit und ihrem umfangreichen Netzwerk unterstützte. Ein großer Dank geht auch an unsere Kolleg·innen am Fachbereich für Urban Studies der Universität Basel, insbesondere an Patricia Noormahomed für ihr wertvolles Feedback. Unser Dank gilt außerdem Nikolai Brandes, Carlos Fernandes, Heike Pander, Su-Ran Sichling und Eva Wiegert. Für ihr umfassendes Wissen und die Zeit, die sie uns zur Unterstützung unserer Forschung bereitgestellt haben, danken wir ihnen sehr herzlich.

2. Lea Marie Nienhoff, „Mankew Valente Mahumana", in: *Revolutionary Romances? Globale Kunstgeschichten in der DDR*, Ausst.-Kat. Staatliche Kunstsammlungen Dresden, Mathias Wagner, Hilke Wagner, Kerstin Schankweiler, Kathleen Reinhardt, Leipzig: Spector Books 2024, S. 98; Lea Marie Nienhoff und Ambre Alfredo. „Der mosambikanische Maler Mankeu V. Mahumana und die DDR: Künstlerfreundschaften und Kulturpolitik" (Teil 1 & Teil 2).

NOTES ON THE VISUAL GRAMMAR OF "SOCIALIST INTERNATIONALISM"

CULTURAL PRODUCTIONS BETWEEN THE GDR AND THE PRM

Lea Marie Nienhoff

KAMERADSCHAFT IN DEN KÜNSTEN

ANMERKUNGEN ZUR VISUELLEN GRAMMATIK DES „SOZIALISTISCHEN INTERNATIONALISMUS"

KULTURELLE PRODUKTIONEN ZWISCHEN DER DDR UND DER VRM

1. See Kathleen Reinhardt, Kerstin Schankweiler, and Mathias Wagner, "Internationalismus in der DDR – Kunst und visuelle Kultur zwischen Idealen und Widersprüchen," in *Revolutionary Romances? Globale Kunstgeschichten in der DDR*, ed. Staatliche Kunstsammlungen Dresden (Spector Books, 2024), 23–31.

Let us begin with images.

Images tell us something when they become a collage—then they appear as fragments whose meaning only accrues from their parallel existence. The forms of artistic and cultural exchange between the two countries defy simple categorization. The vocabulary in which the governments' exchange contracts were clothed, the invocation of "brotherhood" and "anti-imperial solidarity," denies their service. These phrases have peppered too many agreements that led to renewed economic dependence and exploitative work relations. By telling the stories of the photographs, the sculptures, the films, the performances, and the paintings that traveled between the German Democratic Republic (GDR) and the People's Republic of Mozambique (PRM), the chapter seeks to visualize the collaboration in its multiplicity. For all those who had participated in the exchanges within the arts, the practice and discourse of international solidarity were the seeds for building a decolonizing world. When we reflect on what lasted of this collaboration, we find a sense of proximity that existed in the imagination and visual worlds—a closeness that has been preserved in some of the artworks created and displayed across this transnational horizon.[1] However, the power asymmetries between the two countries resulted in a "proximity" without equality.

This chapter provides an initial overview of the cultural-political relations of the GDR with Mozambique in the late 1970s and 1980s. The approach for this piece of writing is that of a camera skimming through the documents and images held in the archives of the Ministry of Culture, the Liga für Völkerfreundschaft (International Friendship League), and the personal archive of Harald Heinke. For selected sequences, the lens is focused on delving into the contexts in which the images and documents were produced.

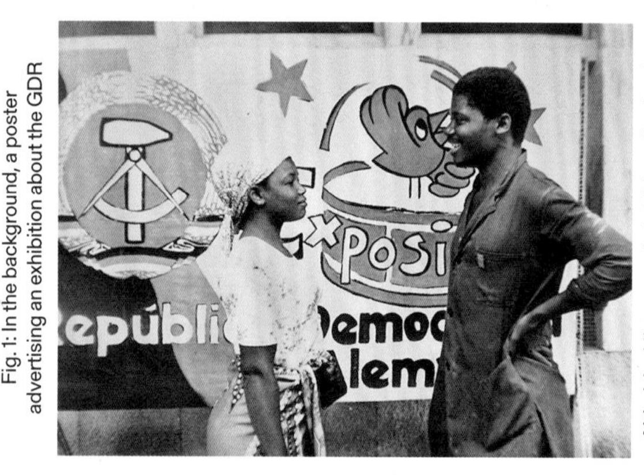

Fig. 1: In the background, a poster advertising an exhibition about the GDR

Abb. 1: Im Hintergrund ein Plakat, das für eine Ausstellung über die DDR wirbt

Lassen wir die Bilder sprechen.

Bilder erzählen uns etwas, wenn sie zu einer Collage werden – dann erscheinen sie als Bruchstücke, deren Bedeutung sich erst zeigt, wenn wir sie nebeneinander legen. Ähnlich verhält es sich mit dem künstlerischen und kulturellen Austausch zwischen den beiden Ländern, der sich einer einfachen Kategorisierung entzieht. Das Vokabular von „Brüderlichkeit" und „antiimperialer Solidarität", in das die Austauschverträge der Regierungen gekleidet waren, verweigert seinen Dienst. Zu viele Abkommen wurden damit überschüttet, die zu erneuter wirtschaftlicher Abhängigkeit und ausbeuterischen Arbeitsverhältnissen führten. Dieses Kapitel erzählt die Geschichten der Fotografien, Skulpturen, Filme, Performances und Gemälde, die zwischen der Deutschen Demokratischen Republik (DDR) und der Volksrepublik Mosambik (VRM) hin und her gereist sind, und versucht auf diese Weise, die Zusammenarbeit in ihrer Vielfalt sichtbar zu machen. Für all diejenigen, die am künstlerischen Austausch teilgenommen haben, waren die Praxis und der Diskurs der internationalen Solidarität der Keim für den Aufbau einer sich dekolonialisierenden Welt. Wenn wir darüber nachdenken, was von dieser Kollaboration geblieben ist, finden wir ein Gefühl der Verbundenheit, das in der Vorstellungs- und Bildwelt existierte – eine Art politische Nachbarschaft, die sich in einigen der Kunstwerke, die vor diesem transnationalen Horizont geschaffen und ausgestellt wurden, bewahrt hat.[1] Und dennoch führten die ungleichen Machtverhältnisse zwischen den beiden Ländern nur zu einer „Nähe" ohne Gleichheit.

Dieses Kapitel gibt einen ersten Überblick über die kulturpolitischen Beziehungen der DDR zu Mosambik in den späten 1970er und 1980er Jahren. Der Text folgt dem Lauf einer Kamera, die durch die Dokumente und Bilder aus den Archiven des Ministeriums für Kultur, der Liga für Völkerfreundschaft und aus dem persönliche Archiv von Harald Heinke streift. In ausgewählten Sequenzen stellt die Kameralinse die Hintergründe und Kontexte scharf, vor denen die Bilder und Dokumente entstanden sind.

1. Siehe Kathleen Reinhardt, Kerstin Schankweiler und Mathias Wagner, „Internationalismus in der DDR – Kunst und visuelle Kultur zwischen Idealen und Widersprüchen", in: *Revolutionary Romances? Globale Kunstgeschichten in der DDR*, Ausst.-Kat. Staatliche Kunstsammlungen Dresden, Leipzig: Spector Books 2024, S. 23–31.

2. Harald Heinke (1941–2023) was a representative of the International Friendship League and coordinated the League's activities in Mozambique from 1979 to 1985.

3. Samora Moisés Machel, *Organizar a sociedade para vencer o subdesenvolvimento*, Colecção Estudos e orientações 14 (Maputo, 1982), 4.

4. Quoted in Alda Costa, *Arte em Moçambique: Entre a construção da nação e o mundo sem fronteiras 1932–2004* (Verbo, 2013), 248.

Let us begin with images.

A young couple stands in front of a poster announcing an exhibition about the German Democratic Republic in Maputo, the capital of Mozambique. The photograph must have been taken in the early 1980s. The young woman exudes confidence and wit in her pose. Dressed in work clothes, the young man facing her stands with his arms bent and a broad smile on his face. The image encapsulates ambition and hope. We found it in the private archive of Harald Heinke, who was responsible for many of the exhibitions and events through which the GDR presented itself to the people of Mozambique.[2] It was these young peoples' hearts the GDR wanted to win. For their own sake, and in support of their Mozambican partners' aim, the exhibitions, technical fairs, and cultural events were designed to give reassurance to the chosen path of Marxism-Leninism.

Mozambique and East Germany entered the sphere of "global socialism" under highly unequal conditions. Yet, in the challenge of implementing a new economic order and social values, both governments emphasized their likeness. The armed liberation struggle against the colonial army of Portugal was heralded as the beginning of a socialist revolution in Mozambique. Eduardo Mondlane and Samora Machel, the first leaders of the FRELIMO party (Frente de Libertação de Moçambique), declared that liberation could not be attained without dismantling the economic structure established by the Portuguese colonial empire—namely, capitalism. Hence, seizing power after independence began by organizing the country's transition to socialism. The education system and communication media were reorganized with a view to forming the socialist citizen. What the FRELIMO called the "New Man" implied a vision of men and women "liberated from old ideas, from a mentality that was contaminated by the colonial-capitalist mindset, a man educated by the ideas and practices of socialism."[3] Graça Machel, the first Minister of Education and Culture in the PRM, proclaimed that to eradicate the roots of colonial rule and its values, culture had to be redefined "in terms of the revolution," even more, independence required a "revolution in cultural terms."[4] Following independence, great emphasis was placed on enhancing the presence of the arts through public art programs, artist education, and international exchange.

Lassen wir die Bilder sprechen.

Ein junges Paar steht vor einem Werbeplakat für eine Ausstellung über die Deutsche Demokratische Republik in Maputo, der Hauptstadt von Mosambik. Das Foto muss in den frühen 1980er Jahren entstanden sein. Die junge Frau strahlt mit ihrer Haltung Selbstbewusstsein und Weitblick aus. Der ihr gegenüberstehende junge Mann in Arbeitskleidung hat die Hände in die Hüfte gestemmt und trägt ein breites Lächeln im Gesicht. Das Bild strahlt Ehrgeiz und Hoffnung aus. Wir haben es im Privatarchiv von Harald Heinke gefunden, der für viele der Ausstellungen und Veranstaltungen verantwortlich war, mit denen sich die DDR den Menschen in Mosambik präsentierte.[2] Es waren die Herzen der jungen Menschen, die die DDR gewinnen wollte. Die Ausstellungen, Fachmessen und Kulturveranstaltungen sollten in ihrem eigenen Interesse und zur Unterstützung der Ziele ihrer mosambikanischen Partner dazu dienen, den eingeschlagenen Weg des Marxismus-Leninismus zu bekräftigen.

Mosambik und die DDR traten unter höchst ungleichen Bedingungen in die Sphäre des „globalen Sozialismus" ein. Doch bei der Herausforderung, eine neue Wirtschaftsordnung und neue soziale Werte einzuführen, betonten beide Regierungen ihre Gemeinsamkeiten. Der bewaffnete Befreiungskampf gegen die portugiesische Kolonialarmee wurde in Mosambik als der Beginn einer sozialistischen Revolution gefeiert. Eduardo Mondlane und Samora Machel, die ersten Anführer der FRELIMO-Partei (Frente de Libertação de Moçambique), erklärten, dass die Befreiung ohne die Zerschlagung der vom portugiesischen Kolonialreich geschaffenen kapitalistischen Wirtschaftsstruktur nicht zu erreichen sei. Die neuen Machthaber begannen daher nach der Unabhängigkeit sofort mit der Gestaltung des Übergangs zum Sozialismus. Das Bildungssystem und die Medien erfuhren eine tiefgreifende Neugestaltung mit dem Ziel, den sozialistischen Bürger zu formen. Was die FRELIMO den „Neuen Menschen" nannte, war eine Vision von Mann und Frau, „die von alten Ideen befreit sind, von einer Mentalität, die durch die kolonial-kapitalistische Denkweise kontaminiert ist, [es ist die Vision] eines Menschen, der in den Ideen und Praktiken des Sozialismus erzogen wurde".[3] Graça Machel, die erste Ministerin für Bildung und Kultur in der VRM, verkündete, dass die Kultur „im Sinne der Revolution" neu definiert werden müsse, um die Wurzeln der Kolonialherrschaft und ihrer Werte zu beseitigen, mehr noch, die Unabhängigkeit erfordere eine „Revolution im Sinne der

2. Harald Heinke (1941–2023) war Vertreter der Liga für Völkerfreundschaft und koordinierte von 1979 bis 1985 die Aktivitäten der Liga in Mosambik.

3. Samora Machel, „Organizar a sociedade para vencer o subdesenvolvimento", in: *Colecçao Estudos e Orientações*, 14 (DTI, 1982), S. 4.

5. On the Mozambican Civil War (1977–1992), see Elísio Macamo and Lothar Berger, "Kriege und Konflikte: Mosambik," bpb, December 1, 2020, https://www.bpb.de/themen/kriege-konflikte/dossier-kriege-konflikte/54793/mosambik/#footnote-target-2.

6. FRELIMO Party Ideological Department, *Xiconhoca el enemigo* (Spanish version) (Fundación Editorial el perro y la rana, 2014), 70.

7. See Lars Buur, "1. Xiconhoca: Mozambique's Ubiquitous Post-Independence Traitor," in *Traitors: Suspicion, Intimacy, and the Ethics of State-Building*, ed. Sharika Thiranagama and Tobias Kelly (University of Pennsylvania Press, 2010). 24–47

Independence had been achieved only in 1975, after ten years of war against the Portuguese colonial army. Subsequently, political power was handed over to FRELIMO without election. In the following years, an anti-communist opposition to FRELIMO was formed under the name RENAMO (Resistência Nacional Moçambicana). RENAMO received military support from South Africa and Rhodesia (present-day Zimbabwe) and initiated an internal war to destabilize the country.[5] In this context, FRELIMO's cultural politics were inseparable from the aim of producing "national unity." And the echo of the Cold War, the sharp distinction between "friends" and "enemies," reverberated into FRELIMO's domestic politics. The cartoon figure Xiconhoca was used as a political tool to expose negative social and moral attitudes, attitudes opposite to that of the "New Man."

In one famous cartoon, Xiconhoca speaks to a man who represents the Portuguese regime but could also very much be read as a general representation of a European "man of culture and science." Xiconhoca comments on the group of dancers: "Culture, this? This is the dance of wild men. True culture is European culture. Nothing else."[6] The character of the "European" responds with a validating smile. The cartoon depicts the depreciation of Mozambican popular culture, a core strategy and characteristic of colonialism. It further underlines that FRELIMO had no interest in copying from European artistic creations of the time but instead entered a period of rediscovering local art forms and aesthetics that would encompass traditional dances such as Xigubo (from Maputo and Gaza), Tufo (from Ilha de Moçambique), and Mapiko (from the Makonde in the North).[7]

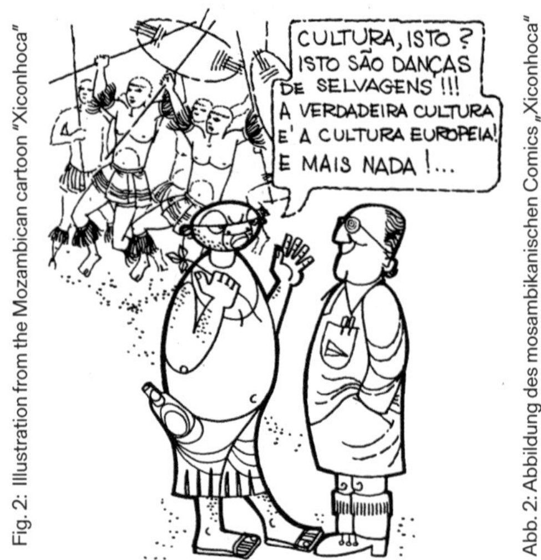

Fig. 2: Illustration from the Mozambican cartoon "Xiconhoca"

Abb. 2: Abbildung des mosambikanischen Comics „Xiconhoca"

Kultur".[4] Nach der Unabhängigkeit wurde großer Wert darauf gelegt, die Präsenz der Kunst durch öffentliche Kunstprogramme, künstlerische Ausbildung und internationalen Austausch zu stärken.

Die Unabhängigkeit war erst 1975 nach einem zehnjährigen Krieg gegen die portugiesische Kolonialarmee erlangt worden. Daraufhin wurde die politische Macht ohne Wahlen an die FRELIMO übergeben. In den folgenden Jahren bildete sich unter dem Namen RENAMO (Resistência Nacional Moçambicana) eine anti-kommunistische Opposition gegen FRELIMO. Die RENAMO erhielt militärische Unterstützung aus Südafrika und Rhodesien (dem heutigen Simbabwe) und begann einen Bürgerkrieg zur Destabilisierung des Landes.[5] In diesem Kontext war die Kulturpolitik der FRELIMO untrennbar mit dem Ziel verbunden, eine „nationale Einheit" herzustellen. Auch das Echo des Kalten Krieges, die trennscharfe Unterscheidung zwischen „Freunden" und „Feinden", hallte in der Innenpolitik der FRELIMO wider. Die Karikaturfigur Xiconhoca wurde als politisches Instrument entwickelt, um negative soziale und moralische Haltungen zu entlarven, Einstellungen, die denen des „Neuen Menschen" entgegengesetzt waren.

In einer berühmten Karikatur spricht Xiconhoca mit einem Mann, der offensichtlich das portugiesische Regime repräsentiert, aber auch sehr gut als allgemeine Darstellung eines europäischen „Mannes der Kultur und der Wissenschaft" gelesen werden könnte. Xiconhoca kommentiert die Gruppe von Tänzern: „Kultur, das? Das ist der Tanz von wilden Männern. Wahre Kultur ist europäische Kultur. Nichts anderes."[6] Die Figur des „Europäers" antwortet mit einem bestätigenden Lächeln. Die Karikatur kritisiert die Abwertung der mosambikanischen Volkskultur, eine zentrale Strategie und Charakteristik des Kolonialismus. Die FRELIMO, das unterstreicht die Zeichnung, hatte kein Interesse daran,

4. Zitiert nach Alda Costa, *Arte em Moçambique: Entre a construção da nação e o mundo sem fronteiras 1932–2004*, Lissabon: Verbo 2013, S. 248.

5. Zum mosambikanischen Bürgerkrieg (1977–1992) siehe Elísio Macamo und Lothar Berger, „Kriege und Konflikte: Mosambik", bpb, veröffentlicht am 1. Dezember 2020, https://www.bpb.de/themen/kriege-konflikte/dossier-kriege-konflikte/54793/mosambik/#footnote-target-2.

6. Ideologische Abteilung der Partei FRELIMO, *Xiconhoca el enemigo* (spanische Fassung), Caracas: Fundación Editorial el perro y la rana 2014, S. 70.

This prompts the question: How did Mozambique's search for a postcolonial culture shape the cooperation with the GDR? For FRELIMO, the arts were a powerful vehicle for cultivating self-awareness in a society liberated from colonial domination. While Mozambique pronounced its search for a national identity, a way of being and "acting in the world" after the colonialists had left, East German domestic cultural policies were cemented, and artists increasingly faced restrictions and control.[8] The exchanges in art and education were subject to monitoring to align with the economic and political agenda of the GDR.

The handwritten note documents instructions given to members of the East German dance company (Tanzensemble der DDR) prior to their journey to Mozambique. The state secretary of culture, Kurt Löffler himself, seems to have briefed the artists on the state's objectives in staging the performance with the question "Is power secure?"[9]

From the outset of the countries' diplomatic relations, art exhibitions and other cultural events were initiated to enhance the image of East Germany in Mozambique and promote the attractiveness of the socialist sphere. In 1976, just one year after Mozambique's independence, the first initiatives were undertaken to introduce East Germany to the Mozambican public as a model for the transition toward a "socialist way of life"; and as an ally against the interventionist activities and apartheid politics of neighboring South Africa. Members of the first diplomatic corps initiated an exhibition of artworks dedicated to the liberation from Nazism.[10]

8. In 1976, the East German singer-songwriter Wolf Biermann was expelled from the GDR. Following the event, known as the "Biermann-Ausbürgerung," punishments for protest statements (or artworks which could be read as such) became more severe. See Dietmar Keller and Matthias Kirchner, eds., *Biermann und kein Ende: Eine Dokumentation zur DDR-Kulturpolitik* (Dietz, 1991).

9. See the handwritten note printed here. Source: BArch DR 1/11646.

10. Dr. Ulrich Weishaupt, email to author, January 16, 2024. The exhibition displayed the collection of artworks from "Internationale Grafik zum 30. Jahrestag der Befreiung," published by Junge Welt in 1975, featuring works by Willi Sitte, Hap Grieshaber, Arno Mohr, and others. It included twenty-five artworks from artists representing nineteen different countries.

Einweisung
Löffler, VR Mocambique
Gesamtnationales Tanzfestival
Frage = Ist Macht sicher?
viele ausl. Experten
Enge Anlehnung an DDR + SL
Gefährdung der Macht
Propaganda S.A.

Anlaß Besuch
Gemeinsames Kulturzentrum Moatize
Förderung der FRELIMO Kultur durch FRELIMO
Sammlung + Förderung d. Erbes
Infrastruktur d. Kultur
Propaganda S.A.

8.6.82

Fig. 3: Handwritten note from the Mozambique Department in the Ministry of Culture, June 8, 1982 "Briefing, Löffler, VR (People's Republic) Mozambique. National dance festival. Question: Is power secure? Many foreign experts. Close relation to GDR + SL [Socialist Bloc]. Endangerment of power. Propaganda S.A. [South Africa]"

Abb. 3: Notiz aus der Abteilung Mocambique im Ministerium für Kultur, 8.6.1982

europäische Kunstwerke zu kopieren, stattdessen leitete sie eine Periode der Wiederentdeckung lokaler Kunstformen und Ästhetik ein, die traditionelle Tänze wie Xigubo (aus Maputo und Gaza), Tufo (von der Ilha de Moçambique) und Mapiko (von den Makonde im Norden) umfasste.[7]

Das wirft die Frage auf: Wie prägte die Suche Mosambiks nach einer postkolonialen Kultur die Zusammenarbeit mit der DDR? Für die FRELIMO waren die Künste ein mächtiges Mittel zur Kultivierung des Selbstbewusstseins einer von der kolonialen Herrschaft befreiten Gesellschaft. Während Mosambik nach dem Abzug der Kolonialmacht seine Suche nach einer nationalen Identität, den Formen und Farben der Emanzipation zum Ausdruck brachte, wurde die interne Kulturpolitik der DDR zunehmend rigider, Künstler·innen waren immer stärkeren Einschränkungen und Zensurmaßnahmen ausgesetzt.[8] Die Austauschprogramme in Kunst und Bildung unterlagen einer Kontrolle, um mit der wirtschaftlichen und politischen Agenda des Staates in Einklang zu stehen.

Die handschriftliche Notiz dokumentiert Anweisungen, die den Mitgliedern des Tanzensembles der DDR vor ihrer Reise nach Mosambik erteilt wurden. Der Staatssekretär für Kultur Kurt Löffler scheint die Kulturschaffenden mit der Frage „Ist [die] Macht sicher?" persönlich über die staatlichen Ziele der Aufführung informiert zu haben.[9]

Gleich zu Beginn der diplomatischen Beziehungen wurden Kunstausstellungen und andere kulturelle Veranstaltungen ins Leben gerufen, um das Image der DDR in Mosambik aufzubessern und die Attraktivität der sozialistischen Welt zu fördern. 1976, nur ein Jahr nach der Unabhängigkeit Mosambiks,

7. Siehe Lars Buur, „Xiconhoca: Mozambique's Ubiquitous Post-Independence Traitor", in: Sharika Thiranagama und Tobias Kelly (Hg.), *Traitors: Suspicion, Intimacy, and the Ethics of State-Building*, Philadelphia: University of Pennsylvania Press 2010, S. 24–47.

8. Im Jahr 1976 wurde der ostdeutsche Liedermacher Wolf Biermann aus der DDR ausgewiesen. In der Folge des als „Biermann-Ausbürgerung" bekannten Vorfalls wurden die Strafen für Protestäußerungen (oder Kunstwerke, die als solche gelesen werden konnten) verschärft. Siehe Dietmar Keller und Matthias Kirchner (Hg.), *Biermann und kein Ende. Eine Dokumentation zur DDR-Kulturpolitik*, Berlin: Dietz 1991.

9. Siehe die hier abgedruckte handschriftliche Notiz. Quelle: BArch DR 1/11646.

11. See James Mark and Paul Betts, *Socialism goes Global: The Soviet Union and Eastern Europe in the Age of Decolonization* (Oxford University Press, 2022).

12. BArch DY 13/2624, Report on the Week of Friendship, September 16, 1970.

13. Among the fifty-four films that were shown during the week of friendship were movies such as *Die Abenteuer des Werner Holt* and *Der Rat der Götter*. Exhibitions of photographs depicting life and work in East Germany were shown in the main movie halls "Gil Vicente" and "Avenida." Additionally, so-called *Druckausstellungen* (print exhibitions), such as those on the theme of solidarity, were displayed in secondary schools, language schools, and universities. BArch DY 13/2624.

14. BArch DY 13/2624.

15. According to the statistics of the League, BArch DY 13/2624.

After World War II, the East German government positioned itself as a successor to the anti-Nazi resistance. This narrative was partly built on the fact that many of its founding members and leaders were former communists who had been persecuted by the Nazi regime. However, it's important to note that the GDR's portrayal of itself as "representative of the victims of Nazism" was also a political strategy to differentiate itself from West Germany and to outsource the legacies of fascism. The invocation of anti-imperialism and anti-fascism functioned as a legitimation and ideological bridge between European socialist countries and emerging African nations.[11] Thus, it was no coincidence that the exhibition of *International Graphics for the 30th Anniversary of Liberation* showed a selection of prints that would depict East Germany as a country that had recently been liberated from National Socialism and thus knew the challenge of building a new national culture. However, in constructing this historical narrative, the East German state obscured the period of German colonial rule from 1885 to 1918 and the German Empire's active role in colonial expansion in Africa. FRELIMO endorsed the narrative for its own aims, speaking of East Germany as a successful example of building a socialist nation: "The experience that the GDR has gained in its thirty years of development, especially in the early years and in its defence against imperialist attacks, is of great importance for the PRM; what the GDR has achieved is encouraging for the Mozambican people."[12]

DISPLAY AND REPRESENTATION

In 1976, the People's Republic of Mozambique hosted a "Week of Friendship" with the GDR. This festivity, not uncommon in the Socialist Bloc, symbolized the partner countries' unity and shared commitment to advancing socialism. For the PRM, it marked the first such event with another nation. The week, initiated by the International Friendship League and realized in collaboration with the Ministry of Information of Mozambique, featured films, exhibitions, and lectures where East Germany showcased its history, culture, and achievements.[13] Approximately 2,500 people attended the events in Maputo and Chimoio.[14] A few years later, in 1979, the "Week of Friendship" with the GDR drew over 65,000

wurden erste Maßnahmen ergriffen, um der mosambikanischen Öffentlichkeit die DDR als Modell für den Übergang zu einer „sozialistischen Lebensweise" und als Verbündeten gegen die interventionistischen Aktivitäten und die Apartheidpolitik des benachbarten Südafrika vorzustellen. Mitglieder des ersten diplomatischen Korps initiierten eine Ausstellung von Kunstwerken, die der Befreiung vom Nationalsozialismus gewidmet war.[10]

Nach dem Zweiten Weltkrieg stellte sich die ostdeutsche Regierung als Nachfolgerin der Widerstandsbewegung gegen den Nationalsozialismus dar. Diese Darstellung beruhte zum Teil auf der Tatsache, dass viele ihrer Gründungsmitglieder und Funktionäre Kommunisten waren, die vom NS-Regime verfolgt worden waren. Die Selbstdarstellung der DDR als Repräsentantin der NS-Opfer war jedoch auch eine politische Strategie, um sich von Westdeutschland abzugrenzen und das Erbe des Faschismus auszulagern. Die Berufung auf Antiimperialismus und Antifaschismus diente als Legitimation und ideologische Brücke zwischen den europäischen sozialistischen Ländern und den aufstrebenden afrikanischen Nationen.[11] So war es kein Zufall, dass die Ausstellung *Internationale Grafik zum 30. Jahrestag der Befreiung* eine Auswahl von Grafiken zeigte, die die DDR als ein Land darstellten, das gerade erst vom Nationalsozialismus befreit worden war und daher die Herausforderungen des Aufbaus einer neuen nationalen Kultur kannte. Bei der Konstruktion dieses historischen Narrativs blendete die DDR auch die Zeit der deutschen Kolonialherrschaft von 1885 bis 1918 und die aktive Rolle des Deutschen Reiches bei der kolonialen Expansion in Afrika völlig aus. Die FRELIMO machte sich dieses Narrativ für ihre Ziele zu eigen und bezeichnete die DDR als erfolgreiches Beispiel für den Aufbau einer sozialistischen Nation: „Die Erfahrungen, die die DDR in den 30 Jahren ihrer Entwicklung gemacht hat, vor allem in den Anfangsjahren und bei der Verteidigung gegen imperialistische Angriffe, sind für die VRM von großer Bedeutung, und was die DDR erreicht hat, ist Ermutigung für das mosambikanische Volk."[12]

SELBSTDARSTELLUNG UND REPRÄSENTATION

Im Jahr 1976 veranstaltete die Volksrepublik Mosambik eine „Woche der Freundschaft" mit der DDR. Diese im sozialistischen Block nicht unübliche Feierlichkeit symbolisierte die Einheit der Partnerländer und ihr gemeinsames Bekenntnis zur

10. Dr. Ulrich Weishaupt, E-Mail an die Autorin, 16.1.2024. Die Ausstellung zeigte die Sammlung *Internationale Grafik zum 30. Jahrestag der Befreiung*, herausgegeben von der *Jungen Welt* im Jahr 1975, mit Werken von Willi Sitte, HAP Grieshaber, Arno Mohr und anderen. Sie enthielt 25 Kunstwerke von Künstler·innen aus 19 verschiedenen Ländern.

11. Siehe James Mark und Paul Betts (Hg.), *Socialism Goes Global: The Soviet Union and Eastern Europe in the Age of Decolonization*, Oxford: Oxford University Press 2022.

12. BArch DY 13/2624, Bericht über die Woche der Freundschaft, 16.9.1979.

16. Letters from Ulrich Makosch to Konrad Wolf (AdK President from 1965–1982) and Manfred Wekwerth (AdK President from 1982–1990), AdK-O 3998.

visitors in various cities around the country.[15] The titles of the displays and events show the broad scope of topics that were captured: "Woman in Socialism," "Fight Against Racism," "Labor Law in East Germany," and more. The week's activities ranged from German and Mozambican youth groups planting trees together in Chimoio, to a forum on "The Responsibility of Mass Media in Educating the Masses" for selected FRELIMO members and journalists. The forum was led by Ulrich Makosch, the GDR's most renowned foreign correspondent. In addition to reporting on events in Mozambique in the East German press, Makosch served on the board of the GDR-Mozambique Friendship Committee and played a pivotal role in facilitating encounters between artists, politicians, and journalists from both countries. Between 1980 and 1984, Ulrich Makosch sent several personal letters to the president of the East German Academy of Arts, in which he praised the artworks and political commitment of Mankew V. Mahumana, making a plea for his nomination as a corresponding member.[16]

The events of the "Week of Friendship" were meticulously chronicled by representatives of the GDR in Mozambique. The reports contain endless lists, documenting the number of visitors to each exhibition and event, further indicating the presence of high-ranking FRELIMO officials and the dissemination of brochures. Thus, we glean from these records that in preparation for the "Week of Friendship" in 1979, there were 430 brochures on "Physical Education and Sports" from East Germany in stock. By means of naming, numbering, and listing, the East German authorities endeavored to quantify the impact of their promotion efforts. Together with the protocols on such events, the logic of such lists suggests that the kind of "cultural transfer" pursued here was deeply embedded in Cold War practices. It reflects the idea of "winning over the country" with a

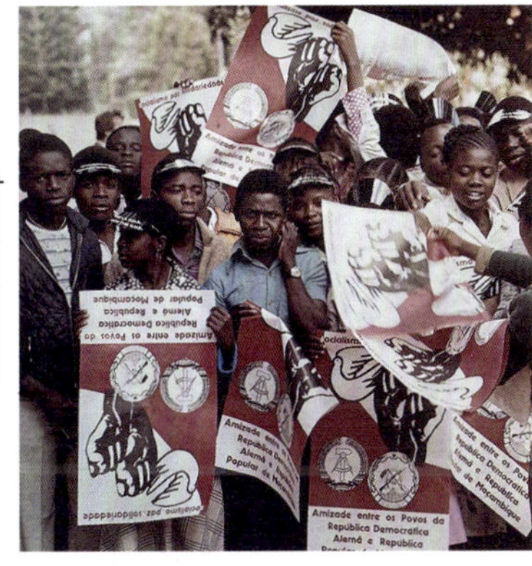

Figs. 4–5: Advertising for the "Week of Friendship"

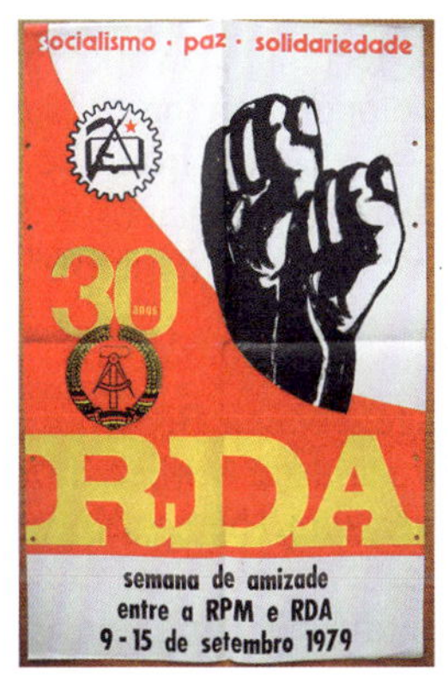

Abb. 4–5: Plakat für die „Woche der Freundschaft"

Förderung des Sozialismus. Für die VRM war es die erste derartige Veranstaltung mit einer anderen Nation. Die von der Liga für Völkerfreundschaft initiierte und in Zusammenarbeit mit dem mosambikanischen Informationsministerium durchgeführte Woche umfasste Filmvorführungen, Ausstellungen und Vorträge, in denen die DDR ihre Geschichte, Kultur und Errungenschaften vorstellte.[13] An den Veranstaltungen in Maputo und Chimoio nahmen etwa 2500 Menschen teil.[14] Einige Jahre später, 1979, zog die „Woche der Freundschaft" mit der DDR über 65 000 Besucher in verschiedenen Städten des Landes an.[15] Die Titel der Ausstellungen und Veranstaltungen zeigen die große Bandbreite der Themen, die aufgegriffen wurden: „Die Frau im Sozialismus", „Kampf gegen Rassismus", „Arbeitsrecht in der DDR" und mehr. Die Aktivitäten der Woche reichten von deutschen und mosambikanischen Jugendgruppen, die in Chimoio gemeinsam Bäume pflanzten, bis hin zu einem Forum zum Thema „Die Verantwortung der Massenmedien bei der Erziehung der Massen" für ausgewählte FRELIMO-Mitglieder und Journalist·innen. Geleitet wurde das Forum von Ulrich Makosch, dem bekanntesten Auslandskorrespondenten der DDR. Makosch berichtete nicht nur in der ostdeutschen Presse über die Ereignisse in Mosambik, sondern war auch im Vorstand des Freundschaftskomitees DDR-Mosambik tätig. Dabei spielte er eine zentrale Rolle bei der Vermittlung von Begegnungen zwischen Künstler·innen, Politiker·innen und Journalist·innen aus beiden Ländern. Zwischen 1980 und 1984 richtete Ulrich Makosch mehrere persönliche Briefe an den Präsidenten der Akademie der Künste der DDR, in denen er die Kunstwerke und das politische Engagement von Mankew V. Mahumana lobte und für seine Ernennung zum korrespondierenden Mitglied der Akademie warb.[16]

Die Veranstaltungen der „Woche der Freundschaft" wurden von Vertretern der DDR in Mosambik akribisch protokolliert. Die Berichte enthalten endlose Listen, die die Besucherzahlen jeder Ausstellung und Veranstaltung dokumentieren. Ferner wird auf die Anwesenheit hochrangiger FRELIMO-Funktionäre und

13. Unter den 54 Filmen, die während der Woche der Freundschaft gezeigt wurden, waren Filme wie *Die Abenteuer des Werner Holt* und *Der Rat der Götter*. In den großen Kinosälen „Gil Vicente" und „Avenida" wurden Fotoausstellungen gezeigt, die das Leben und Arbeiten in der DDR darstellten. Darüber hinaus wurden an weiterführenden Schulen, Sprachschulen und Universitäten sogenannte „Druckausstellungen" gezeigt, beispielsweise zum Thema Solidarität. BArch DY 13/2624.

14. BArch DY 13/2624.

15. Nach den Statistiken der Liga, BArch DY 13/2624.

16. Briefe von Ulrich Makosch an Konrad Wolf (AdK-Präsident von 1965 bis 1982) und Manfred Wekwerth (AdK-Präsident von 1982 bis 1990), AdK-O 3998.

17. Marcus Andrew Hurtig, "The International Aspirations of the Museum der bildenden Künste Leipzig with Regard to Its Collection and Exhibition Programme between 1949 and 1989," in *Re-Connect: Art and Conflict in Brotherland*, exh. cat., MdbK, Leipzig (Hirmer, 2023), 48. See also the oral history interview with Giselher Blesse, researcher at Leipzig Museum of Ethnography during the 1980s, "From Leipzig to Maputo, Mozambique," https://artinnetworks.webspace.tu-dresden.de/en/beitraege/von-leipzig-nach-maputo-mosambik.

18. Until the mid-twentieth century, the collections in European ethnographic museums were administered by anthropologists, and artworks were regarded as an expression of tribal identity and culture.

proliferation of media outlets, a strategy used by the Eastern and Western blocs alike to strengthen their presence and influence. We think of the picture (fig. 4) as a commentary—an abundance of posters held by a group of young people. The posters, designed by Harald Heinke, promote the *Semana de Amizade* (Week of Friendship) in 1979. Curiosity is evident in some of the faces, others appear uninterested. They realize the camera is pointed at them, while hands reach out to grasp the posters. To us, the picture embodies some of the complexities of cultural dissemination amidst ideological tension.

THE GRAMMAR OF EXHIBITIONS

At the "Week of Friendship" and on other occasions, East Germany showcased its social and political achievements, a format which was also common in the GDR itself. On the other hand, Mozambique was introduced to the East German public primarily through exhibitions in various museums, which mostly showcased contemporary and historical artworks as well as what was then referred to as "handicrafts" from ethnographic collections. At Leipzig's ethnographic museum, the GRASSI Museum für Völkerkunde zu Leipzig, several exhibitions on Mozambican art were curated: *Moçambique: Kunst und Kunsthandwerk einer jungen Volksrepublik* (1977, in collaboration with the Solidarity Committee of the GDR), *Moderne Kunst aus Moçambique* (1980), and *Moderne Makonde-Plastik: Kunst aus Ostafrika,* presented at the Kulturhaus Mölkau (1984).[17] The exhibitions were developed in consultation with the Mozambican Ministry of Culture. Yet apart from contemporary Mozambican art, they also drew on the extensive collection of Makonde sculptures held by the museum itself. The titles of the exhibitions signal a shift toward recognizing works from Mozambique as modern art.[18] However, the fact that the exhibitions were displayed in the ethnographic museum reflect that artworks from the continent were still seen as peripheral to art, as not belonging in the citadel of modern art.

Apart from the exhibitions in Leipzig, Mozambican art was presented on different occasions in East Berlin. In October 1980, artworks from Mozambique were shown at the Berlin Television Tower. The East German news agency, ADN,

auf die Anzahl der ausgegebenen Broschüren hingewiesen. So geht aus diesen Aufzeichnungen hervor, dass zur Vorbereitung der „Woche der Freundschaft" im Jahr 1979 430 Broschüren zum Thema „Körpererziehung und Sport" aus der DDR vorrätig waren. Durch Benennung, Nummerierung und Auflistung versuchten die ostdeutschen Behörden, die Wirkung ihrer Werbemaßnahmen zu quantifizieren. Zusammen mit den Protokollen über solche Veranstaltungen deutet die Logik solcher Listen darauf hin, dass die hier verfolgte Art des „Kulturtransfers" in die Praktiken des Kalten Krieges eingebettet war. Sie spiegelt die Idee wider, das Land mit einer Vielzahl von Medien zu „erobern", eine Strategie, die sowohl vom Ost- als auch vom Westblock zur Stärkung ihrer Präsenz und ihres Einflusses eingesetzt wurde. Wir können das Foto (Abb. 4) als einen Kommentar begreifen – es zeigt eine Vielzahl von Plakaten, die von einer Gruppe junger Menschen gehalten werden. Die von Harald Heinke gestalteten Plakate werben für die *Semana de Amizade* (Woche der Freundschaft) im Jahr 1979. In einigen Gesichtern ist Neugierde zu erkennen, andere wirken desinteressiert. Während ihre Hände nach den Plakaten greifen, bemerken sie, dass die Kamera auf sie gerichtet ist. Das Bild symbolisiert für uns die Komplexität interkultureller Veranstaltungen, die vor dem Hintergrund ideologischer Konflikte stattfanden.

AUSSTELLUNGSGRAMMATIKEN

In der „Woche der Freundschaft" und bei anderen Gelegenheiten stellte die DDR ihre gesellschaftlichen und politischen Errungenschaften vor, ein Format, das auch in der DDR selbst üblich war. Umgekehrt wurde Mosambik der ostdeutschen Öffentlichkeit vor allem durch Ausstellungen in verschiedenen Museen vorgestellt, in denen in erster Linie zeitgenössische und historische Kunstwerke sowie sogenanntes „Kunsthandwerk" aus ethnografischen Sammlungen gezeigt wurden. Im Leipziger GRASSI Museum für Völkerkunde wurden mehrere Ausstellungen zur mosambikanischen Kunst kuratiert: *Moçambique. Kunst und Kunsthandwerk einer jungen Volksrepublik* (1977, in Zusammenarbeit mit dem Solidaritätskomitee der DDR), *Moderne Kunst aus Moçambique* (1980) und *Moderne Makonde-Plastik. Kunst aus Ostafrika*, präsentiert im Kulturhaus Mölkau (1984).[17] Die Ausstellungen wurden in Absprache mit dem mosambikanischen Kulturministerium entwickelt. Neben zeitgenössischer mosambikanischer Kunst wurden aber auch

17. Marcus Andrew Hurtig, „Der internationale Anspruch des Museums der bildenden Künste Leipzig in Bezug auf seine Sammlung und sein Ausstellungsprogramm zwischen 1949 und 1989", in: *Re-Connect. Kunst und Kampf im Bruderland*, Ausst.-Kat. Museum der bildenden Künste Leipzig, München: Hirmer 2023, S. 36–53, hier S. 48. Siehe auch das Oral-History-Interview mit Giselher Blesse, Wissenschaftler am Leipziger Museum für Völkerkunde in den 1980er Jahren: http://artinnetworks.gsw.tu-dresden.de/public/de/beitraege/von-leipzig-nach-maputo-mosambik.

19. ADN, "Ausstellung mit Kunst aus Afrika in Berlin eröffnet," *Neues Deutschland*, October 1, 1980, BArch DR 123/143.

promoted the exhibition as the first extensive display of fine art originating from African nations – comprising a total of 750 works.[19] The exhibition with the title *Art from Africa* took place during the Days of the Culture of Liberated Peoples of Africa (Tage der Kultur befreiter Völker Afrikas), which were specifically dedicated to Mozambique, Angola, and Ethiopia. Invited to contribute artworks, Mozambique chose to present itself with political poster art articulating the ideals of socialist citizenship, signaling a new beginning in art and aesthetics following independence.

The photographs from the exhibition *Art from Africa* were taken by Ingrid Hänse at the opening event. We don't know the names of the people in the picture. But we can study the scene depicted. We see a group of people whose looks rest firmly on the objects under a glass cabinet. Notwithstanding that the picture gives the impression of a staged scene, we can establish that the man in the center of the picture (fig. 6), dressed in a fine suit, is being listened to. When studying the second photograph of the exhibition (fig. 7), however, we might notice with unease the undifferentiated compilation of objects—from ancient Ethiopian pottery and traditional garments to Mozambican graphics rich in symbols of the political and cultural revolution. Until then, artworks from the African continent had been confined to ethnographic museums, where objects from their collection were displayed.

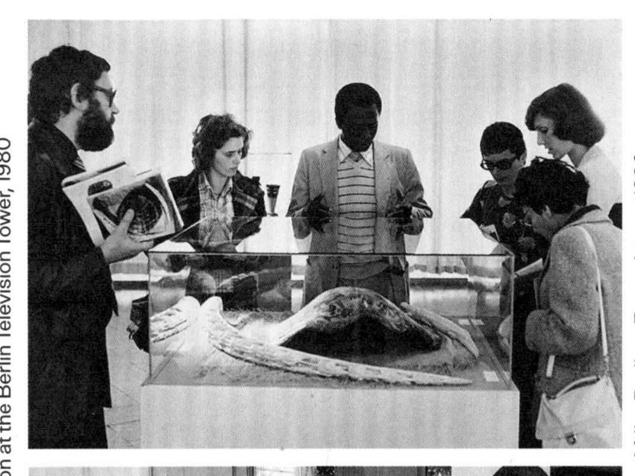
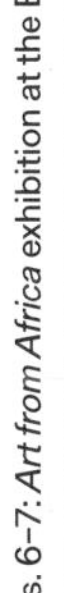

Figs. 6–7: *Art from Africa* exhibition at the Berlin Television Tower, 1980

Abb. 6–7: Ausstellung *Kunst aus Afrika*, Berliner Fernsehturm, 1980

Makonde-Skulpturen aus der umfangreichen Sammlung des Museums ausgestellt. Die Titel der Ausstellungen signalisieren einen Wandel hin zur Anerkennung von Kunstwerken aus Mosambik als moderne Kunst.[18] Die Tatsache, dass die Ausstellungen im ethnografischen Museum stattfanden, spiegelt jedoch wider, dass Kunstwerke vom afrikanischen Kontinent vorerst weiterhin als peripher zur Kunst und zu den Zentren der modernen Kunst betrachtet wurden.

Neben den Ausstellungen in Leipzig wurde mosambikanische Kunst bei verschiedenen Gelegenheiten in Ost-Berlin präsentiert. Im Oktober 1980 wurden im Berliner Fernsehturm Kunstwerke aus Mosambik gezeigt. Die ostdeutsche Nachrichtenagentur ADN bewarb die Ausstellung als die erste umfassende Schau bildender Kunst aus afrikanischen Ländern, mit insgesamt 750 Werken.[19] Die Ausstellung mit dem Titel *Kunst aus Afrika* fand im Rahmen der „Tage der Kultur befreiter Völker Afrikas" statt, die speziell Mosambik, Angola und Äthiopien gewidmet waren. Mosambik, das eingeladen war, Kunstwerke beizusteuern, entschied sich dafür, sich mit politischer Plakatkunst zu präsentieren, die die Ideale des sozialistischen Weges zum Ausdruck brachte und einen künstlerischen und ästhetischen Neuanfang nach der Unabhängigkeit signalisierte.

Die Fotos der Ausstellung *Kunst aus Afrika* wurden von Ingrid Hänse bei der Eröffnungsveranstaltung aufgenommen. Wir kennen die Namen der Menschen auf dem Bild (Abb. 6) nicht. Aber wir können die abgebildete Szene studieren. Wir sehen eine Gruppe von Menschen, deren Blicke fest auf den Objekten in einer

18. Bis Mitte des 20. Jahrhunderts wurden die Sammlungen in europäischen ethnografischen Museen von Anthropologen verwaltet, und die Kunstwerke wurden als Ausdruck von Stammesidentität und -kultur betrachtet.

19. „Ausstellung mit Kunst aus Afrika in Berlin eröffnet", in: *Neues Deutschland*, 1.10.1980, BArch DR 123/143.

20. Message to the author (May 5, 2024)

21. Letter to the East German embassy in the People's Republic of Mozambique, March 10, 1980, BArch DR 1/17805.

22. Barbara Fuchs, "Von der Kamelglocke bis zum Agitationsposter," *BZ am Abend*, October 16, 1980, BArch 123/143.

23. Ibid.

In the 1980 exhibition, artworks were selected by the partner countries and loaned from institutions such as the National Museum of Ethiopia. Ingrid Hänse, who took the photograph of the exhibition, recalls that the Cameroonian anthropologist Dr. Yalla Eballa who worked at the GRASSI Museum in Leipzig at the time was involved in curating the exhibition.[20] From what we can reconstruct of the exhibition in East Berlin, it appears to have been an initial attempt to cooperate with formerly colonized nations in exhibition practices and to recognize them as authorities on their own cultures.

Despite the effort to recognize "modern African art," letters and reports accompanying the exhibition are rife with phrases that categorize the artworks as "traditional" objects, thereby perpetuating an understanding of African art as craft. The German side harbored reservations regarding Mozambique's sole display of political posters in the exhibition. "We would be pleased if the exhibition could be extended by the addition of handicraft exhibits (carvings, wickerwork, weaving, etc.),"[21] states a letter from the East German Ministry of Culture addressing the Mozambican partners. When studying the media coverage, the exoticizing gaze that shaped the curation and perception of artworks stands out. "From the camel bell to the agitation poster," ran the *Berliner Zeitung* headline announcing the exhibition.[22] Yet, the article also criticized the exhibition for exposing the works without explanatory notes: "It is regrettable, however, that the Center for Art Exhibitions, as the organizer, failed to include some absolutely essential explanations regarding the cultural traditions and history of these countries, as well as the function of the everyday objects, which are crucial for our understanding."[23] The international art exhibition "Art from Africa" (1980) demonstrates that the new East-South relations among socialist-leaning countries also shaped the exhibition politics and visual culture in East Germany. However, it would still take a long time to overcome the hegemonic discourses that view artworks from the continent through an "ethnographic" lens.

Beyond the art exhibition, the festival hosted performance groups from Ethiopia, Mozambique, Angola, the Congo, and Benin. The National Dance and Music Ensemble of the People's Republic of Mozambique presented a dance that re-enacted the people's fight for independence and the liberation from the

Glasvitrine ruhen. Auch wenn das Bild inszeniert sein könnte, sehen wir, dass die Menschen dem Mann in der Mitte, der ein elegantes Sakko trägt, aufmerksam zuhören. Wenn wir das zweite Foto (Abb. 7) der Ausstellung betrachten, wird jedoch auch die undifferenzierte Zusammenstellung von Objekten deutlich – von alten äthiopischen Töpferwaren und traditionellen Gewändern bis hin zu mosambikanischen Grafiken, die reich an Symbolen der politischen und kulturellen Revolution sind. Bis dahin waren Ausstellungen mit Kunstwerken vom afrikanischen Kontinent auf die Sammlungen der ethnografischen Museen beschränkt.

Für die Ausstellung 1980 hingegen wurden die Kunstwerke von den Partnerländern ausgewählt und wurden als Leihgaben von Institutionen wie zum Beispiel dem Nationalmuseum von Äthiopien zur Verfügung gestellt. Ingrid Hänse, die die Ausstellung fotografiert hat, erinnert sich, dass der kamerunische Anthropologe Dr. Yalla Eballa, der damals am GRASSI Museum für Völkerkunde in Leipzig arbeitete, als Kurator an der Ausstellung beteiligt war.[20] Soweit wir die Ausstellung in Ost-Berlin rekonstruieren können, handelt es sich um einen ersten Versuch, gemeinsam mit ehemaligen Kolonien Ausstellungen zu gestalten und sie als Autoritäten ihrer eigenen Kulturen anzuerkennen.

Trotz des Bemühens, „moderne afrikanische Kunst" als solche vorzustellen, wimmelt es in Briefen und Berichten zu der Ausstellung von Formulierungen, die die Werke als „traditionelle" Objekte einordnen und ein Verständnis von afrikanischer Kunst als Handwerk reproduzieren. Zudem erhob die deutsche Seite Einwände gegen die ausschließliche Präsentation von politischen Plakaten aus Mosambik. „Wir wären sehr froh, wenn die Ausstellung noch durch Zugabe von Kunsthandwerk-Exponaten (Schnitzereien, Flecht- und Webarbeiten o. ä.) erweitert werden könnte", heißt es in einem Schreiben des ostdeutschen Kulturministeriums an die mosambikanischen Partner.[21] Bei der Betrachtung der Medienberichterstattung fällt der exotisierende Blick auf, der die Kuratierung und Wahrnehmung der Kunstwerke prägte. „Von der Kamelglocke bis zum Agitationsposter" betitelte die *Berliner Zeitung* eine Ankündigung der Ausstellung.[22] In dem Artikel wurde aber auch kritisiert, dass die Ausstellung die Werke ohne Erläuterungen präsentierte: „Schade nur, daß es das Zentrum für Kunstausstellungen als Veranstalter versäumte, einige für das Verständnis unbedingt wichtige Erläuterungen zur kulturellen Tradition und Geschichte dieser

20. Nachricht an die Autorin (5.5.2024).

21. Brief an die Botschaft der DDR in der Volksrepublik Mosambik, 10.3.1980, BArch DR 1/17805.

22. Barbara Fuchs, „Von der Kamelglocke bis zum Agitationsposter", in: *BZ am Abend*, 16.10.1980, BArch 123/143.

24. Assessment of the guest performance, October 2, 1980, BArch DR1/17805.

25. Ibid.

26. See Monica Popescu, "The Battle of Conferences: Cultural Decolonization and Global Cold War," in *Inventing the Third World: In Search of Freedom for the Postwar Global South*, ed. Jeremy Adelman and Gyan Prakash (Bloomsbury Academic, 2022), 163–82.

27. Submission to the Secretariat of the Central Committee of the SED, BArch DR1/21056.

28. Ibid.

29. ADN, "Ausstellung mit Kunst aus Afrika in Berlin eröffnet."

colonial force.[24] To the East German public, the National Dance and Music Ensemble was promoted as a "Folklore Ensemble." However, the performance of the Mozambican dance company had little to do with a conception of traditional dance. A member of the audience described it as a praise of proletarian internationalism, expressed in the movements and choreographies from Mozambique. The choir sang working-class songs specially rehearsed for the tour, in German, such as the song "Brüder, zur Sonne zur Freiheit,"[25] originally a hymn of the Russian Revolution. Now, in 1980, it was sung by a group of Mozambicans on the stages of East Berlin, Magdeburg, and Erfurt. While the East German public's faith in socialism had been eroded over more than three decades and the hopes of many had been dashed, the Mozambican performance must have conveyed a lost sense of euphoria for the socialist project. Before performing in East Berlin, the same group had been on tour in Cuba and the Caribbean, promoting the People's Republic of Mozambique as an emerging socialist nation.

It was no coincidence that the exhibition of artworks from Mozambique, Angola, and Ethiopia took place in the television tower—symbol of the country's economic strength and the power of communication. Berlin was divided by the wall, and, like no other city, it was the battleground of a "Cultural Cold War." International festivals and exhibitions on both sides of the wall were linked with the intention of expanding spheres of influence.[26] The Days of the Culture of Liberated Peoples of Africa aimed at "solidifying" the political bonds to recently independent African nation states.[27] The preparatory document, from the office of the Minister of Culture, emphasizes the need to compete with West Berlin in embracing contemporary arts from the South. It states, "The weeks also gain significance in view of the fact that the class enemy is preparing to establish a new center for the culture of developing countries in West Berlin, as demonstrated by the 'Horizonte' festival of world cultures."[28]

The events and exhibitions on African cultures in 1980 not only served East German foreign policy but also targeted the East German audience. In his opening speech at the exhibition, Horst Schneider, director of the Center of Art Exhibitions in the GDR, emphasized the significance of "understanding the

Länder wie auch zur Funktion der Gebrauchsgegenstände beizugeben."[23] Die internationale Kunstausstellung *Kunst aus Afrika* (1980) zeigt, dass die neuen Ost-Süd-Beziehungen der sozialistisch geprägten Länder auch die Ausstellungspolitik und die visuelle Kultur in der DDR prägten. Allerdings sollte es noch lange dauern, bis die hegemonialen Diskurse überwunden waren, die die Kunstwerke des Kontinents nur durch eine „ethnografische" Brille betrachteten.

Neben der Kunstausstellung waren auf dem Festival Performancegruppen aus Äthiopien, Mosambik, Angola, dem Kongo und Benin vertreten. Das Nationale Tanz- und Musikensemble der Volksrepublik Mosambik präsentierte einen Tanz, der den Kampf des Volkes um die Unabhängigkeit und die Befreiung von der Kolonialmacht darstellte.[24] In der ostdeutschen Öffentlichkeit wurde das Nationale Tanz- und Musikensemble als „Folklore-Ensemble" beworben. Die Vorstellung der mosambikanischen Tanzkompanie hatte jedoch wenig mit einer Darbietung von traditionellem Tanz zu tun. Ein Zuschauer bezeichnete sie als einen Lobgesang auf den proletarischen Internationalismus. Der Chor sang eigens für die Tournee einstudierte Arbeiterlieder in deutscher Sprache, wie das Lied „Brüder, zur Sonne, zur Freiheit",[25] ursprünglich eine Hymne der russischen Revolution. Jetzt, 1980, wurde es von einer Gruppe von Mosambikaner·innen auf den Bühnen von Ost-Berlin, Magdeburg und Erfurt gesungen. Während der Glaube der ostdeutschen Öffentlichkeit an den Sozialismus in mehr als drei Jahrzehnten erodiert und die Hoffnungen vieler Menschen enttäuscht worden waren, könnte der Auftritt der Mosambikaner·innen ein verlorenes Gefühl der Euphorie für das sozialistische Projekt vermittelt haben. Vor dem Auftritt in Ost-Berlin war dieselbe Gruppe auf Kuba und in der Karibik unterwegs gewesen, um für die Volksrepublik Mosambik als aufstrebende sozialistische Nation zu werben.

Es war kein Zufall, dass die Ausstellung von Kunstwerken aus Mosambik, Angola und Äthiopien im Fernsehturm stattfand. Dieser galt als Symbol für die wirtschaftliche Stärke des Landes und die Macht der Kommunikation. Berlin war durch die Mauer geteilt und wie keine andere Stadt Austragungsort eines „Kalten Kulturkrieges". Internationale Festivals und Ausstellungen auf beiden Seiten der Mauer wurden mit der Absicht verbunden, die Einflusssphären zu erweitern.[26] Die „Tage der Kultur befreiter Völker Afrikas" zielten darauf ab, die politischen Bindungen zu den kürzlich unabhängig gewordenen afrikanischen Nationalstaaten

23. Ebd.

24. Bewertung des Gastspiels, 2.10.1980, BArch DR1/17805.

25. Ebd.

26. Siehe Monica Popescu, „The Battle of Conferences: Cultural Decolonisation and Global Cold War", in: Jeremy Adelman und Gyan Prakash (Hg.), *Inventing the Third World: In Search of Freedom for the Postwar Global South*, London: Bloomsbury Academic 2022, S. 163–182.

30. Maritta Tkalec and Klaus Ullrich, "Eine Tür zur Begegnung mit Freunden: Kunstausstellung aus Moçambique," *Neues Deutschland*, January 12, 1982, BArch DR 1 123/77.

31. Ministry of Education and Culture of Mozambique, ed., "Artistas de Moçambique," 1981, BArch N 2841.

32. In 1986, the painter Malangatana Valente Ngwenya was honored with a solo exhibition at the GRASSI Museum in Leipzig. A catalog was published in conjunction with the exhibition: Renate Schmidt, ed., *Malangatana Valente Ngwenya: Malerei, Grafik, Zeichnungen; Personalausstellung im Museum für Völkerkunde Leipzig / Ministerium für Kultur der DDR* (Zentrum für Kunstausstellungen der DDR, 1986).

cultural achievements of these peoples and stimulating active solidarity."[29] The term "active" support was hinting at the monetary fund collected by the Solidarity Committee. In factories, on the streets, and at public festivities, people were regularly encouraged to donate in solidarity with the "sister countries" in Africa, Latin America, and Asia.

Two years later, in January 1982, an exhibition was installed in the Berlin Television Tower exclusively showing contemporary paintings and sculptures by Mozambican artists. The exhibition had been curated by the Ministry of Education and Culture of Mozambique and was traveling to various countries. Before arriving in Berlin, the artworks had been on display in Moscow and Sofia. The painter Malangatana Valente Ngwenya, who was present at the opening (fig. 9), expressed his hopes of forging new connections through art in an interview with East German journalists: "Malangatana also calls the exhibition,… a door that he wishes to open on both sides."[30] The "contact with Mozambican art," he hopes, will open the door wide for a mutual exchange between the two countries. Mankew V. Mahumana, to whom we dedicate a chapter in this book, was present with five artworks in the exhibition.[31] Perhaps for the first time in the two Germanies, Mozambican artworks were taken out of the context of an ethnographic exhibition and shown as contemporary positions and comments of the time.[32]

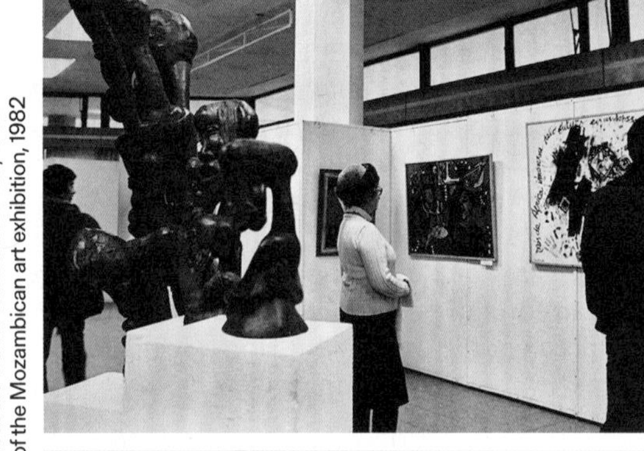

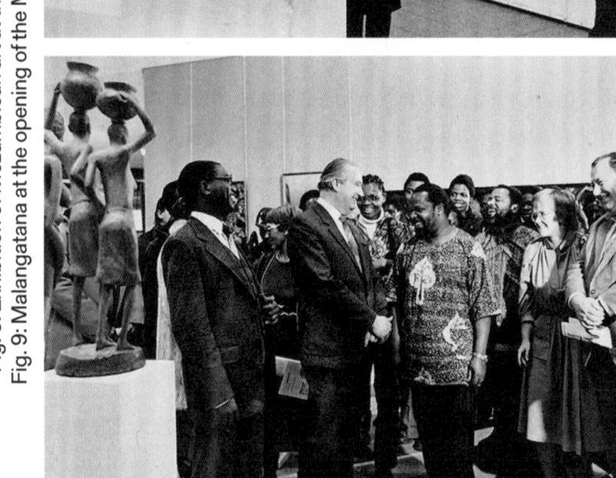

Fig. 8: Exhibition of Mozambican art at the Berlin Television Tower, 1982
Fig. 9: Malangatana at the opening of the Mozambican art exhibition, 1982

Abb. 8: Ausstellung mosambikanischer Kunst im Berliner Fernsehturm, 1982
Abb. 9: Malangatana bei der Eröffnung der Ausstellung mosambikanischer Kunst, 1982

zu „festigen".[27] Das vorbereitende Dokument aus dem Büro des Kulturministers unterstreicht die Notwendigkeit, in Bezug auf die zeitgenössische Kunst aus dem Süden mit West-Berlin zu konkurrieren. Darin heißt es: „Die Wochen gewinnen auch an Bedeutung angesichts der Tatsache, daß der Klassengegner sich anschickt, in Westberlin ein neues Zentrum der Kultur der Entwicklungsländer aufzubauen, wie das mit dem Festival der Weltkulturen ‚Horizonte' demonstriert wurde."[28]

Die Veranstaltungen und Ausstellungen zu den Kulturen Afrikas im Jahr 1980 dienten nicht nur der Außenpolitik, sie richteten sich auch an das ostdeutsche Publikum. In seiner Eröffnungsrede zur Ausstellung verwies Horst Schneider, Direktor des Zentrums für Kunstausstellungen der DDR, auf die „freundschaftlichen Beziehungen, die das Verständnis für die kulturellen Leistungen dieser Völker vertiefen und die aktive Solidarität stimulieren".[29] Mit dem Begriff der „aktiven" Solidarität spielte er auf die Spendengelder an, die das Solidaritätskomitee sammelte. In den Betrieben, auf den Straßen und bei öffentlichen Festen wurden die Menschen regelmäßig zu solidarischen Spenden für die „Bruderländer" in Afrika, Lateinamerika und Asien aufgefordert.

Zwei Jahre später, im Januar 1982, wurde im Berliner Fernsehturm eine Ausstellung eingerichtet, die ausschließlich zeitgenössische Gemälde und Skulpturen mosambikanischer Künstler zeigte. Die Ausstellung war vom Ministerium für Bildung und Kultur Mosambiks kuratiert worden und reiste durch verschiedene Länder. Bevor sie nach Berlin kamen, waren die Kunstwerke in Moskau und Sofia zu sehen.

27. Vorlage an das Sekretariat des ZK der SED, BArch DR1/21056.

28. Ebd.

29. „Ausstellung mit Kunst aus Afrika in Berlin eröffnet", in: *Neues Deutschland*, 1.10.1980, BArch 123/143.

33. "House memo" to Kurt Löffler, August 4, 1983; letter to Kurt Löffler from the GDR embassy in Mozambique, Maputo, September 1, 1982, BArch DR1/11646.

34. In the twelve years of co-operation between the GDR mining companies and CAR-BOMOC, around 600 East German citizens worked in Moatize. See Walter Grabner, "DDR-Beteiligung am Steinkohleprojekt Moatize," in *Wir haben Spuren hinterlassen! Die DDR in Mosambik. Erlebnisse, Erfahrungen und Erkenntnisse aus drei Jahrzehnten,* ed. Matthias Voß (LIT Verlag, 2005), 268.

35. According to Walter Grabner, who worked at the CARBOMOC mine, the solidarity committee supported the social care of the workforce with materials and services worth 22 million East German marks. See Grabner, "DDR-Beteiligung am Steinkohleprojekt Moatize," 259.

36. Landolf Scherzer, *Bom dia weißer Bruder: Erlebnisse am Sambesi* (Greifenverlag zu Rudolstadt, 1984), 167.

37. Ibid.

The PRM actively used artistic expressions to present the country in the socialist world. Typically, this form of cultural lobbying was organized by state-run institutions. In some instances, however, exhibitions were arranged through personal contacts between Maputo and Berlin. One such case is a photographic exhibition by the Mozambican photographer Ricardo Rangel, displayed in the foyer of the Palace of the Republic in Berlin in September 1983. Letters from the archive suggest that Kurt Löffler, the State Secretary at the Ministry of Culture, had personally invited Rangel and his wife, Beatrice, to visit East Germany, in connection with an exhibition of his photography in Berlin. Ricardo transported the photographs with him in his luggage; the GDR handled the appropriate framing and the creation of an exhibition catalog according to the photographer's specifications.[33]

COLLABORATIONS

Since 1978, East German staff were present in Moatize, the site of Mozambique's largest coal mining industry.[34] Through the implementation of new technologies and a transfer of know-how, Mozambique aimed to improve working conditions for miners and increase production. A direct collaboration had been established between the state-owned companies, the East German combine VEB Schwarze Pumpe, the VEB August Bebel Werk Zwickau and the coal mine CARBOMOC E.E. in Moatize. Beyond setting up new mining infrastructure, the VEB Schwarze Pumpe also planned and constructed a cultural center for the mine workers. The order for the construction came from the Solidarity Committee. In this way, East German donors' money financed the workers' cultural center.[35] The architecture resembled similar institutions across East German factories. The center consisted of a space for educational training, a bowling alley, a large canteen kitchen, and rooms for a drawing club and a photography club.[36] Even the wallpapers and pictures that decorated the Moatize cultural center came from the GDR.[37] In the spacious patio of the building, a brick barbeque was installed, a space of encounter removed from the infrastructures of mining.

While the design of the patio space and passageways may loosely be called "modernist," the primary focus in planning the center did not lie in its

---

Der Maler Malangatana Valente Ngwenya, der bei der Eröffnung anwesend war (Abb. 9), drückte in einem Interview mit ostdeutschen Journalisten seine Hoffnung aus, durch die Kunst neue Beziehungen zu knüpfen. Im Artikel heißt es: „Malangatana nennt auch die Ausstellung, […], eine Tür, von der er sich wünscht, daß sie nach beiden Seiten aufgehen soll."[30] Der „Kontakt mit mosambikanischer Kunst", so hoffe er, werde die Tür weit öffnen für einen gleichberechtigten Austausch zwischen beiden Ländern. Mankew V. Mahumana, dem wir in diesem Buch ein eigenes Kapitel widmen, war mit fünf Kunstwerken in der Ausstellung vertreten.[31] Vielleicht zum ersten Mal in beiden deutschen Staaten wurden mosambikanische Kunstwerke aus dem Kontext einer ethnografischen Sammlung herausgelöst und als zeitgenössische Positionen und Kommentare auf die damalige Zeit gezeigt.[32]

Die VRM nutzte künstlerische Ausdrucksformen, um das Land in der sozialistischen Welt zu präsentieren. In der Regel waren es staatliche Institutionen, die diese Form der kulturellen Lobbyarbeit organisierten. In einigen Fällen kamen Ausstellungen jedoch auch durch persönliche Kontakte zwischen Maputo und Berlin zustande. Ein solcher Fall ist eine Fotoausstellung des mosambikanischen Fotografen Ricardo Rangel, die im September 1983 im Foyer des Palastes der Republik in Berlin gezeigt wurde. Briefe aus dem Archiv deuten darauf hin, dass Kurt Löffler, der Staatssekretär im Ministerium für Kultur, Rangel und seine Frau Beatrice Rangel persönlich eingeladen hatte, die DDR zu besuchen und seine Fotografien in einer Ausstellung in Berlin zu zeigen. Ricardo Rangel transportierte die Fotografien in seinem Gepäck. Die DDR kümmerte sich um die Rahmung der Bilder und die Erstellung eines Ausstellungskatalogs nach Vorgaben des Fotografen.[33]

KOLLABORATIONEN

Seit 1978 waren Arbeiter·innen aus der DDR in Moatize, dem größtem Standort der Kohleindustrie Mosambiks tätig.[34] Durch die Einführung neuer Technologien und den Transfer von Know-how strebte Mosambik an, die Arbeitsbedingungen der Bergleute zu verbessern und die Produktion zu steigern. Zwischen den Staatsbetrieben, dem Kombinat VEB Schwarze Pumpe, dem VEB August Bebel Werk Zwickau und dem Kohlebergwerk CARBOMOC E. E. in Moatize war eine direkte Zusammenarbeit entstanden. Neben dem Aufbau einer neuen bergbaulichen Infrastruktur plante und errichtete der VEB Schwarze Pumpe auch ein

30. Maritta Tkalec und Klaus Ullrich, „Eine Tür zur Begegnung mit Freunden. Kunstausstellung aus Moçambique", in: *Neues Deutschland,* 12.1.1982, BArch DR 1 123/77.

31. „Artistas de Moçambique", hg. vom Ministerium für Bildung und Kultur von Mosambik (1981), BArch N 2841.

32. Außerdem wurde 1986 der Maler Malangatana Valente Ngwenya mit einer Einzelausstellung im GRASSI Museum für Völkerkunde geehrt. Zur Ausstellung wurde ein Katalog veröffentlicht: Renate Schmidt (Hg.), *Malangatana Valente Ngwenya: Malerei, Grafik, Zeichnungen,* Einzelausstellung im Museum für Völkerkunde Leipzig / Ministerium für Kultur der DDR, Zentrum für Kunstausstellungen der DDR, 1986.

33. „Hausnotiz" an Kurt Löffler, 4.8.1983; Schreiben der DDR-Botschaft in Mosambik, Maputo, an Kurt Löffler, 1.9.1982, BArch DR1/11646.

34. In den zwölf Jahren der Zusammenarbeit zwischen den DDR-Bergbauunternehmen und CARBOMOC arbeiteten rund

38. Łukasz Stanek, *Architecture in Global Socialism: Eastern Europe, West Africa, and the Middle East in the Cold War* (Princeton University Press, 2020), 15.

39. Letter from VEB Gaskombinat Schwarze Pumpe to the Ministry of Culture of the GDR, November 11, 1980, BArch DR 106/17.

40. Stephen A. Emerson, *The Battle for Mozambique: The FRELIMO-RENAMO Struggle, 1977–1992* (Helion, 2014), 38.

41. Ros Gray, *Cinemas of the Mozambican Revolution: Anti-Colonialism, Independence and Internationalism in Filmmaking, 1968–1991* (Boydell and Brewer, 2020).

architecture. It was not the type of showpiece building donated under Khrushchev's "gift diplomacy," as described by Łukasz Stanek with respect to the architecture exported in the 1960s.[38] A letter found in the archive suggests that "the Solidarity Committee of the GDR" had "defined key measures to improve social welfare and raise the level of intellectual and cultural work" in Moatize.[39] We need to bear in mind that the construction coincided with RENAMO's growing presence in the region. The coal mine and the surrounding area were a key battlefield in the civil war. Beginning in 1979, with the destruction of major bridges around the Tete-Moatize area by the colonial army of Rhodesia in support of RENAMO forces, insurgent activities in the region escalated throughout the 1980s.[40] The challenge of sustaining the mining industry was compounded by FRELIMO's concerns over potential loss of popular support. The cultural center, built and funded by East German institutions, undoubtedly conveyed a symbolic message that could bolster trust in the East German partnership and thus strengthen the geopolitical alignment. Beyond symbolism, it served as a space for political education under the auspices of FRELIMO. Accommodating 250 people, the main hall of the building functioned as a movie theater, which was also financed by the Solidarity Committee.

CINEMA AS CIRCULATION

Cinema was one of the most important cultural projects of FRELIMO.[41] Delving into the collaborations between the GDR and the PRM in the realm of film production would exceed the scope of this publication. Yet, we want to briefly pause to address the circulation of images. Images, whether in films, paintings, or murals, operated as a resource on the "cultural front" of both national and

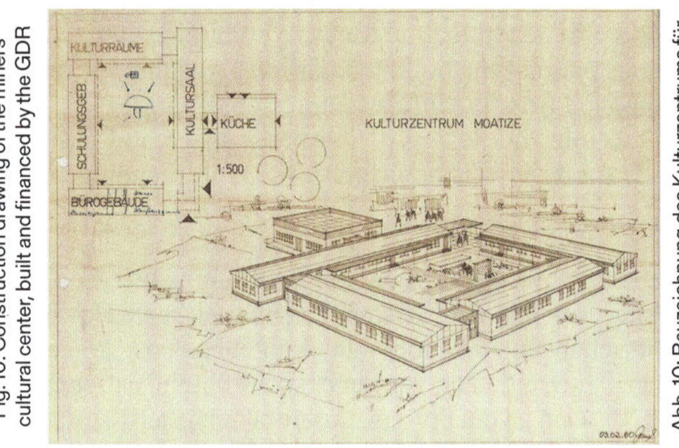

Fig. 10: Construction drawing of the miners' cultural center, built and financed by the GDR

Abb. 10: Bauzeichnung des Kulturzentrums für Bergarbeiter, gebaut und finanziert durch die DDR

Kulturzentrum für die Bergarbeiter. Der Bau entstand im Auftrag des Solidaritätskomitees. Das Kulturzentrum wurde also von Spendengeldern aus der DDR finanziert.[35] Die Architektur ähnelte den entsprechenden Einrichtungen in ostdeutschen Betrieben (Abb. 10). Das Zentrum bestand aus einem Schulungsraum, einer Kegelbahn, einer Großküche sowie Räumen für einen Zeichen- und einen Fotoclub.[36] Selbst die Tapeten und Bilder, die das Kulturzentrum Moatize schmückten, stammten aus der DDR.[37] Im großzügigen Innenhof des Gebäudes wurde ein gemauerter Grill installiert. Hier sollte ein Begegnungsraum abseits der Bergbauanlagen entstehen.

Die Gestaltung des Innenhofs und der Verbindungselemente können zwar als „moderne Architektur" gelesen werden, doch lag der Schwerpunkt bei der Planung des Zentrums nicht auf der Architektur. Es war nicht die Art von Vorzeigegebäude, die Łukasz Stanek erfasst hat und die im Zuge von Chruschtschows „Geschenkdiplomatie" in den 1960er Jahren entstanden.[38] Aus einem im Archiv entdeckten Brief geht hervor, dass „das Solikomitee der DDR" in Moatize „wesentliche Maßnahmen zur Verbesserung der sozialen Betreuung und zur Hebung des Niveaus der geistig-kulturellen Arbeit" veranlasst habe.[39] Der Bau des Gebäudes fiel mit der wachsenden Präsenz der RENAMO in der Region zusammen. Im sich verschärfenden Bürgerkrieg waren die Kohlemine und das umliegende Gebiet ein zentraler Kampfplatz. Ab 1979, mit der Zerstörung wichtiger Brücken im Gebiet von Tete-Moatize durch die rhodesische Kolonialarmee zur Unterstützung der RENAMO-Truppen, verschärften sich die Kampfhandlungen in der Region in den 1980er Jahren.[40] Die Herausforderung, die Bergbauindustrie aufrechtzuerhalten, wurde durch die Besorgnis der FRELIMO über den möglichen Verlust der Unterstützung seitens der Bevölkerung noch verstärkt. Das von DDR-Institutionen errichtete und finanzierte Kulturzentrum vermittelte zweifellos eine symbolische Botschaft, die das Vertrauen in die Partnerschaft stärken und damit

600 DDR-Bürger·innen in Moatize. Siehe Walter Grabner, „DDR-Beteiligung am Steinkohleprojekt Moatize", in: Matthias Voß (Hg.), *Wir haben Spuren hinterlassen! Die DDR in Mosambik. Erlebnisse, Erfahrungen und Erkenntnisse aus drei Jahrzehnten*, Münster: LIT Verlag 2005, S. 216–269, hier S. 268.

35. Laut Walter Grabner, der in der CARBOMOC-Mine arbeitete, unterstützte das Solidaritätskomitee die soziale Betreuung der Belegschaft mit Materialien und Dienstleistungen im Wert von 22 Millionen DDR-Mark. Siehe Grabner, „DDR-Beteiligung am Steinkohleprojekt Moatize", S. 259.

36. Landolf Scherzer, *Bom dia weißer Bruder: Erlebnisse am Sambesi*, Rudolstadt: Greifenverlag 1984, S. 167.

37. Ebd.

38. Łukasz Stanek, *Architecture in Global Socialism: Eastern Europe, West Africa, and the Middle East in the Cold War*, Princeton: Princeton University Press 2020, S. 15.

39. Brief des VEB Gaskombinat Schwarze

42. Doreen Mende, "The Image-Complex of Modernity's Grandchildren," in *Changes in Motion: A Journal,* ed. Laura Horelli (Archive Books, 2021), 155.

43. *Fünf Patronenhülsen* (Five Cartridges), directed by Frank Beyer (DEFA-Studio für Spielfilme, 1960). Statistics of the first "TKW" events, December 5, 1979, BArch DY13/2624.

transnational campaigns against the Western Bloc. Images brought closer a world that had not yet fully materialized and thus strengthened hopes and moral concepts that were worth fighting for—a future socialist Mozambique.

> All these aspects compose the condition for an "image-complex" that demands from us to enter the image beyond vision, connecting media with circulation, politics, lived experience, potential history and infrastructures: Instead of speaking about the image as an object, it is helpful to consider the image as a complex, both in infrastructural as well as transgenerational terms.[42]

The infrastructure provided by the GDR was not only of a technical nature. In line with Doreen Mende's conceptualization of the image-complex, film technology presents itself as an infrastructure that bound together East Germany and Mozambique in the image itself. In their depiction of a communist war hero, East German films screened in Mozambique asked the viewer for an emotional response, an emotional alliance with the struggle for a socialist society, just as the films from and about Mozambique screened in the GDR asked for the East German audience's active solidarity and empathy.

On November 24, 1979, around 4,000 people watched the DEFA (the GDR's state-owned film studios) film *Fünf Patronenhülsen* (Five Cartridges) in the rural area around Manhiça.[43] The film depicts the fight of the communist militia in the Spanish Civil War. The German leader of the battalion sacrifices himself to save others, leaving a final message for his comrades urging them to persevere and not surrender. Thousands of Mozambicans, not only in Manhiça but in many other towns and villages, watched the East German film in the early 1980s. DEFA

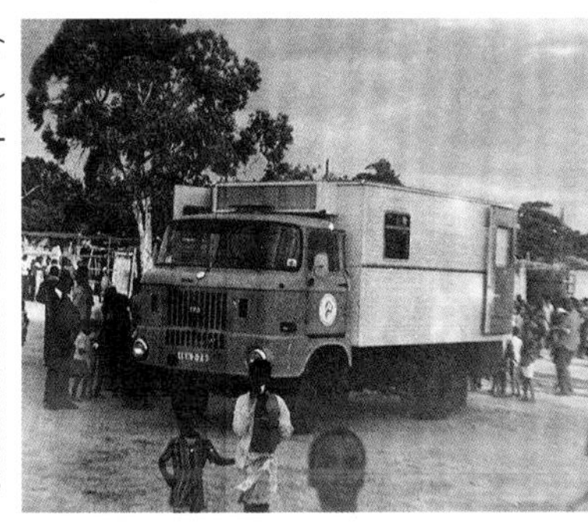

Fig. 11: The GDR's mobile cinema truck in Mozambique
Fig. 12: Drawing by Mankew V. Mahumana on an invitation card from the National Cinema Institute of Mozambique (INC)

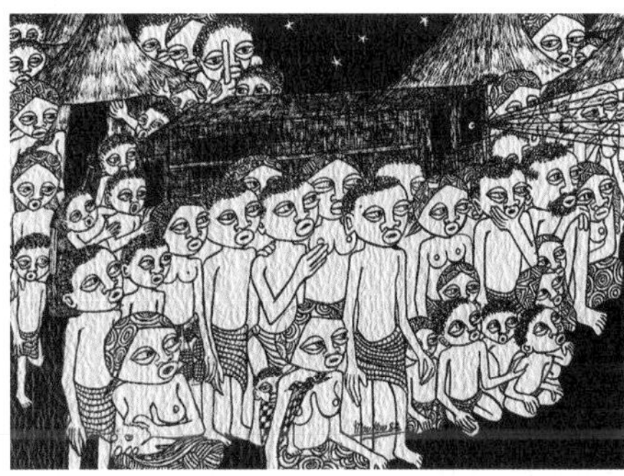

Abb. 11: Der Ton-Kino-Wagen der DDR in Mosambik
Abb. 12: Zeichnung von Mankew V. Mahumana auf der Einladungskarte des Mosambikanischen Filminstituts (INC)

die geopolitische Ausrichtung bekräftigen sollte. Über die Symbolik hinaus diente es als Raum für politische Bildung unter der Ägide der FRELIMO. Der Hauptsaal des Gebäudes bot Platz für 250 Personen und konnte als Kinosaal genutzt werden, dessen Ausstattung ebenfalls vom Solidaritätskomitee finanziert wurde.

KINO ALS MITTEL DER VERBREITUNG

Das Kino war eines der wichtigsten kulturellen Projekte der FRELIMO.[41] Ein tiefergehender Blick auf die Kooperationen zwischen der DDR und der VRM im Bereich der Filmproduktion würde den Rahmen sprengen. Dennoch wollen wir kurz innehalten und uns der Zirkulation von Bildern zuwenden. Bilder, ob in Filmen, Gemälden oder Wandmalereien, dienten als Ressource an der „kulturellen Front" der nationalen und transnationalen Kampagnen gegen den Westblock. Bilder brachten eine Welt näher, die sich noch nicht vollständig verwirklicht hatte, und waren auf diese Weise Rückenwind für Hoffnungen und Moralvorstellungen, für die es wert war zu kämpfen – ein zukünftiges sozialistisches Mosambik.

> „All diese Aspekte bilden die Voraussetzung für einen ‚Bildkomplex', der uns auffordert, das Bild über das Visuelle hinaus zu erfassen und Medien im Zusammenhang mit ihrer Verbreitung, der Politik, der gelebten Erfahrung, der möglichen Geschichte und den Infrastrukturen zu betrachten: Anstatt über das Bild als Objekt zu sprechen, ist es hilfreich, das Bild als einen Komplex zu betrachten, sei es in infrastruktureller oder in generationenübergreifender Hinsicht."[42]

Die von der DDR bereitgestellte Infrastruktur war nicht nur technischer Natur. In Anlehnung an Doreen Mendes Konzept des Bildkomplexes stellt sich die Filmtechnologie als eine Infrastruktur dar, die die DDR und Mosambik über das Bild selbst miteinander verband. Die in Mosambik gezeigten DDR-Filme verlangten

Pumpe an das Zentrum für kulturelle Auslandsarbeit, 11.11.1980, BArch DR 106/17.

40. Stephen A. Emerson, *The Battle for Mozambique: The FRELIMO-RENAMO Struggle, 1977–1992*, Warwick: Helion and Company 2014, S. 38.

41. Ros Gray, *Cinemas of the Mozambican Revolution: Anti-Colonialism, Independence and Internationalism*, Martlesham: Boydell & Brewer 2020.

42. Doreen Mende, „Der Bildkomplex der Enkelinnen und Enkel der Moderne", in: Laura Horelli (Hg.), *Changes in Direction. A Journal*, Berlin: Archive Books 2021, S. 249–257, hier S. 252.

44. Agreement between the ideological work department of FRELIMO's central committee and the International Friendship League, May 1978, BArch DR1/17805.

45. Ibid.

46. *Für den Frieden ist keine Anstrengung zu groß* [No Effort Is Too Great for Peace] (Camera DDR, 1983); *Genügt es, besorgt zu sein?* [Is It Enough to Be Worried?] (DEFA-Studio für Dokumentarfilme, 1982). Annual Report for 1983, BArch DY13/2881.

47. Interview with Dr. Ulrich Weishaupt and Wolfgang Wagner on Harald Heinke's activities in Maputo, Berlin, June 28, 2022.

movies were screened with the mobile cinema truck that traveled across the country and was managed by the International Friendship League in cooperation with the Instituto Nacional de Cinema (National Cinema Institute of Mozambique, INC), based in Maputo (fig. 11). A contract between the two institutions specified that the East German side would provide, "free of charge," the truck, screening technology, and training for Mozambican projectionists to operate the technology independently.[44] Additionally, the contract stated that the Liga für Völkerfreundschaft "will make available films and publications in Portuguese that lend themselves to supporting FRELIMO's political-ideological work."[45] In reports, Harald Heinke, representative of the Liga in Maputo, reflected on the political impact of the different films. In the documentary *Für den Frieden ist keine Anstrengung zu groß,* he concluded: "This movie is not suitable…. The passivity of the people in the film (listening) makes it hard to motivate viewers to get involved" and instead proposed using the film *Genügt es, besorgt zu sein?*, which included scenes of mass demonstrations.[46]

Did Mozambican spectators find themselves represented in these movies, did they feel called upon to act, watching German communists fight? The assessments of the impact of DEFA films in Mozambique can hardly be taken as an account of the feelings and sensations that the films elicited. Rather, the above quote gives us an idea of the nature of the cultural-political activities of East German institutions in Mozambique. The use of East German cultural products, in particular film and the underlying technology, could be interpreted as quasi-military infrastructure aimed at supporting FRELIMO forces and politics in the civil war. Film was conceived of as a technique of psychological warfare by both superpowers of the Cold War. The distribution of media was a core element used by both sides to bolster either anti-capitalist or anti-communist sentiments. Yet, when we read between the lines of the reports, it is also the very personal voice of Harald Heinke who speaks through the letters—the voice of someone who practiced his solidarity with the young nation through his daily encounters and activities.[47] Beyond serving the national interests of the GDR, Heinke identified his own mandate with the needs of FRELIMO. His writing reflects a deep

in ihrer Darstellung eines kommunistischen Kriegshelden eine emotionale Reaktion des Zuschauers, eine emotionale Verbundenheit mit dem Kampf für eine sozialistische Gesellschaft. Genauso forderten auch die in der DDR gezeigten Filme aus und über Mosambik die aktive Solidarität und Empathie des ostdeutschen Publikums ein.

Am 24. November 1979 sahen rund 4000 Menschen in der ländlichen Umgebung von Manhiça den DEFA-Film *5 Patronenhülsen*.[43] Der Film schildert den Kampf der kommunistischen Miliz im Spanischen Bürgerkrieg. Der deutsche Anführer des Bataillons opfert sich, um andere zu retten, und hinterlässt seinen Kameraden eine letzte Botschaft, in der er sie auffordert, durchzuhalten und nicht zu kapitulieren. Nicht nur in Manhiça, sondern auch in vielen anderen Städten und Dörfern sahen Anfang der 1980er Jahre Tausende Menschen in Mosambik diesen Film. Die DEFA-Filme wurden mit einem mobilen Kinowagen vorgeführt, der durch das Land reiste und von der Liga für Völkerfreundschaft in Zusammenarbeit mit dem INC (Instituto Nacional de Cinema) mit Sitz in Maputo betrieben wurde (Abb. 11). In einem Vertrag zwischen den beiden Institutionen wurde festgelegt, dass vonseiten der DDR der Lastwagen, die Vorführtechnik und die Ausbildung der mosambikanischen Filmvorführer zur selbstständigen Bedienung der Technik kostenlos zur Verfügung gestellt wurden.[44] Außerdem stellte die Liga für Völkerfreundschaft laut Vertrag „Filme und Publikationen in portugiesischer Sprache zur Verfügung, die geeignet sind, die politisch-ideologische Arbeit der FRELIMO zu unterstützen".[45] In Berichten zog Harald Heinke, Vertreter der Liga in Maputo, Bilanz über die politische Wirkung der verschiedenen Filme. Sein Fazit zu dem Dokumentarfilm *Für den Frieden ist keine Anstrengung zu groß*: „Dieser Film ist nicht geeignet […] die Passivität der Menschen im Film (zuhören) kann die Zuschauer kaum zu Engagement motivieren". Er schlug stattdessen den Film *Genügt es, besorgt zu sein?* vor, der Szenen von Massendemonstrationen enthält.[46]

Fühlten sich die mosambikanischen Zuschauer·innen in diesen Filmen repräsentiert, fühlten sie sich zum Handeln aufgerufen, wenn sie deutsche Kommunist·innen kämpfen sahen? Die Einschätzungen zur Wirkung der DEFA-Filme in Mosambik können nicht die Gefühle und Empfindungen reflektieren, die die Filme hervorgerufen haben. Das obige Zitat vermittelt uns vielmehr eine Vorstellung von der Art der kulturpolitischen Aktivitäten von DDR-Institutionen in Mosambik. Die

43. *5 Patronenhülsen* (DEFA-Studio für Spielfilme, 1960), Regie: Frank Beyer. Statistik der ersten „TKW"-Veranstaltungen, 5.12.1979, BArch DY13/2624. Die Deutsche Film Aktiengesellschaft (DEFA) war das staatseigene Filmstudio der DDR.

44. Abkommen zwischen der Abteilung für ideologische Arbeit des Zentralkomitees der FRELIMO und der Liga für Völkerfreundschaft, Mai 1978, BArch DR1/17805.

45. Ebd.

46. Jahresbericht für 1983, BArch DY13/2881. *Für den Frieden ist keine Anstrengung zu groß* (Camera DDR, 1983); *Genügt es, besorgt zu sein?* (DEFA-Studio für Dokumentarfilme, 1982), Regie: Rolf Hempel.

48. Inês Cordeiro Dias, "Filming the Nation in Post-Independence Mozambique," *Third Text* 34, no. 4 (2020): 540.

49. See Ros Gray, introduction to *Cinemas of the Mozambican Revolution*, 1–14.

50. Interview conducted by Harald Heinke, archived in BArch N 2841.

respect, and sometimes an admiration, for the work of the Mozambican Film Institute directed toward realizing the "cultural revolution" that Graça Machel called for. In fact, through FRELIMO's investment in the INC, Mozambique became the first African country to become completely independent in terms of film production.[48] In the early 1980s, the INC was a space of knowledge sharing and creative experimentation focused on unleashing the emancipatory potential of film and decolonizing filmmaking.[49]

Pedro Pimenta, deputy director of the INC, was interviewed by Heinke on January 20, 1982.[50] We print an excerpt from the conversation here:

> Mozambican cineasts currently face the problem of how to create the conditions necessary to produce a truly Mozambican cinema that is part of Mozambican culture. This requires a new language, new forms of communication in cinema, a new rhythm, a real transformation of cinema. And that is a long process…. In 1975, 95 percent of the population was illiterate. Cinema therefore has a role to play within the country's information media, because cinema reaches an audience that other information media do not…. This is the only form that exists to reach the population in the community villages, in the state farms in the countryside…. Since colonialism, people have known no alternative, and now the ideological conflict continues in the same areas. The people of these areas often discover through cinema that Mozambique is independent.

From the same interview, we learn that in 1982 six mobile cinema units from the Soviet Union and one mobile cinema truck from the GDR were operated to screen Mozambican and foreign films in rural areas. "Two to three thousand viewers attend each screening, a significant number. And that proves the importance of cinema, its popularity, and the need for more mobile cinema technology," Pedro Pimenta concludes. The movies themselves, the film posters, the screening technology, and the training to operate it were subsidized by East Germany for FRELIMO's information campaign in Mozambique. The infrastructure around the mobile

kulturellen Mittel, insbesondere Filme und Filmtechnik aus der DDR, können mitunter als militärische Infrastruktur zur Unterstützung der FRELIMO-Kräfte und der Politik im Bürgerkrieg interpretiert werden. Kinofilme wurden von beiden Supermächten im Kalten Krieg als Technik der psychologischen Kriegsführung gesehen. Die Verbreitung von Medien war ein Kernelement, das von beiden Seiten eingesetzt wurde, um entweder antikapitalistische oder antikommunistische Stimmungen zu verstärken. Doch wenn wir zwischen den Zeilen lesen, spricht auch die ganz persönliche Stimme von Harald Heinke aus den Berichten: jemand, der in seinen täglichen Begegnungen und Aktivitäten seine Solidarität mit der jungen Nation praktizierte.[47] Heinke vertrat zwar die nationalen Interessen der DDR in Mosambik, darüber hinaus hatte er allerdings auch die Bedürfnisse der FRELIMO im Blick. Seine Schriften zeugen von einem tiefen Respekt und manchmal auch von Bewunderung für die Arbeit des mosambikanischen Filminstituts, das die von Graça Machel geforderte „kulturelle Revolution" verwirklichen wollte. Tatsächlich wurde Mosambik durch die Investitionen der FRELIMO in das INC zum ersten afrikanischen Land, das im Bereich der Filmproduktion völlige Unabhängigkeit erlangte.[48] In den frühen 1980er Jahren war das INC ein Ort des Wissensaustauschs und des kreativen Experimentierens mit dem Ziel, das emanzipatorische Potenzial des Films zu nutzen und das Filmschaffen zu dekolonisieren.[49]

Pedro Pimenta, stellvertretender Direktor des INC, wurde von Harald Heinke am 20. Januar 1982 interviewt.[50] Wir drucken hier einen Auszug aus dem Gespräch ab:

> „Das Problem, das sich gegenwärtig den moçambikanischen Cineasten stellt ist, wie man die Bedingungen schaffen kann, um ein wirklich moçambikanisches Kino zu schaffen, welches Bestandteil der moçambikanischen Kultur ist. Das bedingt eine neue Sprache, neue Kommunikationsformen im Kino, einen neuen Rhythmus, eine wirkliche Umgestaltung des Kinos. Und das ist ein langer Prozeß. […] 1975 waren 95 % der Bevölkerung Analphabeten. Das Kino hat also eine Rolle zu spielen innerhalb der Informationsorgane des Landes, weil das Kino ein Publikum erreicht, welches andere Informationsmedien nicht erreichen […]. Das ist die einzige Form, die existiert, um die

47. Interview mit Dr. Ulrich Weishaupt und Wolfgang Wagner über die Aktivitäten von Harald Heinke in Maputo (Berlin, 28.6.2022).

48. Inês Cordeiro Dias, „Filming the Nation in Post-Independence Mozambique", in: *Third Text*, 34 (2020), No. 4–5, S. 538–550, hier S. 540.

49. Siehe Gray, „Introduction", in: dies., *Cinemas of the Mozambican Revolution*, S. 1–14.

50. Interview geführt von Harald Heinke (ins Deutsche übersetzt), archiviert in BArch N 2841.

cinema truck could turn a flat plain into a lively cinema space where films from both countries were shown. Regardless of how we assess these and similar cultural events, they established a socialist visual culture with revolutionary ambitions and thus laid the groundwork for a shared political identity. In our conversations with people from Mozambique and the former GDR who experienced the countries' collaborations firsthand, this commonality remains present in how they speak of the other.

"Why study the cultural byproducts of a failed political alliance?" This is the question with which Rossen Djagalov introduces his book, *From Internationalism to Postcolonialism: Literature and Cinema Between the Second and the Third Worlds* (2020). Djagalov argues that what used to be called the "Second" and the "Third World" have been mutually constitutive. He observed that the circulation of literature and film allowed readers in the "Third World" to inhabit the "world revolution" and creatively appropriate narratives of socialist success for their own purposes. When we examine how Mozambican realities were reported in East Germany and how East German realities were reported in Mozambique, hierarchies between the "knowledgable" and the "learner" were reproduced. Nevertheless, each country highlighted the other's accomplishments. The work of East German authors, journalists, and artists who engaged with the situation in Mozambique cultivated empathy. Examples include the travel reportages by Ursula Püschel, Landolf Scherzer, and Walter Michel, as well as the works of the sculptor Wolfgang Eckardt. In 1979, Reclam (Leipzig) published the book *Gedichte aus Moçambique*. Before independence, it was all but impossible for Mozambican literary works to find distribution channels. The anthology was the first of its kind in the German-speaking world. It presents poems that worship the land and condemn subjugation, that dream of freedom and fear the deadly work in the mines.

In 1979, when the East German journalist Walter Michel was traveling through Mozambique, Samora Machel was attending the 6th Summit Conference of Non-Aligned States in Havana. The military conflicts in Africa and the Middle East, fueled by the struggle of the superpowers for spheres of influence in resource-rich countries, became the central theme of the conference. In his speech,

> Bevölkerung in den Gemeinschaftsdörfern zu erreichen, in den Staatsbetrieben auf dem Land […]. Seit dem Kolonialismus haben die Leute keine Alternative gekannt und jetzt geht der ideologische Konflikt in denselben Zonen weiter. Die Leute dieser Gebiete entdecken oft durch das Kino, daß Moçambik unabhängig ist."

Aus demselben Interview erfahren wir, dass 1982 sechs mobile Kinoeinheiten aus der Sowjetunion und ein mobiler Kinowagen aus der DDR eingesetzt wurden, um mosambikanische und ausländische Filme in ländlichen Gebieten vorzuführen. „In jede Veranstaltung kommen zwei- bis dreitausend Zuschauer, was sehr viel ist. Und das beweist die Bedeutung des Kinos, seine Popularität und die Notwendigkeit, die technischen Mittel des Mobilen Kinos zu erhöhen", so Pedro Pimenta abschließend. Mit den Filmen selbst, den Filmplakaten, der Vorführtechnik und der Ausbildung der Filmvorführer subventionierte die DDR die Kampagne der FRELIMO in Mosambik. Die Technik des mobilen Kinowagens konnte eine flache Ebene in einen lebendigen Kinoraum verwandeln, in dem Filme aus beiden Ländern gezeigt wurden. Unabhängig davon, wie wir diese und ähnliche Kulturveranstaltungen bewerten, beförderten sie eine sozialistische visuelle Kultur mit revolutionären Ambitionen, die den Beginn einer gemeinsamen politischen Identität markierte. In unseren Gesprächen mit Menschen aus Mosambik und der ehemaligen DDR, die die Zusammenarbeit der beiden Länder persönlich miterlebt haben, bleiben die Gemeinsamkeiten präsent, wenn sie von der jeweiligen Partnerseite sprechen.

„Wozu die kulturellen Nebenprodukte eines gescheiterten politischen Bündnisses untersuchen?" Mit dieser Frage leitet Rossen Djagalov sein Buch *From Internationalism to Postcolonialism: Literature and Cinema Between the Second and the Third Worlds* (2020) ein. Djagalov argumentiert, dass das, was früher als „Zweite" und „Dritte Welt" bezeichnet wurde, sich wechselseitig geprägt hat. Er stellte fest, dass sich Leser·innen in der „Dritten Welt" durch die Verbreitung von Literatur und Film die „Weltrevolution" und die Erzählungen über den sozialistischen Aufbau kreativ aneignen konnten. Wenn wir genau hinschauen, wie über die mosambikanischen Realitäten in der DDR und wie über ostdeutsche Realitäten in Mosambik berichtet wurde, sehen wir, dass die Hierarchie zwischen den „Wissenden" und den „Lernenden" reproduziert wurde.

Samora Machel made a plea for the socialist camp. Describing the reaction of GDR citizens to Machel's speech, Walter Michel writes: "We members of the small FDJ delegation were also enthusiastic about his speech, which spoke of passion and confidence in victory, as well as internationalism and solidarity with other states and peoples."[51] Michel's reportage is written in alignment with the official East German position and may not necessarily reflect individual perceptions. However, the empathy of East German youth toward Mozambican losses in the war was also shared by many East German citizens whom we interviewed for the book. They had worked in Mozambique during the 1980s, and their stories underscored a genuine connection to the country's struggles.

DEEPENING ASYMMETRIES

If one were to come up with a periodization of global socialism, 1979, the year in which the PRM and the GDR intensified their relations on all levels, was paralleled by the dwindling force of socialist internationalism and the "Third Worldist movement." Collective strategies from the "Third World" demanding a broad international transformation that encompassed decolonization and modernization—a call for a new world order—had reached its climax. When the Havana summit took place in September 1979, ninety-three countries participated. Yet not only did Afghanistan become the site of a proxy war between the superpowers in the months that followed but armed conflicts in Nicaragua, Angola, Ethiopia, Mozambique, and other countries turned into the new battlegrounds on which the Cold War was fought in the 1980s. Shortly after Mozambique entered the international diplomatic scene, the room to maneuver contracted from all sides. By the early 1980s, the transnational movement that forged a path towards South-South Cooperation and economic self-determination was

51. Walter Michel, *Lieder vom Sambesi: Impressionen aus der Volksrepublik Moçambique* (Verlag Neues Leben, 1984), 71–72.

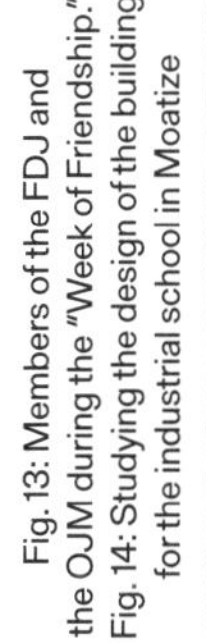

Fig. 13: Members of the FDJ and the OJM during the "Week of Friendship."
Fig. 14: Studying the design of the building for the industrial school in Moatize

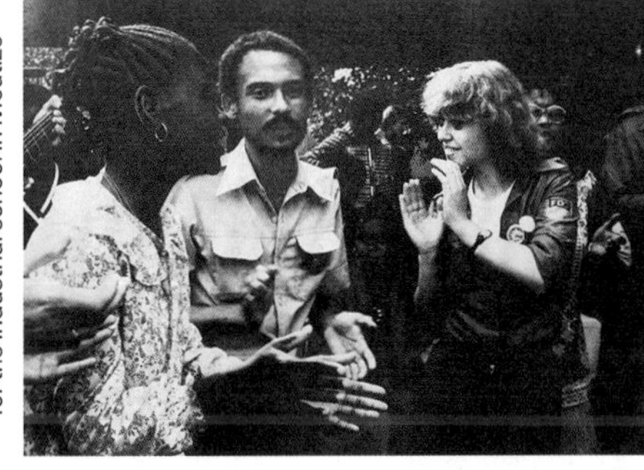

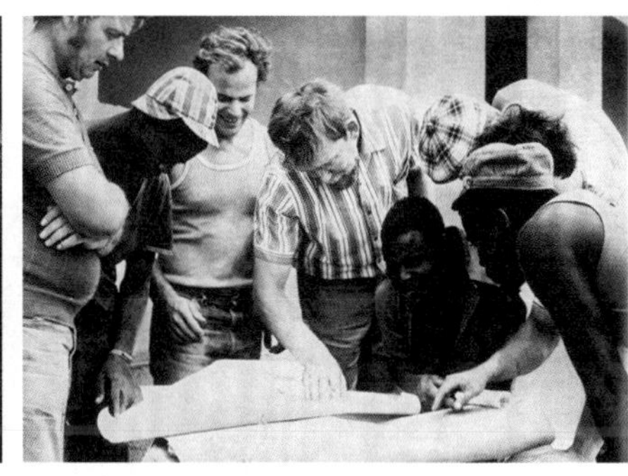

Abb. 13: Mitglieder der FDJ und der OJM während der „Woche der Freundschaft".
Abb. 14: Diskussion über den Entwurfs des Gebäudes für die Industrieschule in Moatize

Nichtsdestotrotz haben beide Länder die Errungenschaften des jeweils anderen Landes hervorgehoben. Ostdeutsche Autor·innen, Journalist·innen und Künstler·innen, die sich in ihren Werken mit der Situation in Mosambik auseinandersetzten, beförderten mit ihren Werken Empathie für das Land. Beispiele sind die Reisereportagen von Ursula Püschel, Landolf Scherzer und Walter Michel sowie die Arbeiten des Bildhauers Wolfgang Eckardt. Im Jahr 1979 erschien bei Reclam (Leipzig) das Buch *Gedichte aus Moçambique*. In der Zeit vor der Unabhängigkeit hatten literarische Werke aus Mosambik kaum Wege der Veröffentlichung gefunden. Die Anthologie war die erste ihrer Art im deutschsprachigen Raum. Darin waren Gedichte versammelt, die das Land als Heimat besingen und die Unterwerfung verurteilen, die von Freiheit träumen und die Furcht vor der mörderischen Arbeit in den Minen zum Ausdruck bringen.

Im Jahr 1979, als der ostdeutsche Journalist Walter Michel durch Mosambik reiste, nahm Samora Machel an dem VI. Gipfeltreffen der Blockfreien Staaten in Havanna teil. Die militärischen Konflikte in Afrika und im Nahen Osten, die durch das Ringen der Supermächte um Einflusssphären in rohstoffreichen Ländern angeheizt wurden, waren das zentrale Thema der Konferenz. Samora Machel plädierte in seiner Rede für das sozialistische Lager. Über die Reaktion der DDR-Bürger·innen auf Samora Machels Rede schreibt Walter Michel: „Auch wir Mitglieder der kleinen FDJ-Delegation begeisterten uns an seinen Ausführungen, aus denen Leidenschaft und Siegeszuversicht, aber auch Internationalismus und solidarische Haltung zu anderen Staaten und Völkern sprachen."[51] Walter Michels Reportage stand im Einklang mit der offiziellen Position der DDR und muss nicht unbedingt individuelle Wahrnehmungen widerspiegeln. Die Empathie der ostdeutschen Jugend gegenüber den Verlusten Mosambiks im Bürgerkrieg wurde jedoch auch von vielen DDR-Bürger·innen geteilt, die wir für dieses Buch interviewt haben. Sie hatten in den 1980er Jahren in Mosambik gearbeitet, und ihre Erzählungen drücken noch heute ihre Verbundenheit mit dem Land aus.

51. Walter Michel, *Lieder vom Sambesi. Impressionen aus der Volksrepublik Moçambique*, Berlin: Verlag Neues Leben 1984, S. 71–72.

52. For background information on this shift, see Odd A. Westad, *The Global Cold War: Third World Interventions and the Making of Our Times* (Cambridge University Press, 2005); Jeremy Friedman, introduction to *Ripe for Revolution: Building Socialism in the Third World* (Harvard University Press, 2021).

53. Marcia C. Schenck, *Remembering African Labor Migration to the Second World: Socialist Mobilities Between Angola, Mozambique, and East Germany* (Springer Nature, 2023).

beginning to fall apart. Many member countries of the Non-Aligned Movement strengthened their ties to the Soviet Union. The "solidarity" of the Socialist Bloc came with strings attached. From 1979 onwards, the Soviet Union faced economic stagnation, and the GDR slid into a severe debt crisis. Hence, partner countries such as Algeria, Angola, Ethiopia, and Mozambique were targeted more and more for the supply of cheap raw materials and a sales market for their own exports.[52]

Imagine the following scene: two high-ranking representatives from the East German delegation visit a metalworking shop in Maputo. The workers are concentrated on the mechanical movement of the machines; they keep working, diligent and dedicated. On the workbench stands a pennant with the GDR flag. Willi Stoph, deputy chief of state of the GDR, presents the workers with a gift: a carpet with the heads of Marx, Engels, and Lenin. The three men's stern gazes point in one direction.

The scene described above is from the film *Begegnungen der Freundschaft Mocambique* (Friendship Encounters in Mozambique), shot in 1979 in Maputo. The DEFA documentary captures the meetings and the agreements made during the visit of the GDR state delegation in February 1979, when bilateral treaties were signed that initiated the placement of Mozambican workers in East German state-owned companies. The PRM expected the workers to return with a vocational training, as exemplary workers, men and women that would represent the ideal of the "New Man"—the *novo homem*.[53]

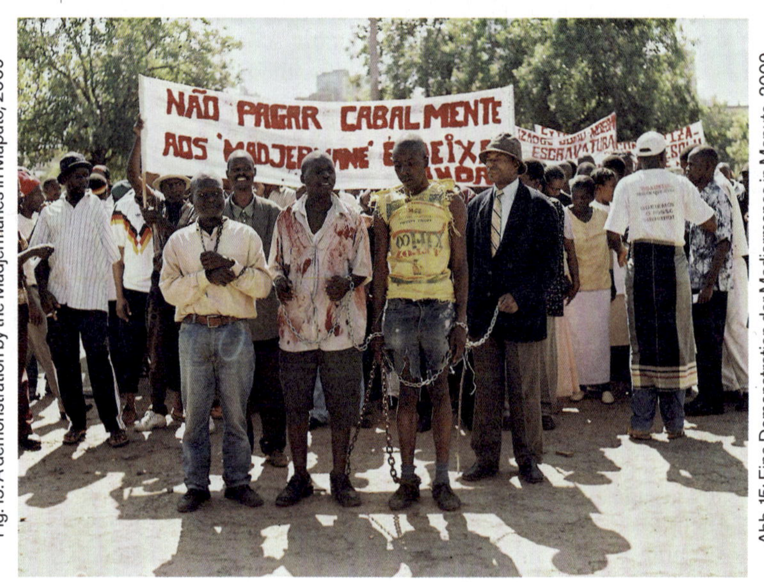

Fig. 15: A demonstration by the Madjermanes in Maputo, 2009

Abb. 15: Eine Demonstration der Madjermanes in Maputo, 2009

ZUNEHMENDE ASYMMETRIEN

Wollte man eine Periodisierung des globalen Sozialismus vornehmen, so zeichnete sich ausgerechnet im Jahr 1979, in dem die VRM und die DDR ihre Beziehungen auf allen Ebenen intensivierten, der schwindende Einfluss des sozialistischen Internationalismus und der „Dritte-Welt-Bewegung" ab. Die kollektiven Strategien aus der „Dritten Welt" mit der Forderung nach einer tiefgreifenden internationalen Transformation, die Dekolonialisierung und Modernisierung umfasste – die Forderung nach einer neuen Weltordnung –, hatten ihren Höhepunkt erreicht. Als im September 1979 in Havanna das sechste Gipfeltreffen der Bewegung der Blockfreien Staaten stattfand, nahmen 93 Länder daran teil. Doch in den darauffolgenden Monaten wurde nicht nur Afghanistan zum Schauplatz eines Stellvertreterkriegs zwischen den Supermächten. Bewaffnete Konflikte in Nicaragua, Angola, Äthiopien, Mosambik und anderen Ländern waren die neuen Schauplätze, auf denen der Kalte Krieg in den 1980er Jahren ausgetragen wurde. Kurz nachdem Mosambik die internationale diplomatische Bühne betreten hatte, wurde der Handlungsspielraum der Regierung von allen Seiten eingeengt. Anfang der 1980er Jahre begann die transnationale Bewegung zu zerfallen, die sich für die Süd-Süd-Kooperation und für eine wirtschaftliche Selbstbestimmung der Länder des globalen Südens eingesetzt hatte. Viele Mitgliedsländer der Bewegung der Blockfreien Staaten verstärkten ihre Bindung an die Sowjetunion. Die „Solidarität" des sozialistischen Blocks brachte aber auch Nachteile mit sich. Ab 1979 stagnierte die Wirtschaft der Sowjetunion und die DDR geriet in eine schwere Schuldenkrise. Daher nahmen sie ihre Partnerländer wie Algerien, Angola, Äthiopien oder Mosambik immer stärker ins Visier, um sich mit billigen Rohstoffen zu versorgen und einen Absatzmarkt für die eigenen Exporte zu schaffen.[52]

52. Für Hintergrundinformationen zu diesem Wandel siehe Odd Arne Westad, *The Global Cold War: Third World Interventions and the Making of Our Times*, Cambridge: Cambridge University Press 2005; Jeremy Friedman, *Ripe for Revolution: Building Socialism in the Third World*, Cambridge, MA: Harvard University Press 2021.

54. On Mozambique's debt to the GDR and the retention of workers' wages, see Almuth Berger, "Vertragsarbeiter: Arbeiter der Freundschaft? Die Verhandlungen in Maputo 1990," in Voß, *Wir haben Spuren hinterlassen!*, 512–29. Ralf Straßburg, "Zahlen und ihre Deutungen: Blicke aus Deutschland", conference presentation, February 23, 2019, https://vertragsarbeit-mosambik-ddr.de/konferenz_video/was-sagen-die-zahlen-und-was-sagen-sie-nicht/.

From 1979 to 1989, around 21,000 young Mozambicans arrived in East Germany to work for state-owned companies and receive a training. A part of their wages (40–60 percent) was held back. They were told that they would receive this sum of money upon their return to Mozambique. Most workers never received the missing part of their incomes. The money they had earned was used to pay off their country's debt. The agreements on "economic cooperation" between the GDR and Mozambique furthered the dependence of Mozambique throughout the 1980s—driven by a growing debt burden, a debt that had risen to a total of DM440 million by 1990.[54] The workers who returned to Mozambique are today known as Madjermanes (the Germans). For the past thirty years, Madjermanes have demonstrated in front of the Labor Ministry of Mozambique to demand the payment of outstanding wages. In one of their protests, four workers put chains around their wrists and ankles and colored their shirts with red paint. Since it was revealed that their money was used to pay the state's debt, workers began to frame their role as "state slaves," accusing their government of having sold their labor to the GDR just as the Portuguese colonial government had sold Mozambicans' labor in the decades before independence.

Many of the Madjermanes struggle daily to make a living in today's Mozambique. Their view back to the 1980s is often accompanied by nostalgia. They retain a strong sympathy for Eastern Germany, where they spent a part of their youth. Joyful memories of this time sit next to memories of the racism they had

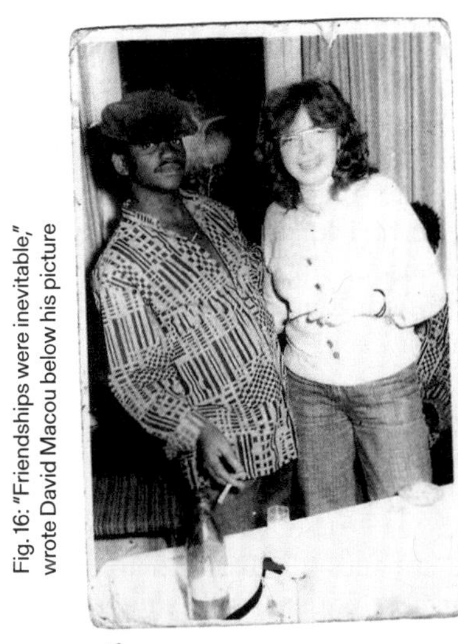

Fig. 16: "Friendships were inevitable," wrote David Macou below his picture

Abb. 16: „Freundschaften waren unvermeidlich", schrieb David Macou unter seinem Bild

Amizades eram enivitaveis na fortificação da cooperação entre os dois povos 1986

Stellen Sie sich die folgende Szene vor:

Zwei hochrangige Vertreter der DDR-Delegation besuchen einen metallverarbeitenden Betrieb in Maputo. Die Arbeiter konzentrieren sich auf die mechanische Bewegung der Maschinen, sie arbeiten fleißig und engagiert weiter. Auf der Werkbank steht ein DDR-Wimpel. Willi Stoph, der Stellvertreter des Staatsoberhaupts der DDR, überreicht den Arbeitern ein Geschenk: einen Teppich mit den Köpfen von Marx, Engels und Lenin. Ihre ernsten Blicke sind in eine Richtung gerichtet.

Die oben beschriebene Szene stammt aus dem Film *Begegnungen der Freundschaft Moçambique*, der 1979 in Maputo gedreht wurde. Die DEFA-Produktion dokumentiert die Begegnungen und die Vereinbarungen, die im Februar 1979 während des Besuchs der DDR-Staatsdelegation getroffen wurden, als bilaterale Verträge über den Einsatz mosambikanischer Arbeiter·innen in ostdeutschen Staatsbetrieben unterzeichnet wurden. Die VRM erwartete, dass die Arbeiter·innen mit einer Berufsausbildung zurückkehren würden, als Vorbilder, die das Ideal des „Neuen Menschen" – des novo homem – repräsentieren würden.[53]

Von 1979 bis 1989 kamen rund 21 000 junge Mosambikaner·innen in die DDR, um in volkseigenen Betrieben zu arbeiten und eine Ausbildung zu erhalten. Ein Teil ihrer Löhne (40 bis 60 %) wurde einbehalten, mit der Zusicherung, dass sie diesen Betrag bei ihrer Rückkehr nach Mosambik erhalten würden. Doch sie haben den fehlenden Lohn nie gesehen. Das Geld, das sie verdient hatten, wurde stattdessen zur Tilgung der Schulden ihres Landes verwendet. Die Vereinbarungen zur „wirtschaftlichen Zusammenarbeit" zwischen der DDR und Mosambik

53. Vgl. Marcia C. Schenck, *Remembering African Labor Migration to the Second World: Socialist Mobilities Between Angola, Mozambique, and East Germany*, Berlin: Springer Nature 2023.

55. Christian Saehrendt, *Kunst im Kampf für das "Sozialistische Weltsystem": Auswärtige Kulturpolitik der DDR in Afrika und Nahost* (Franz Steiner Verlag, 2017), 103.

56. Carlos Fernandes, "Intellectual Legacies, Political Morality, and Disillusionment: Connections Between Two Mozambique Research Institutions, 1967-2017," *The Journal of African History* 64, no. 1 (2023): 119.

to endure in the public space. Mozambicans who went to work in East Germany were sometimes seen as part of Samora Machel's new elite, as quasi-military; later they regarded themselves as slaves, and yet they often see themselves as friends of the GDR. Such are the conflicting narratives that the cooperation between Mozambique and East Germany has engendered.

While the number of Mozambican workers in East German factories continued to increase until 1989, the close collaboration in the field of education and cultural activities dwindled from 1985 on.[55] When the FRELIMO government obtained loans from the International Monetary Fund and opened up its economy accordingly, the activities of "cultural lobbying" receded together with the financial support from the GDR. Hence, the discrepancy between the proclaimed brotherhood, people's expectations, and the fulfillment of these expectations grew. Tapping the resources of East Germany and the Soviet Union in the field of education had been crucial in the years after independence. This, however, should not obscure the fact that the education by East German professors was considered rather narrow, dogmatic, and orthodox. Students at the University Eduardo Mondlane, in Maputo, preferred the curricula taught by the teaching staff of anglophone and francophone Europe. A student protest in 1983 was directed against the dogmatic teachings of Marxism. The rigidity of "dialectical and historical materialism" demanded by East German and Soviet teachers was disapproved of as "diabolical and hysterical materialism."[56]

By the mid-1980s, the collaboration between the People's Republic of Mozambique and the German Democratic Republic in the field of arts also transformed, and the partnership became more heavily driven by transactions. Since independence, Makonde sculptures had been placed in the foreground as representative of Mozambican artistic culture. Now, Makonde sculptures were offered as decorative "exotic" objects for East German living rooms. In 1985, the Studio-Galerie in East Berlin had two thousand objects from Mozambique on sale. The newspaper announced: "In November, the Berlin office of the State Art Trade surprised lovers of non-European art with something special: the Studio-Galerie on Strausberger Platz sold paintings and prints, folk art carvings and jewelry from

führten in den 1980er Jahren zu einer verstärkten Abhängigkeit Mosambiks, die auf einer steigenden Schuldenlast basierte. Bis 1990 war die Verschuldung auf insgesamt 440 Millionen DM angestiegen.[54] Die Arbeiter, die nach Mosambik zurückkehrten, werden heute als Madjermanes (die Deutschen) bezeichnet. Seit 30 Jahren demonstrieren die Madjermanes vor dem Arbeitsministerium von Mosambik und fordern die Zahlung ausstehender Löhne. Bei einem ihrer Proteste legten sich vier Arbeiter Ketten um die Hand- und Fußgelenke und färbten ihre Hemden rot (Abb. 15). Nachdem ans Licht gekommen war, dass ihr Geld zur Begleichung der Staatsschulden verwendet worden war, bezeichneten sie sich als „Staatssklaven" und warfen der Regierung vor, ihre Arbeitskraft an die DDR verkauft zu haben, wie es zuvor die portugiesische Kolonialregierung in den Jahrzehnten vor der Unabhängigkeit getan hatte.

Viele der Madjermanes kämpfen im heutigen Mosambik täglich um ihren Lebensunterhalt. Ihr Rückblick auf die 1980er Jahre ist oft von Nostalgie geprägt. Sie hegen eine starke Sympathie für Ostdeutschland, wo sie immerhin einen Teil ihrer Jugend verbracht haben. Fröhliche Erinnerungen an diese Zeit stehen neben den Erfahrungen von Rassismus, dem sie im öffentlichen Raum ausgesetzt waren. Mosambikaner·innen, die in der DDR gearbeitet haben, galten damals als Teil von Samora Machels neuer Elite, ähnlich wie Mitglieder des Militärs. Später identifizierten sie sich als Sklavenarbeiter·innen und zugleich betrachten sie sich oft auch als Freund·innen der DDR. Es sind solche widersprüchlichen Narrative, die von der Kooperation zwischen Mosambik und der DDR bleiben.

Während die Zahl der mosambikanischen Arbeiter·innen in ostdeutschen Betrieben bis 1989 weiter anstieg, reduzierte sich die Zahl der Kollaborationen in Bildung und Kultur ab 1985 merklich.[55] Die FRELIMO-Regierung nahm Kredite vom Internationalen Währungsfonds an und öffnete ihre Wirtschaft entsprechend. Parallel dazu gingen die Aktivitäten der „kulturellen Lobbyarbeit" und die dazugehörige finanzielle Unterstützung durch die DDR zurück. Dadurch vergrößerte sich die Diskrepanz zwischen der proklamierten Brüderlichkeit, den Erwartungen und deren tatsächlicher Erfüllung. In den Jahren nach der Unabhängigkeit war die Unterstützung im Bildungsbereich, die die DDR und die Sowjetunion bereitstellten, von großer Bedeutung. Dabei muss aber auch erwähnt werden, dass die Ausbildung durch Lehrkräfte aus der DDR als recht eng, dogmatisch und

54. Zu den Schulden Mosambiks bei der DDR und der Einbehaltung der Löhne der Arbeiter siehe Almuth Berger, „Vertragsarbeiter: Arbeiter der Freundschaft? Die Verhandlungen in Maputo 1990", in: Voß (Hg.), *Wir haben Spuren hinterlassen!*, S. 512–529; Ralf Straßburg, „Zahlen und ihre Deutungen – Blicke aus Deutschland", Vortrag, 23.2.2019, https://vertragsarbeit-mosambik-ddr.de/konferenz_video/was-sagen-die-zahlen-und-was-sagen-sie-nicht/

55. Christian Saehrendt, *Kunst im Kampf für das „Sozialistische Weltsystem". Auswärtige Kulturpolitik der DDR in Afrika und Nahost*, Stuttgart: Franz Steiner Verlag 2017, S. 103.

Mozambique. You could, for example, take home … wood-carved animal sculptures with a peculiarly "naive" charm—painted in bright colors."[57] But works by famous Mozambican painters such as Sansão Cossa, Naguib Elias Abdula Jacob, and Estevão Macambaco were also sold to private buyers by the GDR's state art trade.[58] In the GDR, the artworks were popular and valued, as they connected an East German home to a different, unknown cultural world beyond the wall. And for the PRM, the massive selling of artworks became a new source of export revenue, as their industry had completely dwindled under the conditions of civil war.

In the homes of those I interviewed—diplomats, experts, and workers who had traveled to Mozambique in the 1980s—I discovered paintings by Mankew and other Mozambican artists displayed on the walls. These artworks are another archive, a tangible reminder of Mozambique and East Germany's brief but significant period of shared history. The global connectedness of the East German art scene and the close institutional relations to "sister countries" on all levels had

57. Lutz Presch, "Shetani-Skulpturen in Berlin," *Neue Berliner Illustrierte* 50 (1985), AdK-O 2385.

58. Interview with Dr. Ulrich Weishaupt, and Wolfgang Wagner, Berlin, June 28, 2022. Ulrich Weisshaupt paid 1,900 East German marks, the sum of a rather high monthly salary, when he bought a painting by Sensão Cossa.

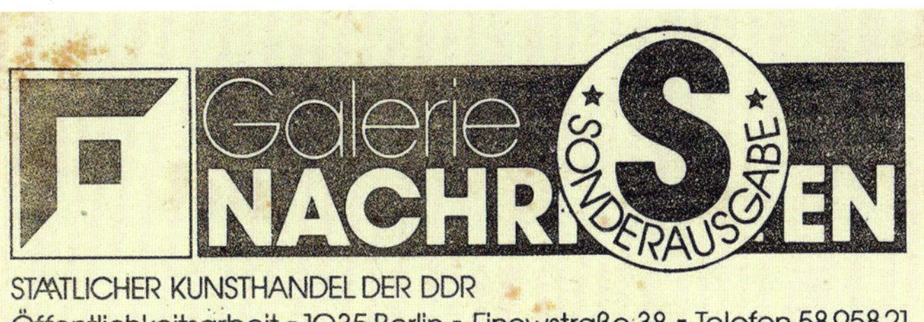

Fig. 17: Promotional material for the sales exhibition of Mozambican art

Abb. 17: Ankündigung der Verkaufsausstellung mosambikanischer Kunst

orthodox angesehen wurde. Die Studierenden der Universität Eduardo Mondlane in Maputo bevorzugten jene Lehrinhalte, die von Dozent·innen aus dem anglophonen und frankophonen Europa unterrichtet wurden. Im Jahr 1983 gab es einen Studierendenprotest, der sich gegen die dogmatischen Lehren des Marxismus richtete. Das starre Festhalten am „dialektischen und historischen Materialismus" der sowjetischen und ostdeutschen Dozent·innen wurde als „teuflisch und hysterisch" abgelehnt.[56]

Mitte der 1980er Jahre wandelte sich die Zusammenarbeit zwischen der Volksrepublik Mosambik und der Deutschen Demokratischen Republik auch auf dem Gebiet der Kunst, wobei die Partnerschaft zunehmend geschäftliche Züge annahm. Seit der Unabhängigkeit wurden Makonde-Skulpturen als Vorzeigeobjekte der mosambikanischen Kunst in den Vordergrund gerückt. Makonde-Skulpturen wurden nun als „exotische" Dekorationsobjekte für ostdeutsche Wohnzimmer angeboten. Im Jahr 1985 bot die „Studio-Galerie" in Ost-Berlin 2000 Kunstobjekte aus Mosambik zum Verkauf an. Die *Neue Berliner Illustrierte* meldete: „Mit einer Besonderheit überraschte im November die Bezirksdirektion Berlin des Staatlichen

56. Carlos Fernandes, „Intellectual Legacies, Political Morality, and Disillusionment: Connections Between Two Mozambique Research Institutions, 1967–2017", in: *The Journal of African History*, 64 (2023), No. 1, S. 112–125, hier S. 119.

59. Bonaventure Soh Bejeng Ndikung, introduction to *Echos der Bruderländer: Was ist der Preis der Erinnerung und wie hoch sind die Kosten der Amnesie? Oder: Visionen und Illusionen antiimperialistischer Solidarität* (HKW, 2024), 11.

been brushed aside in the first decade of East German historiography. Speaking of a collective "amnesia" emphasizes the willful erasure of such histories, which implies the erasure of socialist internationalism as an alternative to the capitalist globalization we inhabit.[59] Only now, by starting to ask other questions, by widening the gaze beyond the guarded wall that surrounded East Germany, we find that all those stories were already there—stored in institutional and private archives, in personal memories. Once we fully recognize them with the ambivalences they contain, what influence will they have on the evaluation of the East German art sphere? How will they change our understanding of 1989 as a global rupture and end to socialist connectivity? Such are the questions that need further debate and can only be answered in conversation and partnership with actors in former "sister countries."

Kunsthandels die Liebhaber aussereuropäischer Kunst: Die Studio-Galerie am Strausberger Platz verkaufte Gemälde und Grafiken, Volkskunstschnitzereien und Schmuck aus Mocambique. Man konnte beispielsweise […] holzgeschnitzte Tierskulpturen von eigentümlich ‚naivem' Reiz – in leuchtenden Farben bemalt – mit nach Hause nehmen."[57] Aber auch Werke berühmter mosambikanischer Maler wie Sansão Cossa, Naguib Elias Abdula und Jacob Estevão Macambaco wurden über den staatlichen Kunsthandel der DDR an private Käufer verkauft.[58] In der DDR waren die Kunstwerke beliebt, denn sie verbanden ihr Zuhause mit einer anderen, unbekannten kulturellen Welt jenseits der Mauer. Der großangelegte Verkauf von Kunstwerken aus der Volksrepublik Mosambik in Deutschland wurde zudem zu einer neuen Export-Einnahmequelle, während sich die Industrie des Landes durch die Bedingungen des Bürgerkriegs im freien Fall befand.

In den Wohnungen der Diplomat·innen, Expert·innen und Arbeiter·innen, die in den 1980er Jahren nach Mosambik gereist waren, entdeckte ich während der Interviews oft Gemälde von Mankew und anderen mosambikanischen Künstler·innen an den Wänden. Auch diese Kunstwerke sind eine Art von Archiv, eine greifbare Erinnerung an die kurze, aber bedeutende Periode der gemeinsamen Geschichte von Mosambik und der DDR. Die globale Verflechtung der ostdeutschen Kunstszene und die engen institutionellen Beziehungen zu den „Bruderländern" auf allen Ebenen sind im ersten Jahrzehnt der Aufarbeitung der DDR-Geschichte ausgeblendet worden. Wird in diesem Zusammenhang von einer kollektiven „Amnesie" gesprochen,[59] so wird die gezielte Verdrängung solcher Geschichten betont – dies schließt auch die Verdrängung der Ideale eines sozialistischen Internationalismus als mögliche Alternative zum globalen Kapitalismus ein. Erst jetzt, da wir beginnen, andere Fragen zu stellen und unseren Blick über die Mauer, die die DDR umschloss, hinaus zu weiten, stellen wir fest, dass all diese Geschichten bereits vorhanden waren – gespeichert in öffentlichen und privaten Archiven und in persönlichen Erinnerungen. Welchen Einfluss werden sie auf die Bewertung der ostdeutschen Kunstwelt haben, wenn wir sie mitsamt ihrer Ambivalenzen vollständig anerkennen? Werden sie unser Verständnis von 1989 verändern, als einen globalen Bruch und das Ende einer sozialistischen Vernetzung? Das sind Fragen, die weiter diskutiert werden müssen und nur im Gespräch und in der Partnerschaft mit Akteur·innen aus den ehemaligen „Bruderländern" beantwortet werden können.

57. Lutz Presch, „Shetani-Skulpturen in Berlin", in: *Neue Berliner Illustrierte*, 50, 1985, AdK-O 2385.

58. Interview mit Dr. Ulrich Weishaupt und Wolfgang Wagner (Berlin, 28.6.2022). Ulrich Weishaupt zahlte 1900 ostdeutsche Mark, die Summe eines recht hohen Monatsgehalts, für ein Gemälde von Sensão Cossa.

59. Bonaventure Soh Bejeng Ndikung, „Introduction", in: *Echos der Bruderländer: Was ist der Preis der Erinnerung und wie hoch sind die Kosten der Amnesie? Oder: Visionen und Illusionen antiimperialistischer Solidarität*, Berlin: HKW 2024, S. 8–25, hier S. 11.

MANKEW VALENTE

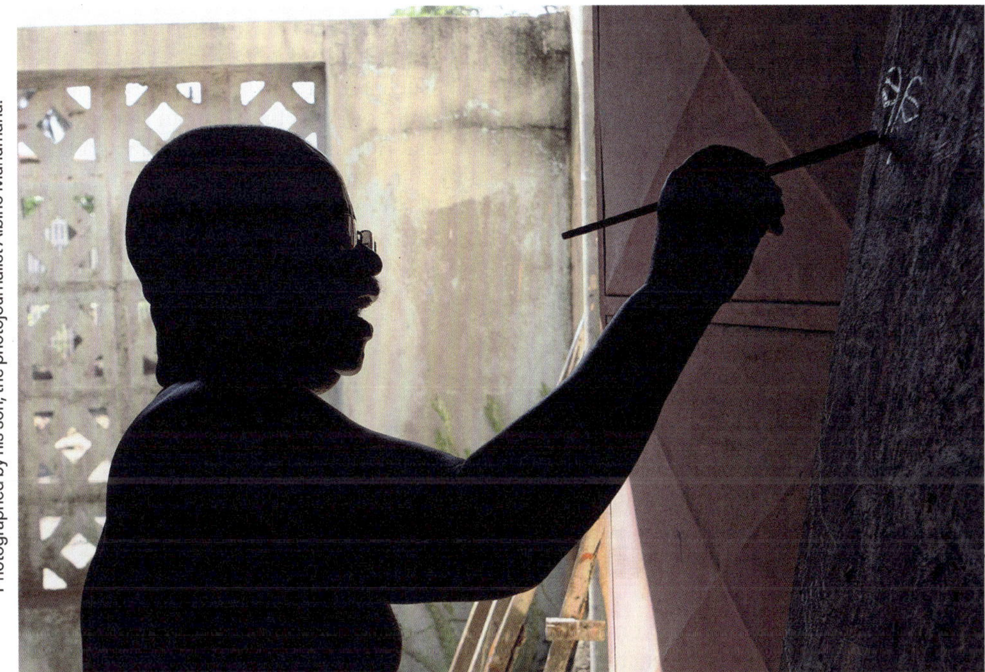

MAHUMANA

Fig. 18: The painter in his studio.
Photographed by his son, the photojournalist Albino Mahumana.

Abb. 18: Der Maler in seinem Atelier. Fotografiert von seinem Sohn, dem Fotojournalisten Albino Mahumana

1. Letter to the East German Academy of Arts, December 19, 1984, AdK-O 8529.

2. Interview with Mankew V. Mahumana, *Domingo*, January 22, 1984, N 2841/24.

LEA MARIE NIENHOFF

PAINTING FOR SOCIAL TRANSFORMATION AND CONNECTION

"The freedom of the people depends on the new relationships among us people; only a relationship of equality and cooperation can make freedom possible."[1] These are the words of Mankew Valente Mahumana, renowned Mozambican artist and former member of the East German Academy of Arts. His work as a painter was a project of emancipation. Mankew was a member of FRELIMO. After independence, he became a member of the city council of Maputo, and for some time he held the presidency of the Mozambican Association of Friendship and Solidarity Between Peoples (AMASP). An active participant in the process of building post-independence Mozambique, Mankew never separated his art from his politics: "For me, painting is a reflection of the life of our people. Through my art, I denounce colonialism, and today I am committed to the development of my country and the African continent. My art is meant to mobilize people."[2]

The idea for this book's research started with Mankew, or more precisely with the discovery that a Mozambican painter had been a member of the East German Academy of Arts. We began tracing Mankew's links to the GDR in various personal and official archives, such as Harald Heinke's private archive, the Archives of the East German Academy of Arts, the German Federal Archives, and the Stasi Records Archive. The stories that started to surface portrayed him as a staunch supporter of close diplomatic and economic relations with the GDR. Mankew was depicted in several books by authors such as Landolf Scherzer, Walter Michel, and Ursula Püschel and was regularly visited by groups from the GDR who arrived in Maputo: from workers to engineers and from diplomats to artists, East German citizens who traveled to Mozambique in the 1980s retain personal

LEA MARIE NIENHOFF

MALEREI FÜR SOZIALE TRANSFORMATION UND VERBINDUNG

„Die Freiheit des Volkes ist abhängig von den neuen Beziehungen unter uns Menschen, eine Beziehung von Gleichberechtigung und Kooperation erst kann die Freiheit möglich machen."[1] Dies sind die Worte von Mankew Valente Mahumana, dem bekannten mosambikanischen Künstler und Mitglied der Akademie der Künste der DDR. Sein malerisches Schaffen war ein Projekt der Emanzipation. Mankew war Mitglied der FRELIMO. Nach der Unabhängigkeit wurde er Mitglied des Stadtrats von Maputo und hatte eine Zeit lang den Vorsitz der Gesellschaft für Freundschaft und Solidarität zwischen den Völkern (AMASP) in Mosambik inne. Mankew, der aktiv am Aufbau des postkolonialen Mosambik beteiligt war, hat seine Kunst stets mit politischer Arbeit verbunden: „Für mich ist die Malerei ein Spiegel des Lebens unseres Volkes. Mit meiner Kunst prangere ich den Kolonialismus an, und heute engagiere ich mich für die Entwicklung meines Landes und des afrikanischen Kontinents. Meine Kunst soll die Menschen mobilisieren."[2]

Die Idee für die Recherchen zu diesem Buch entstand durch die Entdeckung, dass ein mosambikanischer Maler Mitglied der Akademie der Künste der DDR war. Wir begannen, Mankews Verbindungen zur DDR in verschiedenen privaten und öffentlichen Archiven nachzugehen, etwa im Privatarchiv von Harald Heinke, im Archiv der Akademie der Künste, im Bundesarchiv und im Stasi-Unterlagen-Archiv. Die Geschichten, die wir zusammentrugen, zeigten ihn als entschiedenen Befürworter enger diplomatischer und wirtschaftlicher Beziehungen zur DDR. Mankew wurde in mehreren Büchern von Autor·innen wie Landolf Scherzer, Walter Michel und Ursula Püschel porträtiert und in Maputo regelmäßig von Delegationen aus der DDR besucht: Von Arbeiter·innen bis zu Ingenieur·innen, von Diplomat·innen bis zu Künstler·innen – die meisten DDR-Bürger·innen, die in den 1980er Jahren nach Mosambik reisten, haben persönliche Erinnerungen an den Künstler. Viele von ihnen kauften

1. Brief an die Akademie der Künste der DDR, 19.12.1984, AdK-O 8529.

2. Interview mit Mankew V. Mahumana, *Semanário Domingo*, 22.1.1984, N 2841/24.

3. See n. 1.

memories connected to the artist. Many of them purchased his works. To this day, paintings by Mankew and other Mozambican artists such as Malangatana, Naguib, Samate Mulungo, and Sansão Cossa hang on the walls of their living rooms, preserving the memory of a time when sympathy for Mozambique's struggle shaped their perception of world politics.

One could retell the story of Mankew's relationship with the GDR in simple terms: loyal to the political aims of Marxism-Leninism, he benefited from the esteem bestowed upon him by the GDR, while the GDR, in turn, was able to profit from Mankew's public support for East German activities in Mozambique. Mankew became the figurehead of a political friendship that was, in fact, not only flawed but also tightly controlled.

But what if this story glossed over how the artist leveraged his position to redefine the relationship between the two nations? What if reducing Mankew to a mere state artist, entirely loyal to the system, is misleading? We started this text with a quote from a letter that Mankew sent to the president of the East German Academy of Arts in 1984. The letter was his contribution to a series in the journal *Neue Berliner Illustrierte*, which published reflections by corresponding Academy members on "political and artistic issues of our time." In his letter addressed to the German public, Mankew reminds the reader of the European powers' violent division of Africa—lines drawn on a map of the African continent that charted plunder and legitimized oppression. His letter continues: "It has gradually become the map of a region of freedom where humans and material resources have become the preserve of the people themselves."[3] In a very concrete manner, Mankew's artistic endeavors in fostering international connections and recognition were aimed at advancing the cause of decolonization.

Through his hospitality—akin to what some might term "comradeship"—Mankew aimed to build bridges between both societies. His atelier and family home in the Xipamanine neighborhood in Maputo, where he regularly welcomed guests from the GDR, stood out as one of the rare venues where personal encounters could occur on equal terms—a dynamic often absent in other realms of cooperation, such as technical aid, consulting, and economic collaboration.

Werke von Mankew. Gemälde von Mankew und anderen mosambikanischen Künstlern wie Malangatana, Naguib, Samate Mulungo und Sansão Cossa hängen bis heute an den Wänden ihrer Wohnzimmer und bewahren die Erinnerung an eine Zeit, in der ihre Unterstützung für den Kampf in Mosambik ihre Sicht auf die Weltpolitik prägte.

Man könnte das Verhältnis zwischen Mankew und der DDR mit einfachen Worten beschreiben: Mankew, der den politischen Zielen des Marxismus-Leninismus treu verbunden war, profitierte von der Wertschätzung, die ihm die DDR entgegenbrachte. Im Gegenzug kam der DDR Mankews öffentliche Unterstützung ihrer Aktivitäten in Mosambik zugute. Mankew avancierte zum Symbol einer politischen Freundschaft.

Aber was, wenn diese Erzählung ausblendet, in welchem Maße der Künstler die Möglichkeit nutzte, die Beziehung zwischen den beiden Nationen neu zu gestalten? Was, wenn es zu kurz gegriffen ist, Mankew als reinen Staatskünstler zu sehen, der dem System uneingeschränkte Loyalität entgegenbrachte? Dieser Text beginnt mit einem Zitat aus einem Brief, den Mankew 1984 an den Präsidenten der Akademie der Künste der DDR geschrieben hat. Der Brief war sein Beitrag zu einer Serie in der Zeitschrift *Neue Berliner Illustrierte*, in der Betrachtungen von Akademiemitgliedern zu „politischen und künstlerischen Fragen unserer Zeit" veröffentlicht wurden. In seinem an die deutsche Öffentlichkeit gerichteten Brief erinnert Mankew an die gewaltsame Aufteilung Afrikas durch die europäischen Mächte – Linien, die auf einer Landkarte des afrikanischen Kontinents gezogen wurden, um die gewaltsame Aneignung und Unterdrückung zu legitimieren. Sein Brief fährt fort: Der afrikanische Kontinent „verwandele sich [nun] allmählich in eine Region der Freiheit, in der die menschlichen und natürlichen Ressourcen den eigenen Völkern dienen".[3] Mankews Bemühungen um internationale Beziehungen und Anerkennung waren darauf gerichtet, die Dekolonialisierung voranzutreiben.

Durch seine große Gastfreundschaft – die man auch als „Kameradschaftlichkeit" bezeichnen könnte – wollte Mankew Brücken zwischen beiden Gesellschaften bauen. Sein Atelier und sein Wohnhaus im Stadtteil Xipamanine in Maputo, wo er regelmäßig Gäste aus der DDR empfing, waren zwei der wenigen Orte, an denen persönliche Begegnungen auf Augenhöhe möglich waren, eine Dynamik, die in anderen Bereichen der Zusammenarbeit – wie technischer Hilfe, Beratung und wirtschaftlicher Kooperation – oft fehlte.

3. Brief an die Akademie der Künste der DDR, 19.12.1984, AdK-O 8529.

What about Mankew's reception in the GDR? How was he received?

Let us look at the photo below. It was taken in Wolfgang Eckardt's atelier in Rostock during Mankew's first visit to the GDR in 1984. In it, we see Mankew in a three-piece suit, hands clasped together at the front, looking at a bust made by Eckardt, who, in turn, is looking at Mankew.[4] On the right, standing next to Mankew, is a young Mozambican student whose name we do not know, only that he was studying in the GDR at the time and accompanied Mankew as an interpreter. They are surrounded by a group of students who were living in Rostock in 1984. Despite the formality and stiffness of the visit—and the photo—Mankew and Eckardt developed a friendship that lasted through the years. In an interview for the Mozambican newspaper *Notícias* after his return, Mankew emphasized that he came back with greater openness to different aesthetics and techniques he had experimented with in the atelier of his friend Eckardt.[5]

The journey was organized and financed through the International Friendship League.[6] His four-week stay came as a result of invitations from the Rostock Fishing Combine, the Schwarze Pumpe Gas Combine near Cottbus, and the league itself.[7] After a first stop in Weimar, where the league facilitated Communal Politics courses for international cadres, Mankew stayed with Eckardt in Rostock for two weeks.[8] The visit's schedule was filled with official engagements, including the opening of the exhibition *Moderne Makonde-Plastik* at the GRASSI Museum, the museum of ethnography in Leipzig. Three years later, when Mankew visited the GDR in 1987, he asked whether it would be possible to meet with friends and get to know the country better "outside the official program."[9] During his stays in the GDR, Mankew not only had an interpreter but was also

4. Wolfgang Eckardt also created a bronze sculpture of Mankew V. Mahumana. One copy of the sculpture is in the private collection of Arno Schnorrenberg, while the second copy was presented as a gift to Mankew himself and remains in the family's collection.

5. "O pintor Mankew na RDA pela paz e pela amizade," *Notícias*, May 22, 1984, N 2841/22.

6. The PRM lacked the financial resources to cover the travel expenses. The first visit in 1984 was funded by the League, while the second visit in 1987 was financed by the East German Academy of Arts. Note in AdK-O 2385.

7. Both combines had commissions in Mozambique. "Mankew Troca Experiências na RDA," *Revista Tempo*, May 27,

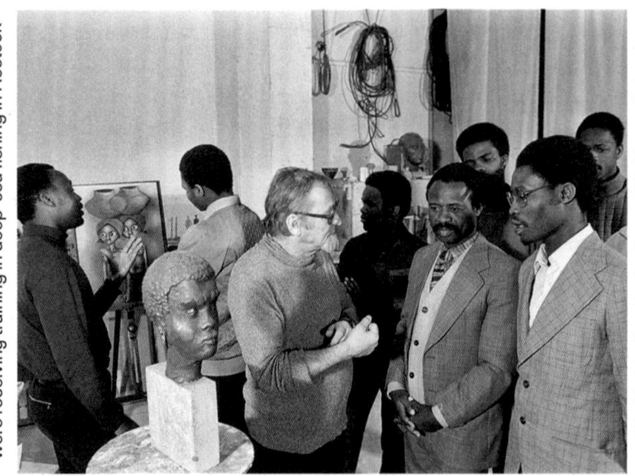

Fig. 19: Mankew in the studio of Wolfgang Eckardt, accompanied by a group of Mozambicans who were receiving training in deep-sea fishing in Rostock

Abb. 19: Mankew im Atelier von Wolfgang Eckardt, begleitet von einer Gruppe Mosambikaner, die in Rostock eine Ausbildung in der Hochseefischerei absolvierten

Wie wurde Mankew in der DDR empfangen?

Betrachten wir das obenstehende Foto. Es wurde während Mankews erstem Besuch in der DDR im Jahr 1984 im Atelier von Wolfgang Eckardt in Rostock aufgenommen. Wir sehen Mankew in Anzug und Weste, die Hände vorne zusammengelegt, mit Blick auf eine Büste von Eckardt, der seinerseits Mankew anschaut.[4] Rechts neben ihm steht ein junger mosambikanischer Student. Seinen Namen kennen wir nicht. Er muss zu dieser Zeit in der DDR studiert haben und hat Mankew als Dolmetscher begleitet. Sie sind umgeben von einer Gruppe von Studenten, die damals in Rostock lebten. Trotz der formellen Atmosphäre des Besuchs – und des Fotos – entstand zwischen Mankew und Eckardt eine Freundschaft, die über die Jahre hinweg Bestand hatte. In einem Interview der mosambikanischen Zeitung *Notícias* betonte Mankew nach seiner Rückkehr, dass er mit einer neuen Offenheit für unterschiedliche Ästhetiken und Techniken zurückgekehrt sei, die er im Atelier seines Freundes Wolfgang Eckardt erprobt habe.[5]

Die Reise wurde von der Liga für Völkerfreundschaft organisiert und finanziert.[6] Mankews vierwöchiger Aufenthalt erfolgte auf Einladung des Fischereikombinats Rostock, des Gaskombinats Schwarze Pumpe bei Cottbus und der Liga selbst.[7] Nach einer ersten Station in Weimar, wo die Liga „Kommunalpolitik"-Kurse für internationale Kader durchführte,[8] blieb er zwei Wochen lang bei Wolfgang Eckardt in Rostock. Das Besuchsprogramm war mit offiziellen Terminen gefüllt, darunter die Eröffnung der Ausstellung *Moderne Makonde-Plastik* im GRASSI Museum für Völkerkunde in Leipzig. Als Mankew drei Jahre später, 1987, erneut die DDR besuchte, äußerte er den Wunsch, Freunde zu treffen und das Land „außerhalb des offiziellen Programms" besser kennenzulernen.[9] Während seiner Aufenthalte in der DDR hatte Mankew nicht nur einen Dolmetscher, sondern auch einen sogenannten „ständigen Begleiter".[10]

4. Wolfgang Eckardt schuf auch ein Porträt von Mankew V. Mahumana in Form einer Bronzeskulptur. Ein Exemplar der Skulptur befindet sich in der Privatsammlung von Arno Schnorrenberg; das zweite Exemplar wurde Mankew selbst geschenkt und befindet sich in der Sammlung seiner Familie.

5. *Notícias*, 22.5.1984, „O pintor Mankew na RDA pela paz e pela amizade", N 2841/22.

6. Die VRM verfügte nicht über die finanziellen Mittel, um die Reisekosten zu decken. Der erste Besuch im Jahr 1984 wurde von der Liga finanziert, der zweite Besuch im Jahr 1987 von der Akademie der Künste der DDR. Vermerk in AdK-O 2385.

7. Beide Kombinate hatten Aufträge in Mosambik. *Revista Tempo*, 27.5.1984, „Mankew Troca

1984, BArch 2841/22; note in AdK-O 2385.

8. The courses took place at the Institut für Kommunalpolitik in Weimar. Their content was adjusted in coordination with the partner countries. See BArch DY 13/2881.

9. Note from a call recorded by Ms. Nagengast, October 30, 1987, AdK-O 2385.

10. Translation of "ständiger Begleiter." In a letter to the East German Academy of Arts, April 3, 1984, AdK-O 2385.

11. The *Medalha Nachingwea* is a medal awarded by the President of Mozambique in recognition of significant contributions made for the benefit of society.

accompanied by a "permanent attendant."[10] However, the institutions coordinating the exchange in the GDR were not so keen on letting him have private exchanges such as the ones he organized at home in Maputo.

In this chapter on Mankew, we have assembled a collection of materials: a portrait of Mankew written by his friend Harald Heinke, letters, quotes, excerpts, and images from various archives. An interview with Mankew's son Albino Mahumana and a text by Ambre Alfredo give voice to perspectives from Mozambique, opening up new insights into the exchange. The archival material, in return, also enables readers today to follow their own questions as they navigate the pages and rest their gaze on his paintings.

MEDALHA NACHINGWEA (1985)

Excerpt from a newspaper article reporting on Mankew's acceptance of the Medalha Nachingwea award, which he received in Maputo in 1985:[11]

> "Receiving the medal also means that we need to do more work to ensure that what we create is, objectively speaking, in line with the wishes of our people. For me, in particular, it means that I need to change something, change what I might do better in a different way." …
> Mankew spoke of the need for visual artists to acquaint the general public with their work, saying that everything should be done to bring artists closer to the people, to teach people to read their work. …
> He pointed out that nowadays, as in the past, it tends to be foreigners,

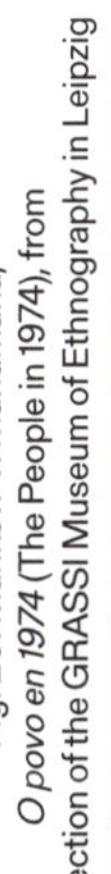
Fig. 20: Mankew V. Mahumana, *O povo en 1974* (The People in 1974), from the collection of the GRASSI Museum of Ethnography in Leipzig

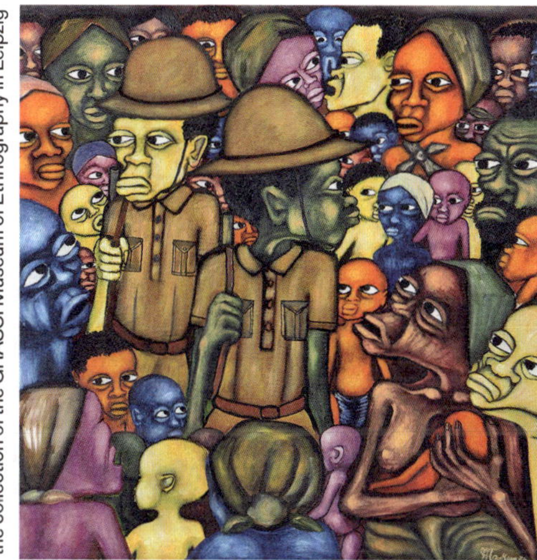
Abb. 20: Mankew V. Mahumana, *O povo en 1974* (Das Volk im Jahr 1974), aus der Sammlung des GRASSI Museums für Völkerkunde zu Leipzig

Die Institutionen, die den Austausch in der DDR koordinierten, zeigten jedoch wenig Interesse daran, ihm private Begegnungen zu ermöglichen, wie sie bei ihm zu Hause in Maputo möglich gewesen waren.

Für dieses Kapitel über Mankew haben wir eine Sammlung von Materialien zusammengestellt: ein Porträt von Mankew, verfasst von seinem Freund Harald Heinke, sowie Briefe, Zitate, Auszüge und Bilder aus verschiedenen Archiven. Ein Interview mit Mankews Sohn Albino Mahumana und ein Text von Ambre Alfredo lassen Stimmen aus Mosambik zu Wort kommen, die neue Perspektiven auf den Austausch eröffnen. Das Archivmaterial hingegen lädt die Leser·innen ein, ihren eigenen Fragen nachzugehen, während sie durch die Seiten blättern.

MEDALHA NACHINGWEA (1985)

Ausschnitt aus einem Zeitungsartikel anlässlich der Verleihung der Auszeichnung Medalha Nachingwea,[11] die Mankew 1985 in Maputo entgegennahm:

> „,Diese Medaille zu erhalten, heißt auch, dass wir weiterarbeiten müssen, und zwar in dem Sinne, dass wir in unserem Schaffen den Wünschen unseres Volkes objektiv entgegenkommen. Das bedeutet insbesondere für mich, dass ich etwas verändern muss, dass ich etwas anders und besser machen kann.' …
> Mankeu sprach darüber, dass es notwendig sei, die Werke der bildenden Künstler der breiten Öffentlichkeit zur Kenntnis zu bringen, und sagte weiter, dass alles getan werden müsse, damit eine größere Annäherung zwischen den Künstlern und dem Volk stattfinde, damit den Menschen beigebracht werde, die Kunstwerke zu lesen. … Er wies darauf hin, dass heute genauso wie früher hauptsächlich Ausländer unsere Kunstwerke am meisten schätzen

Experiências na RDA", BArch 2841/22; Anmerkung in AdK-O 2385.

8. Die Kurse fanden am Institut für Kommunalpolitik in Weimar statt. Ihre Inhalte wurden mit den Partnerländern abgestimmt. Siehe BArch DY 13/2881.

9. Vermerk aus einem Anruf von Frau Nagengast, 30.10.1987, AdK-O 2385.

10. In einem Brief an die Akademie, 3.4.1984, AdK-O 2385.

11. Die Medalha Nachingwea ist eine Medaille, die vom Präsidenten von Mosambik in Anerkennung bedeutender Beiträge zum Wohle der Gesellschaft verliehen wird.

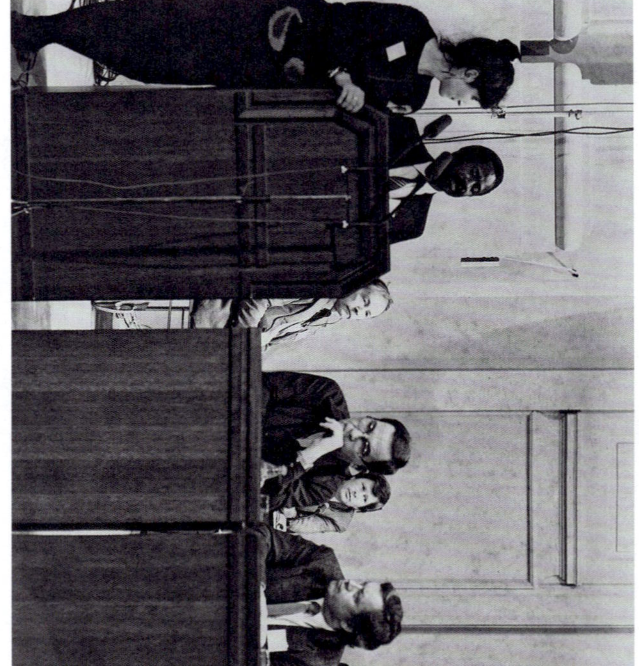

Fig. 22: International Artists' Gathering
at the Nicaraguan Embassy in 1982. Mankew V. Mahumana with fellow artists
Moises Simbine, Leonicio Saénz, Alejandro Canales, and Rafael Castellón

Abb. 22: Internationales Künstlertreffen in der nicaraguanischen Botschaft 1982.
Mankew V. Mahumana mit seinen Künstlerkollegen Moises Simbine,
Leoncio Saénz, Alejandro Canales und Rafael Castellón

Fig. 21: As a corresponding member,
Mankew V. Mahumana speaks at the International Plenary
Session of the East German Academy of Arts on November 19, 1987

Abb. 21: Als korrespondierendes Mitglied spricht Mankew V. Mahumana
auf der Internationalen Plenartagung der Akademie der
Künste der DDR am 19. November 1987

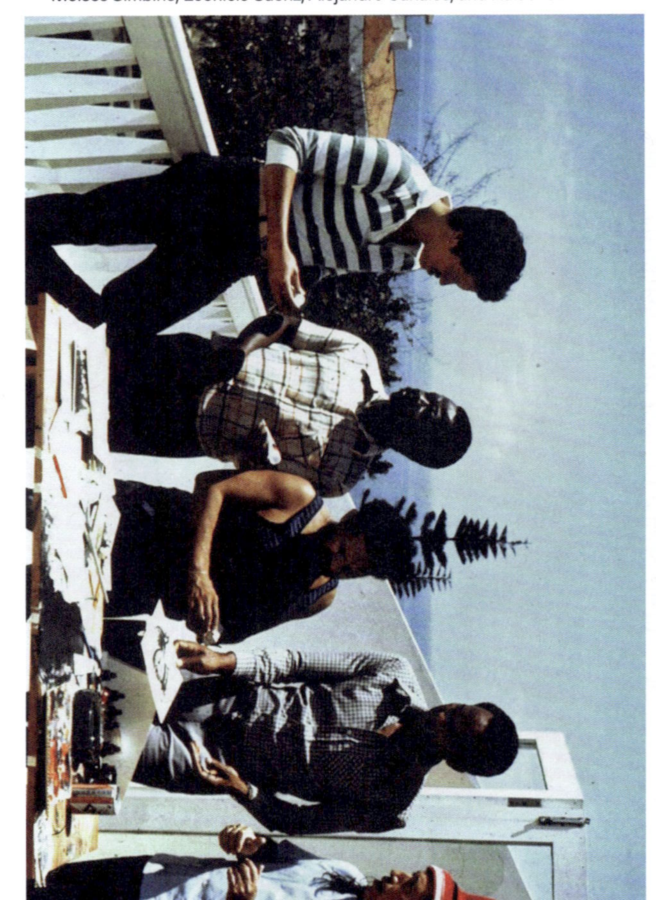

Fig. 23: Mankew V. Mahumana, *O mãe tenho fome* (Mom, I'm Hungry), 1975,
from the collection of GRASSI Museums für Völkerkunde zu Leipzig

Abb. 23: Mankew V. Mahumana, *O mãe tenho fome* (Mutter ich habe Hunger), 1975,
aus der Sammlung des GRASSI Museums für Völkerkunde zu Leipzig

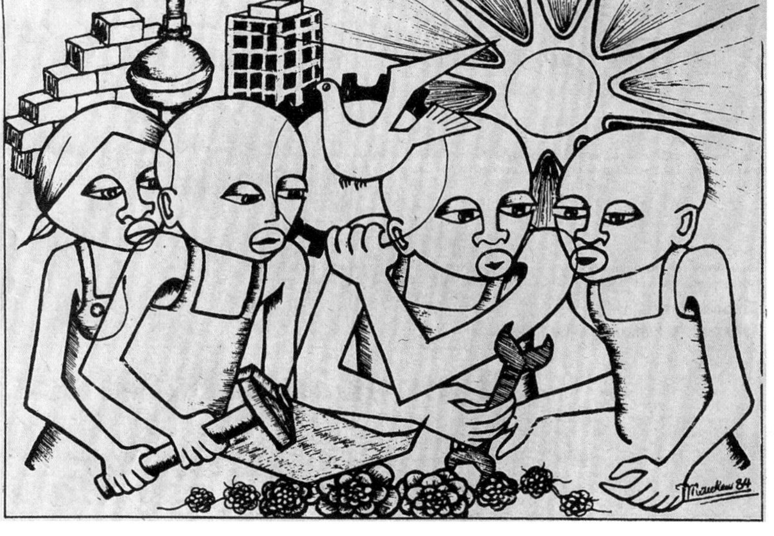

Fig. 24: Mankew V. Mahumana, *Workers in Front of the Television Tower*, published in the magazine *Novidades*, December 11, 1984

Abb.24: Mankew V. Mahumana, *Arbeiter vor dem Fernsehturm*, veröffentlicht in der Zeitschrift *Novidades*, 11. Dezember 1984

<u>Übersetzung</u>

An den Präsidenten
der Akademie der Künste
der Deutschen Demokratischen
Republik
S.E. Manfred Wekwerth

<u>B e r l i n</u>

Sehr geehrter Herr Präsident Manfred Wekwerth!

Durch unsere Presseorgane erfuhr ich zuerst von meiner Berufung zum korrespondierenden Mitglied der Akademie der Künste der DDR.

Ich bin sehr gerührt über die hohe Ehre, die mir damit zuteil wurde.

Für Ihre Glückwünsche im Namen des Präsidiums der Akademie, die Sie mir am 1.7.1983 übermittelten, möchte ich mich ganz herzlich bedanken. Ich versichere Ihnen, mit ganzer Kraft und persönlichem Engagement mit meinen bescheidenen Mitteln, die mir durch die Kunst gegeben sind, für die Völkerverständigung und die Erhaltung des Weltfriedens einzutreten.

In jüngster Zeit verarbeite ich in meinen Werken die Probleme unserer neuen Gesellschaft, so das tägliche Ringen zur Bekämpfung des Hungers, die Verteidigung der Familie vor der Konterrevolution, die gemeinsame Arbeit der Bauern in den Gemeinschaftsdörfern und nicht zuletzt die Sehnsucht nach Frieden unseres Volkes. Als Mitglied der Moçambiquanischen Gesellschaft für Freundschaft und Solidarität mit den Völkern (AMASP) und langjähriger Freund der DDR ist es mir ein Bedürfnis gewesen, die Freundschaftsorganisation bei der Gestaltung eines Kalenders zu unterstützen.

Im November 1983 organisierte die AMASP mit dem Büro der Liga für Völkerfreundschaft der DDR in Maputo einen Künstlerabend, bei dem ich viele Glückwünsche von Persönlichkeiten meines Landes zur Berufung zum korrespondierenden Mitglied der Akademie erhielt.

Mit großem Interesse verfolgte ich die Berichte über den jüngsten Kongreß der Bildenden Künstler der DDR und die Friedensmanifestation Ihrer Akademie, an der der amerikanische Künstler Harry Belafonte teilnahm.

In nächster Zeit widme ich mich der Gestaltung des Themas der Freundschaft der Menschen unserer beiden Länder am Beispiel der Zusammenarbeit der Bergarbeiter in der Steinkohleregion Moatize. Dies soll mein Beitrag zum 35. Jahrestag der DDR, meines Freundeslandes, sein.

Der Kampf geht weiter

gez. Mankeu

Fig. 25: A letter of thanks (translated) from Mankew V. Mahumana to Manfred Wekwerth, president of the East German Academy of Arts, following his appointment as a corresponding member

Abb. 25: Dankschreiben (übersetzt) von Mankew V. Mahumana an Manfred Wekwerth, Präsident der Akademie der Künste der DDR, nach seiner Ernennung zum korrespondierenden Mitglied

12. Augusto de Jesus, "O artista nunca sabe tudo: Mankeu, pintor e … 'Medalha Nachingweya,'" *Domingo*, July 28, 1985, https://www.mozambique-history.net/arts/artes_plasticas/19850728_artista_nunca_sabe_tudo.pdf.

13. Harald Heinke, *Khanimambo Moçambique: Tagebuch und malerische Impressionen einer bewegten Zeit in Mosambik von 1979 bis 1985* (Projekte-Verlag Cornelius, 2012), 140.

14. Landolf Scherzer, *Bom dia, weißer Bruder: Erlebnisse am Sambesi* (Greifenverlag, 1984), 165.

15. Scherzer, *Bom dia*, 166.

16. Scherzer, *Bom dia*, 167.

broadly speaking, who appreciate and buy our works, when it should be Mozambicans. In light of this, he called attention to the fact that Mozambican artworks are constantly being taken abroad, including those that are part of our country's heritage.[12]

"A MURAL OF THE FRIENDSHIP BETWEEN MINERS OF THE PEOPLE'S REPUBLIC OF MOZAMBIQUE AND THE GDR"

Harald Heinke and the writers Walter Michel and Landolf Scherzer wrote accounts of the three-day initiative in which Mankew painted the mural at the Carbomoc cultural center in the early part of 1982. A selection of quotations from their descriptions elucidate the political and historical background against which the mural was interpreted.

To acquaint ourselves with the Moatize coalfield, located northeast of Tete, the three of us—Mankew, Landolf, and I—went down the "Chipanga 7" mine together with the on-duty mining engineer Walter Grabner, who was from Pirna in Saxony.[13]

Mankew fingered the glinting fractures in the coal. "Beauty grows out of the black too," he said…. The aesthetic effect of the coal's beauty was at once destroyed. I saw workers shouting, sweating, groaning. Landolf Scherzer wonders how many workers have died in the Moatize pits already. "There aren't any statistics for the people who've died, only for the coal that's produced and sold."[14]

Three *mineiros* were drilling new blast holes at the end of the seam. . . . Mankeu [*sic*] made drawings of them, as I held his Davy lamp. Drops of black sweat fell on the paper. There was no trace of any beauty.[15]

He was silent on the way back to Moatize.
I asked him, "Was that your first time down a mine?"

und kaufen, während es eigentlich die Mosambikaner sein müssten. Deshalb machte er darauf aufmerksam, dass ständig mosambikanische Kunstwerke ins Ausland gehen, sogar solche, die im Eigentum unseres Landes sind."[12]

„WANDBILD DER FREUNDSCHAFT DER BERGARBEITER DER VOLKSREPUBLIK MOÇAMBIQUE UND DER DDR"

Harald Heinke und die Schriftsteller Walter Michel und Landorf Scherzer haben die dreitägige Aktion, in der Mankew Anfang 1982 das Wandbild am Kulturzentrum der CARBOMOC schuf, geschildert. Ausgewählte Zitate aus ihren Beschreibungen verdeutlichen den politischen und historischen Hintergrund, vor dem das Wandbild interpretiert wurde.

„Zum Kennenlernen der Situation im Kohlegebiet in Moatize, nordöstlich von Tete fuhren wir drei – Mankeu, Landolf und ich – mit dem diensthabenden Bergbau-Diplomingenieur Walter Grabner, aus dem sächsischen Pirna, in die Kohlegrube ‚Chipanga 7' ein."[13]

„Mankeu befühlte die funkelnden Bruchstellen der Kohle. ‚Auch die Schönheit wächst aus dem Schwarz', sagte er … Der ästhetische Eindruck von der Schönheit der Kohle wurde augenblicklich zerstört. Ich sah schreiende, schwitzende, stöhnende Arbeiter." Landolf Scherzer fragt sich, wie viele Arbeiter in den Gruben von Moatize schon umgekommen sind. „Es gibt keine Statistik der Toten, nur eine Statistik der produzierten und verkauften Kohle."[14]

„Am Ende des Flözes bohrten drei Mineiros neue Sprenglöcher …
Mankeu zeichnete sie. Ich hielt seine Grubenlaterne. Schwarzer Schweiß tropfte auf das Papier. Von Schönheit keine Spur."[15]

„Auf dem Weg zurück nach Moatize schwieg er.
Ich fragte ihn: ‚Warst du das erste Mal untertage?'
‚Nein', sagte er, ‚ich kenne Gruben. Nicht die hier am Sambesi, aber andere, schrecklichere, der Hölle ähnlichere.'"[16]

12. *Semanário Domingo*, 28.7.1985, „O artista nunca sabe tudo" – Mankeu, pintor e …"Medalha Nachingweya", Augusto de Jesus, AdK-O 2385 (Übersetzung leicht bearbeitet).

13. Harald Heinke, *Khanimambo Moçambique. Tagebuch und malerische Impressionen einer bewegten Zeit in Mosambik von 1979 bis 1985*, Halle: Projekte-Verlag Cornelius 2010, S. 140.

14. Landolf Scherzer, *Bom dia, weißer Bruder. Erlebnisse am Sambesi*, Rudolstadt: Greifenverlag 1984, S. 165.

15. Ebd., S. 166.

16. Ebd., S. 167.

17. Heinke, *Khanimambo Moçambique,* 141.

18. Walter Michel, *Lieder vom Sambesi: Impressionen aus der Volksrepublik Moçambique* (Verlag Neues Leben, 1984), 195.

"No," he said, "I'm familiar with pits. Not here on the Zambezi, but other, more terrible ones, more like Hell."[16]

After this excursion into the mining underworld, we agreed to start before sunup the next day and begin priming the concrete wall for the mural and doing the outlines of the frieze. We were in accord as to the motif that was to be rendered:
"The self-sacrificing collaboration between the Moatize miners and the [East German] mining experts in a sunny, flowery setting, suggesting an optimistic future." Here, miners from both countries were toiling away to the limits of their resilience.[17]

Mankew sees himself as standing alongside the Mozambican working class. This is why he pointedly went with Harald to Moatize. "As far as I was concerned, it wasn't just about me or art per se. The workers should be able to see that artists and art are their allies," he says enthusiastically.[18]

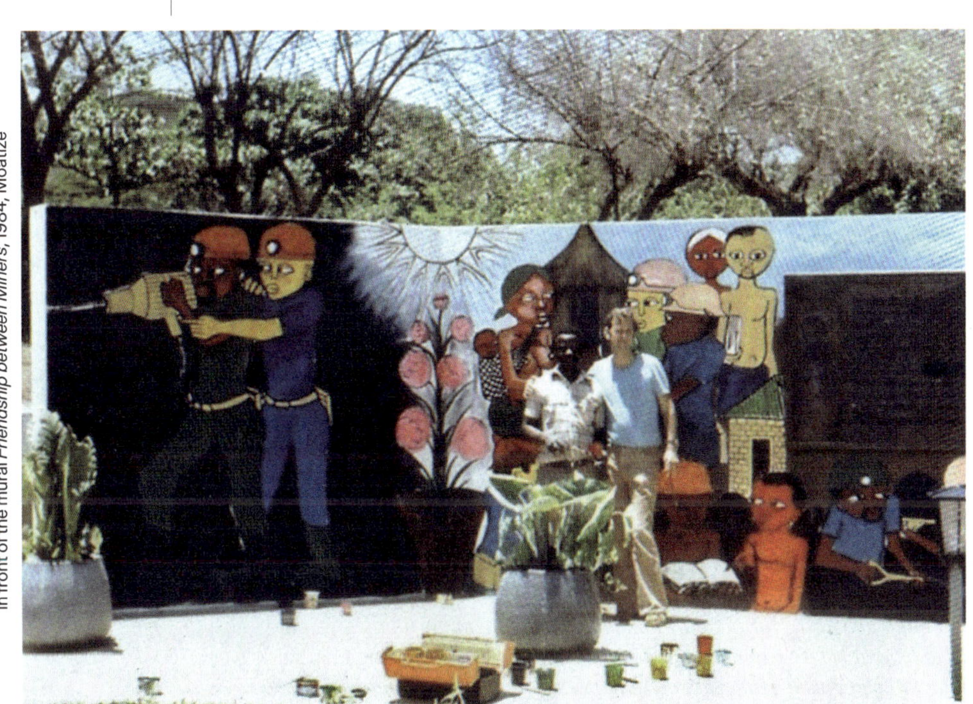

Fig. 26: Mankew V. Mahumana and Harald Heinke in front of the mural *Friendship between Miners,* 1984, Moatize

Abb. 26: Mankew V. Mahumana und Harald Heinke vor dem Wandbild *Freundschaft der Bergarbeiter,* 1984, Moatize

„Nach diesem Ausflug in die Unterwelt des Bergwerks vereinbarten wir, am nächsten Tag vor Sonnenaufgang mit der Grundierung der Beton-Malwand und der Gestaltung der Umrisse des Wandfrieses zu beginnen. Über das zu gestaltende Thema gab es Übereinstimmung:
‚Die aufopferungsvolle Zusammenarbeit der Bergleute aus Moatize und den Bergbau-Spezialisten [aus der DDR] mit einem sonnigen, blumigen Umfeld in einer optimistischen Zukunft.' Hier schufteten Bergleute beider Länder bis an die Grenze der Belastbarkeit."[17]

„Mankeu sieht seinen Platz an der Seite der moçambiquanischen arbeitenden Klasse. Demonstrativ ist er mit Harald gerade deshalb nach Moatize gefahren. ‚Dabei ging es mir nicht nur um mich oder um die Kunst schlechthin. Die Arbeiter sollten sehen, daß Künstler und Kunst ihre Verbündeten sind', sagt er engagiert."[18]

17. Heinke, *Khanimambo Moçambique,* S. 141.

18. Walter Michel, *Lieder vom Sambesi. Impressionen aus der Volksrepublik Moçambique,* Berlin: Verlag Neues Leben 1984, S. 195.

AMBRE ALFREDO AND LEA MARIE NIENHOFF IN CONVERSATION
WITH ALBINO MAHUMANA, SON OF MANKEW V. MAHUMANA

"MY FATHER ALWAYS PAINTED FLOWERS"

Dear Albino,
Could you share a bit about yourself and your experience growing up in
Mozambique with a renowned painter as a father? How has this back-
ground influenced your personal life?

My name is Albino Mahumana. As a child, my father would take me along whenever he went to exhibitions. When I was seven to eight years old, I was already into the arts. He'd go and chat to his friends, Malangatana, Magaia, Samate … I used to play with their children. While they were discussing art, we were playing. My whole life is about art. I was born in the arts, I breathe art, I live art, I think art, I imagine art, and with art, I make the world better.

I'm a photojournalist for a newspaper here in Mozambique. I divide my time between photography and painting. My painting is figurative. I try to portray my experiences, what I see every day, what I imagine my country will become in the future.

You were about ten when Harald Heinke came to Maputo in 1980. Do you
still remember when you first met him?

I remember Harald Heinke very well. He was skinny, tall. I think he had a gold tooth here [points to one of his front teeth]. He was very chatty. Very friendly with the children. He always organized meetings with Mozambican and foreign artists at his house in Rua de Mukumbura. I always went with my father. Harald was a cultural attaché. He created exchanges between artists. He really boosted the culture, the relationship between

AMBRE ALFREDO UND LEA MARIE NIENHOFF IM GESPRÄCH MIT
ALBINO MAHUMANA, SOHN VON MANKEW V. MAHUMANA

„MEIN VATER HAT IMMER BLUMEN GEMALT"

Lieber Albino, wie war es für dich, in Mosambik mit einem berühmten Maler
als Vater aufzuwachsen? Kannst du uns etwas von deinen Erfahrungen erzäh-
len und davon, wie dieser Hintergrund dein persönliches Leben geprägt hat?

Als Kind hat mich mein Vater immer mitgenommen, wenn er zu Ausstellungen ging. Ich habe mich schon für Kunst interessiert, da war ich erst sieben oder acht Jahre alt. Er unterhielt sich mit seinen Freunden Malangatana, Magaia, Samate … Und ich habe mit ihren Kindern gespielt. Während sie über Kunst diskutierten, spielten wir. Mein ganzes Leben dreht sich um Kunst. Ich wurde in die Kunst hineingeboren, ich atme Kunst, ich lebe Kunst, ich denke Kunst, ich stelle mir Kunst vor, mit Kunst mache ich die Welt zu einem besseren Ort.

Ich bin Fotojournalist für eine Zeitung hier in Mosambik. Meine Zeit widme ich sowohl der Fotografie als auch der Malerei. Meine Malerei ist figurativ. Ich versuche, meine Eindrücke und Alltagserfahrungen darzustellen und meine Vorstellung davon, wie mein Land in der Zukunft aussehen könnte, zum Ausdruck zu bringen.

Du warst etwa zehn Jahre alt, als Harald Heinke 1979 nach Maputo kam.
Erinnerst du dich noch daran, wie du ihm zum ersten Mal begegnet bist?

Ich erinnere mich sehr gut an Harald Heinke. Er war schlank, hochgewachsen. Ich glaube, er hatte hier einen Goldzahn [zeigt auf einen seiner Vorderzähne]. Er war sehr gesprächig. Sehr freundlich zu den Kindern. Er organisierte Treffen mit mosambikanischen und ausländischen Künstlern in seinem Haus in der Rua de Mukumbura. Ich bin oft mit meinem Vater dorthin gegangen. Harald Heinke war ein Kulturattaché. Er hat den Austausch zwischen Künstlern gefördert. Er hat die Kultur, die Beziehungen zwischen Mosambik und der ehemaligen DDR wirklich gefördert. Dabei

Mozambique and the former GDR. He was very dynamic. And not just between the two countries, with artists from other countries as well. He was a true ambassador for the arts. He was an uncle to me. Harald was family to us, here at home. He left a great relic with my father, a Lada, the colour of your shirt. A beautiful yellow Lada. I still remember the car very well. With the steering wheel on the left.

My father—I can't remember the year, 2015 or 2016—went to Germany again at Harald's invitation. Harald was very active in the visual arts. I think he didn't just do this with Mozambique, but also with other countries. My father and Harald were like brothers.

In the 1980s, many GDR citizens came to Mozambique. Several artists, such as the sculptor Wolfgang Eckardt, also came during that time. Do you know if your father was friends with them, and if they also came to visit your father in the studio, or was it mainly Harald Heinke?

Yes, yes, I know Wolfgang Eckardt very well. He made a statue of my late father. I know him very well.

They used to come to my father's house, and they also invited my father to their place. There was this exchange. The conversation was always about art. And there's another very important point. They helped a lot in terms of painting materials. Most of the paints my father used came from the former GDR. They were very supportive. Paints. Paper. Ink. They helped a lot.

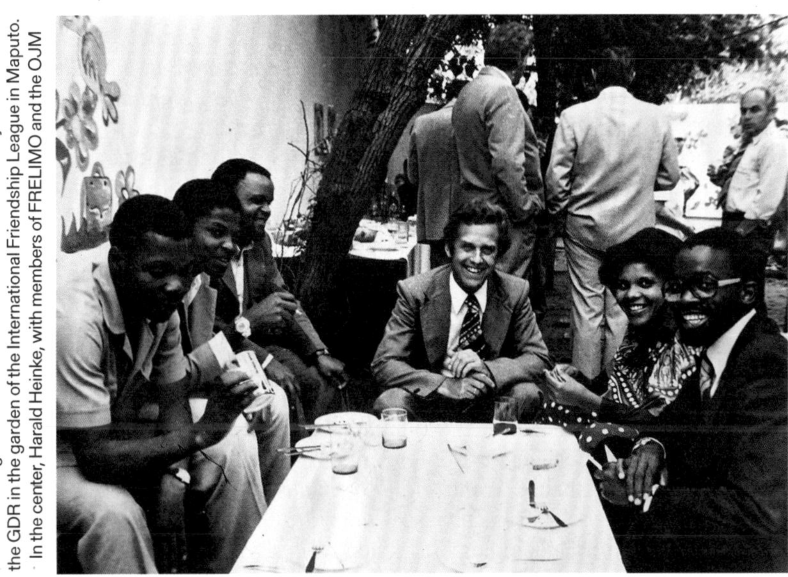

Fig. 27: Celebration of the thirtieth anniversary of the GDR in the garden of the International Friendship League in Maputo. In the center, Harald Heinke, with members of FRELIMO and the OJM

Abb. 27: Feierlichkeiten zum 30. Jahrestag der DDR im Garten der Liga in Maputo. In der Mitte Harald Heinke, neben ihm Mitglieder der FRELIMO und der OJM

war er äußerst dynamisch. Und zwar nicht nur im Austausch zwischen diesen beiden Ländern, sondern auch mit Künstlern aus anderen Ländern. Er war ein echter Botschafter für die Kunst. Für mich war er wie ein Onkel. Harald Heinke gehörte zur Familie. Er hat meinem Vater ein großes Geschenk hinterlassen, einen Lada, in der Farbe von Ihrem Hemd. Ein schöner gelber Lada. Ich erinnere mich noch sehr gut an das Auto. Es hatte das Lenkrad auf der linken Seite.

Mein Vater war auf Einladung von Harald Heinke noch mal in Deutschland, ich weiß nicht mehr genau, in welchem Jahr, 2015 oder 2016. Harald Heinke war sehr aktiv im Bereich der bildenden Kunst. Ich glaube, er hat das nicht nur mit Mosambik gemacht, sondern auch mit anderen Ländern. Mein Vater und Harald Heinke waren wie Brüder.

In den 1980er Jahren kamen viele DDR-Bürger nach Mosambik. Auch einige Künstler, wie der Bildhauer Wolfgang Eckardt, besuchten das Land in dieser Zeit. Weißt du, ob dein Vater mit ihnen befreundet war und ob die Gäste auch deinen Vater im Atelier besuchten? Oder waren sie hauptsächlich bei Harald Heinke anzutreffen?

Ja, ja, ich kenne Wolfgang Eckardt sehr gut. Er hat eine Büste von meinem verstorbenen Vater geschaffen.

Sie kamen zum Haus meines Vaters und luden auch meinen Vater zu sich nach Hause ein. Es gab diesen Austausch. Die Gespräche drehten sich immer um Kunst. Und ein weiterer entscheidender Punkt ist, dass sie bei den Malmaterialien sehr geholfen haben. Die meisten Farben, die mein

Now, almost every day, Harald either went to my father's house, or my father went to his place, so it's easy for us to remember. He didn't have to knock; he'd arrive at our place, open the door, and come in. It was his home. When we went to his house, we felt at ease, it was our home too. It filled us with joy because we were so young. Being in the house of a person of a different race, a white man. We're black, and we're having that freedom. There's no racism. It was extraordinary. We felt different. When he arrived, we hugged. I treasure this memory. Back then? Today, it's easy for this to happen—the relationship between Black and White people— but not then. That inspired me a lot. In terms of freedom, in terms of me as a human being knowing how to value another human being, I learnt a lot back then. It was rare. His humanity transcends borders. I'm talking about the late 1970s, the 1980s … It wasn't normal for a white person to leave Sommerschield and go to Xipamanine. He was a phenomenal person; I've never met anyone like him.

And did your father have similar friendships with artists from other socialist countries—e.g., Cuba or the Soviet Union?

He had relations with all the countries in the Socialist Bloc. There were many relationships between Mozambican artists and the Socialist Bloc. There was no relationship with the other bloc. The relationship between the GDR, Russia, Yugoslavia, and Cuba was strong. But the link with the former GDR was very strong, compared to other countries.

What hopes did Mankew associate with his commitment, including his political commitment through art? What world, what future did he dream of?

My father helped a lot to build this country. The work he did had to do with love and peace. Most of his works had a dove and always a flower, which symbolizes love, symbolizes peace. He dreamed a lot about his own country. He had the opportunity to live abroad. He was invited to live abroad, but he said no, I'm not leaving my country. I'm going to stay

Vater benutzte, kamen aus der ehemaligen DDR. Sie waren sehr hilfsbereit. Farben. Papier. Tinte. Damit haben sie sehr geholfen.

Nun, Harald Heinke kam fast jeden Tag entweder zu meinem Vater nach Hause oder mein Vater ging zu seiner Wohnung, daher können wir uns gut an ihn erinnern. Er brauchte nicht zu klopfen, er kam zu uns, öffnete die Tür und trat ein. Es war sein Zuhause. Wenn wir in sein Haus gingen, fühlten wir uns ebenso wohl, es war auch unser Zuhause. Es erfüllte uns mit Freude – weil wir so jung waren –, im Haus eines Menschen einer anderen Ethnie, eines Weißen, zu sein. Wir sind schwarz und wir erlebten diese Freiheit ohne Rassismus. Das war etwas ganz Besonderes. Wir fühlten uns anders. Wenn er kam, umarmten wir uns. Diese Erinnerung ist mir sehr wichtig. Heute ist so etwas leicht möglich – die Beziehung zwischen Schwarzen und Weißen –, aber damals war das anders. Das hat mich sehr inspiriert. Was die Freiheit angeht, was mich als Mensch betrifft, der anderen Menschen mit Wertschätzung begegnet, habe ich damals sehr viel gelernt. Das war etwas Ungewöhnliches. Seine Menschlichkeit setzte sich über Grenzen hinweg. Ich spreche von den späten 1970ern, den 1980ern … Da war es nicht normal für einen Weißen, Sommerschield zu verlassen und nach Xipamanine zu gehen. Er war ein phänomenaler Mensch; jemanden wie ihn gibt es kein zweites Mal.

Unterhielt dein Vater ähnliche Freundschaften mit Künstlern aus anderen sozialistischen Ländern, zum Beispiel aus Kuba oder der Sowjetunion?

Er unterhielt Beziehungen zu allen Ländern des sozialistischen Blocks. Es gab viele Beziehungen zwischen mosambikanischen Künstlern und dem sozialistischen Block. Mit dem anderen Block gab es hingegen keine Verbindung. Die Beziehungen zwischen der DDR, Russland, Jugoslawien und Kuba waren eng. Aber die Verbindung mit der ehemaligen DDR war im Vergleich zu den anderen Ländern noch einmal besonders ausgeprägt.

Welche Hoffnungen verband Mankew mit seinem Engagement, auch mit seinem politischen Engagement durch die Kunst? Von welcher Welt, von welcher Zukunft hat er geträumt?

here in Mozambique. This epitomizes the love he had for his country. His dream hasn't materialized yet. Democracy has to be consolidated in the country, there have to be more freedoms. We have serious problems. His dream is yet to materialize; it hasn't materialized yet. But he loved the country, just as I love the country. The artist's mission is to fight for the development of their own country. Don't abandon your country. No. Help build your country. Use art to build your country. Promoting peace, promoting freedom through painting. This is our job as artists. That's how we build a society. We need to avoid the brain drain from Africa to Europe. Africans have to stay in Africa. They have to fight to develop their own country, not leave it because it doesn't have good conditions. Fight for your country to have better conditions. Don't abandon it.

In 1984, your father traveled for six weeks in the GDR. Did he tell you about the trip? What impressions did he gather there? What was it like for him?

On one of his trips, I can't remember which one, he was appointed a member of the East German Academy of Arts. He has a document certifying that he is a member of the academy. He brought clothes and toys, but there's one thing that will never fade from memory: he was a member of the East German Academy of Arts. This will never be erased. It's written there. I think that's the biggest memory, but I have several memories. He traveled there a lot. He came with magazines; he came with photographs. We have many memories, as if we had traveled there through those photos, through the magazines, through the gifts. At that time, things weren't so easy here, so he always came with a suitcase full of clothes to give to his children. It was an enormous joy for us.

Did he feel welcome in the GDR?

He felt at home. It was his second home. He went more to the GDR. He also went to Russia, but with the GDR, it was a brotherly relationship.

Mein Vater hat mitgeholfen, dieses Land aufzubauen. Seine Arbeit war von seinem Einsatz für Liebe und Frieden geprägt. Auf den meisten seiner Werke gibt es eine Taube und immer eine Blume, die Liebe und Frieden symbolisieren. Er hatte viele Träume für sein Land. Er hatte durchaus die Möglichkeit, im Ausland zu leben. Er wurde eingeladen, im Ausland zu leben, aber er sagte: Nein, ich verlasse mein Land nicht. Ich werde hier in Mosambik bleiben. Das beweist die Liebe, die er für sein Land empfand. Sein Traum ist noch nicht in Erfüllung gegangen. Die Demokratie muss im Land gefestigt werden, es muss mehr Freiheiten geben. Wir haben ernsthafte Probleme. Aber er hat das Land geliebt, so wie ich das Land liebe. Es ist die Aufgabe eines Künstlers, für die Entwicklung des eigenen Landes zu kämpfen. Lass dein Land nicht im Stich. Nein. Hilf mit, dein Land aufzubauen. Nutze die Kunst, um dein Land aufzubauen. Fördere den Frieden, fördere die Freiheit durch die Malerei. Das ist unsere Aufgabe als Künstler. Auf diese Weise bauen wir eine Gesellschaft auf. Wir müssen den Braindrain von Afrika nach Europa verhindern. Die afrikanische Bevölkerung muss in Afrika bleiben. Sie müssen dafür kämpfen, ihr eigenes Land zu entwickeln, und dürfen es nicht verlassen, auch wenn die Bedingungen ungünstig sind. Kämpfe dafür, dass sich die Bedingungen in deinem Land verbessern. Lass es nicht im Stich.

1984 reiste dein Vater für sechs Wochen in die DDR. Hat er dir von dieser Reise erzählt? Welche Eindrücke hat er dort gesammelt? Wie war es für ihn?

Auf einer seiner Reisen, ich weiß nicht mehr, auf welcher, wurde er zum Mitglied der Akademie der Künste der DDR ernannt. Er erhielt eine Urkunde, die seine Mitgliedschaft in der Akademie der Künste bestätigte. Er brachte Kleidung und Spielzeug mit, aber das ist das, was ich nie vergessen werde: Er war Mitglied der Akademie der Künste der ehemaligen DDR. Das wird nie gelöscht werden. Es steht dort geschrieben. Ich glaube, das ist die schönste Erinnerung. Neben so vielen anderen. Er reiste oft dorthin. Er brachte Zeitschriften mit, er brachte Fotografien mit. Wir haben viele Erinnerungen gesammelt, als wären wir durch diese Fotos, durch die Magazine und durch die Geschenke selbst dorthin gereist. Damals war hier

Then AMASP was created, the Association of Friendship and Solidarity Between Peoples, which served as a link. If we weren't living in Mozambique, we'd be living in the GDR.

Mankew painted a mural with Harald Heinke for the coal miners in Moatize, entitled "Friendship of the Miners." The painting was also dedicated to celebrating the collaboration between East German mining companies and the Mozambican mine. How did Mankew see the role of the GDR in relation to the expansion of the mine in Moatize and this mining work in general? Because he also worked in the mine as a young man in South Africa.

My father went to South Africa to work in the mines. He worked with other brothers from Zimbabwe and neighboring countries. At the time, South Africa was the Eldorado of southern Africa. Now it's not. So, the tendency was to leave your country to go to South Africa to work. My father went there to work and the memories he has are of meeting many good people from other countries, such as Namibia, Botswana, and Eswatini.

As for Moatize, the great memory he always shared was the generosity of the former GDR. The heart of the people and the government to help the countries that were following the socialist line. They received support, including moral support, which is much more important. These are the memories he always shared with us.

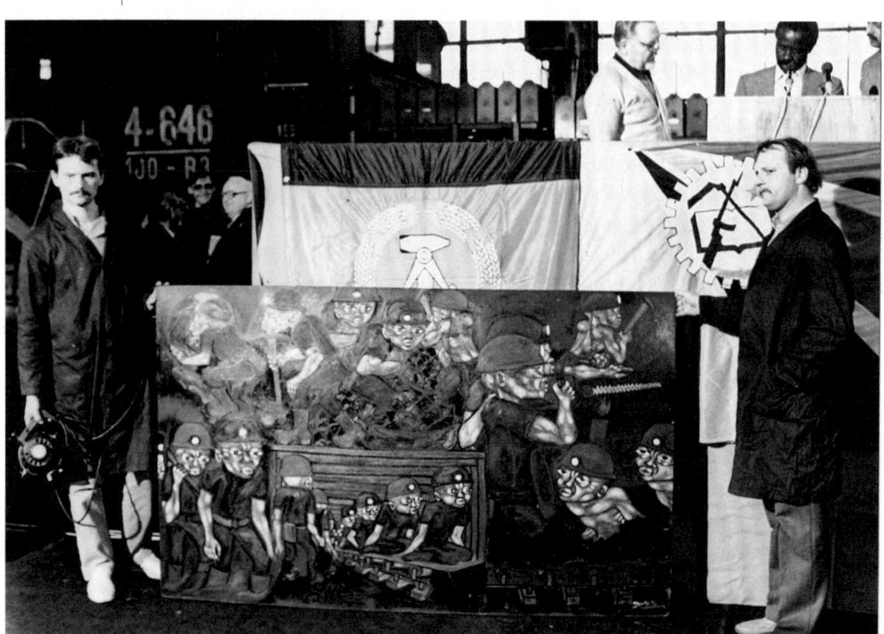

Fig. 28: Mankew V. Mahumana (in the top-right corner of the photograph) presenting his painting as a gift to the brigade "Eduardo Mondlane" at the VEB Gaskombinat Schwarze Pumpe on April 26, 1984

Abb. 28: Mankew V. Mahumana (in der rechten oberen Ecke) überreichte den Arbeitern der Brigade „Eduardo Mondlane" im VEB Gaskombinat Schwarze Pumpe am 26. April 1984 ein Gemälde als Geschenk

alles nicht so einfach, deshalb brachte er immer einen Koffer voller Kleidung mit, um sie seinen Kindern zu schenken. Das war eine große Freude für uns.

Hat er sich in der DDR willkommen gefühlt?

Er fühlte sich zu Hause. Es war seine zweite Heimat. Er reiste öfters in die DDR. Er ging auch nach Russland, aber mit der DDR war es ein brüderliches Verhältnis. Dann wurde die AMASP gegründet, die Mosambikanische Gesellschaft für Freundschaft und Solidarität zwischen den Völkern, die als Bindeglied diente. Wenn wir nicht in Mosambik gelebt hätten, wären wir in die DDR gegangen.

Mankew hat zusammen mit Harald Heinke ein Wandgemälde für die Bergarbeiter in Moatize gemalt mit dem Titel Freundschaft der Bergarbeiter. Das Gemälde sollte auch die Zusammenarbeit zwischen ostdeutschen Bergbauunternehmen und dem mosambikanischen Bergwerk würdigen. Wie sah Mankew die Rolle der DDR in Bezug auf den Ausbau der Mine in Moatize und bei den Bergbauarbeiten im Allgemeinen? Er hat selbst als junger Mann in einer Mine in Südafrika gearbeitet.

Mein Vater ging nach Südafrika, um in den Minen zu arbeiten. Er arbeitete dort mit Brothers aus Simbabwe und den benachbarten Ländern. Damals war Südafrika das Eldorado des südlichen Afrika. Heute ist es das nicht mehr. Die Tendenz ging also dahin, sein Land zu verlassen und nach Südafrika zu

1. Harald Heinke, *Khanimambo Moçambique: Tagebuch und malerische Impressionen einer bewegten Zeit in Mosambik von 1979 bis 1985* (Projekte-Verlag Cornelius, 2010); Walter Michel, *Lieder vom Sambesi: Impressionen aus der Volksrepublik Moçambique* (Verlag Neues Leben, 1984); Ursula Püschel, *Der Schlangenbaum: Eine Reise nach Moçambique* (Mitteldeutscher Verlag, 1984); Landolf Scherzer, *Bom dia, weißer Bruder: Erlebnisse am Sambesi* (Greifenverlag, 1984).

Many GDR writers and others who visited Mozambique got to know your father and wrote about him in books and travelogues. Four different publications exist in which the mural of the "friendship of the miners" is described.[1] One book is by Harald Heinke, describing how your father painted the mural and what it looks like. Harald's writing is full of gratitude and reverence for this work.

My father didn't have the habit of telling us, "I'm going to do this." We didn't know until he had done it. Only after they happened would he surprise us with a book, a catalog, a sculpture from Germany.

It's always a pleasure for us as a family, as children, as Mozambique when a Mozambican artist is recognized in Europe. Especially at a time when it was difficult. Today, it's easy, but back then it was difficult. To have a Mozambican artist who is being recognized in Germany, the former GDR, is a star in Mozambique, and is my father. It's a great source of pride. Great pride.

How did your father experience the changes after the fall of the Berlin Wall? He was removed from the list of the East German Academy of Arts because it was dissolved. I can imagine that it was more difficult to maintain the relationship with Germany after that. How did he experience the change after 1990?

My father loved the socialist regime. So, with the fall of the socialist regime, he felt very bad. He died a socialist. He felt terrible. All that support that was going on—when the Berlin Wall came down, it didn't happen anymore. Nothing happened anymore. All those socialist African countries, I'm sure none of them received any more support. The capitalist regime came in. My father was never in favor of the capitalist regime. He always said so, he never hid it. He's a socialist; he was never a capitalist. He never liked it. He died without liking the capitalist regime. He was always on the socialist side. He always said, I'm not going to hide it. So, when the USSR was dissolved, it was painful for him. He thought that in the socialist

gehen, um dort zu arbeiten. Auch mein Vater ging dorthin, um zu arbeiten, und was er in Erinnerung behalten hat, ist, dass er viele gute Leute aus anderen Ländern wie Namibia, Botswana und Eswatini kennengelernt hat.

Was Moatize betrifft, so betonte er uns gegenüber immer die Großherzigkeit der ehemaligen DDR. Das Herz dieser Menschen und dieser Regierung, den Ländern zu helfen, die sich auf der sozialistischen Linie befanden. Sie erhielten Unterstützung, auch moralische Unterstützung, was noch viel wichtiger ist. Das sind die Erinnerungen, die er immer mit uns geteilt hat.

Viele DDR-Schriftsteller·innen und andere, die Mosambik besuchten, lernten deinen Vater kennen und schrieben über ihn in Büchern und Reiseberichten. Es gibt vier Publikationen, in denen das Wandbild der Freundschaft der Bergarbeiter *beschrieben wird.[1] Eines der Bücher stammt von Harald Heinke, er beschreibt, wie dein Vater dieses Wandbild geschaffen hat und wie es aussieht. Heinkes Text ist von Dankbarkeit und Ehrfurcht für dieses Werk geprägt.*

Mein Vater hatte nicht die Angewohnheit, uns im Vorhinein groß zu erklären: Ich werde dieses und jenes tun. Wir hatten keine Ahnung, bis er es getan hatte. Erst im Anschluss hat er uns mit einem Buch, einem Katalog, einer Skulptur aus Deutschland überrascht.

Es ist immer eine Freude für uns als Familie, als Kinder, als Mosambikaner, wenn ein mosambikanischer Künstler in Europa anerkannt wird. Besonders damals, als es schwierig war. Heute ist es einfach, aber damals war es schwierig. Ein mosambikanischer Künstler, der in Deutschland, der ehemaligen DDR, Anerkennung findet, ist ein Star in Mosambik, und dann war er auch noch mein Vater. Das ist ein Grund, stolz zu sein. Sehr stolz.

Wie hat dein Vater die Veränderungen nach dem Fall der Mauer erlebt? Er wurde von der Liste der Akademie der Künste gestrichen, weil die Akademie der Künste der DDR aufgelöst wurde. Ich kann mir vorstellen, dass es danach schwieriger war, die Beziehungen zu Deutschland aufrechtzuerhalten. Wie hat er die Veränderung nach 1990 erlebt?

1. Harald Heinke, *Khanimambo Moçambique. Tagebuch und malerische Impressionen einer bewegten Zeit in Mosambik von 1979 bis 1985*, Halle: Projekte-Verlag Cornelius 2010; Walter Michel, *Lieder vom Sambesi. Impressionen aus der Volksrepublik Moçambique*, Berlin: Verlag Neues Leben 1984; Ursula Püschel, *Der Schlangenbaum. Eine Reise nach Moçambique*, Halle und Leipzig: Mitteldeutscher Verlag 1984; Landolf Scherzer, *Bom dia, weißer Bruder. Erlebnisse am Sambesi*, Rudolstadt: Greifenverlag 1984.

regime there was fairness, equality in the distribution of wealth. That's
what he always said.

Was it more difficult to make a living from his work after 1990?
It wasn't just difficult for my father. It was difficult for all Mozambicans.
It was a national crisis. But he always made sure there was no shortage of
bread at home. We always had bread. I don't know how he found it. He
was a visual artist; he woke up and worked. He'd be in his studio painting
at 5 am. He always worked hard, always gave us the feeling that things
would get better. We grew up with this kind of spirit, when there's diffi-
culty, we always find an alternative to survive. He didn't give me fish, he
taught me how to fish. That's what he taught me: "My son, in the midst
of difficulties, find a way to survive, don't cry." That's the great legacy
I have from him.

*In terms of recognition of the arts, do you think there has been a change
in the way the state views the arts from the socialist period to the capitalist period?*
Things have become more difficult now. Before it was easy—there used to
be support. Now, it's very difficult to sell works of art here in Mozambique.

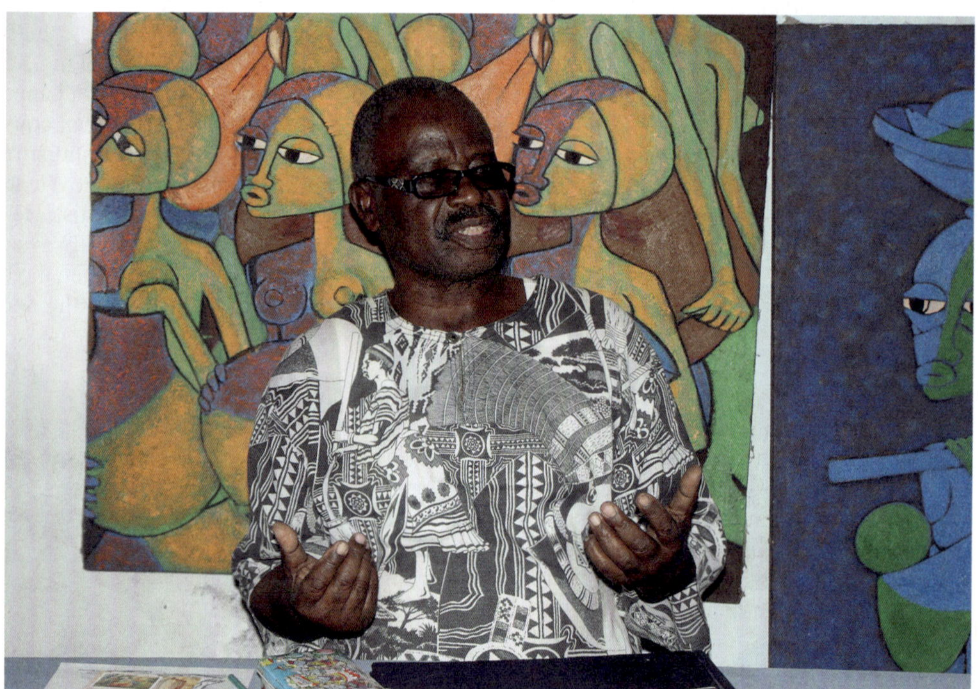

Fig. 29: Mankew conversing with journalists from a Mozambican magazine.
The photograph, taken by Albino Mahumana, was captured in the latter years of his life

Abb. 29: Mankew im Gespräch mit Journalisten eines mosambikanischen Magazins.
Das Foto wurde von Albino Mahumana in Mankews letzten Lebensjahren aufgenommen

Mein Vater liebte den Sozialismus. Deshalb ging es ihm nach dem Zu-
sammenbruch des sozialistischen Regimes sehr schlecht. Er starb als So-
zialist. Er fühlte sich schrecklich. Auch die gesamte Unterstützung, die es
gegeben hatte, endete mit dem Fall der Berliner Mauer. Es geschah einfach
nichts mehr. All die sozialistischen Staaten in Afrika – ich bin sicher, dass
keiner davon noch Unterstützung erhielt. Stattdessen kam das kapitalistische Regime. Mein Vater war nie ein Befürworter des Kapitalismus. Das
hat er immer rundheraus gesagt, er hat es nie verheimlicht. Er starb, ohne
das kapitalistische Regime zu mögen. Er war immer auf der Seite der Sozialisten. Als die UdSSR aufgelöst wurde, war das für ihn sehr schmerz-
haft. Er war überzeugt, dass es im Sozialismus Gerechtigkeit und Gleichheit bei der Verteilung des Wohlstands gab. Das hat er immer gesagt.

War es für ihn nach 1990 schwieriger, von seiner Arbeit zu leben?
Es war nicht nur für meinen Vater schwierig. Es war für alle Mosambikaner
schwierig. Es war eine nationale Krise. Aber er hat immer dafür gesorgt,
dass es zu Hause nicht an Brot fehlte. Ich weiß nicht, wie er es hinkriegte.
Er war ein bildender Künstler; er wachte auf und arbeitete. Um fünf Uhr
morgens stand er in seinem Atelier und malte. Er hat immer hart gearbeitet
und uns stets das Gefühl gegeben, dass es bergauf gehen wird. Wir sind
mit diesem Spirit aufgewachsen: Wenn es auch Schwierigkeiten gibt, wir
finden immer einen Weg zu überleben. Er hat mir keinen Fisch gegeben,

I'm not saying it doesn't sell, but it's difficult to sell. You have to be in some kind of scheme to sell a work of art. I can hardly sell. People don't look at quality; they look at commissions. It used to be easy. In previous governments, exhibitions were organized for the government to buy the artists' works. Today, that's no longer the case. We've fallen a lot. We've been better, but now we've fallen a lot.

We're in a very difficult country, and things aren't easy. But I'm going to keep fighting for a better Mozambique, for a better life for artists. That's what my father taught me. My father taught me that. Peace, harmony, love, work. Four things: peace, harmony, love, work.

er hat mir beigebracht, wie man fischt. Das ist es, was er mich gelehrt hat: Mein Sohn, finde inmitten von Schwierigkeiten einen Weg zu überleben, weine nicht. Das ist das, was ich von ihm als Vermächtnis erhalten habe.

Was den Stellenwert von Kultur und Kunst betrifft, wie hat sich deiner Einschätzung nach durch den Übergang von Sozialismus zu Kapitalismus das Verhältnis des Staats zur Kultur verändert?

Es ist schwieriger geworden. Früher war es einfacher, da hat es noch Unterstützung gegeben. Heute ist es hier in Mosambik sehr schwierig, Kunstwerke zu verkaufen. Ich will damit nicht sagen, dass sie sich gar nicht verkaufen lassen, aber es ist schwierig. Um ein Kunstwerk zu verkaufen, muss man in irgendeine Art von Projekt eingebunden sein. Ich kann kaum etwas verkaufen. Die Leute achten nicht auf die Qualität, sie schauen auf die Aufträge. Früher war es einfach. In der Vergangenheit hat die Regierung Ausstellungen organisiert, damit die Werke der Künstler gekauft werden können. Heute ist das nicht mehr der Fall. Wir haben einen Rückgang erlebt. Es ging uns mal besser, wir sind stark zurückgefallen.

Wir leben in einem sehr schwierigen Land, und die Dinge sind nicht einfach. Aber ich werde weiter für ein besseres Mosambik und ein besseres Leben für die Künstler kämpfen. Das hat mir mein Vater beigebracht. Vier Dinge: Frieden, Harmonie, Liebe, Arbeit.

AMBRE ALFREDO

IF AN APPOINTMENT WITH HISTORY COULD SHELTER DREAMS

PERSONAL REFLECTIONS ON THE INTERVIEW WITH ALBINO MAHUMANA

I have always been curious about and inspired by post-independence Mozambique. I only got to know the Mozambique that came after—the Mozambique of "free elections," of "donors," of structural adjustment programs and public debts. The Mozambique of "deixa-andar."

I only know post-independence Mozambique through stories and anecdotes. People don't talk about it much. It was a difficult time. A time of war and hunger, of restrictions and repression. Of re-education camps. But it was also a time of hopes, dreams, and new possibilities. After all, we were constructing a new country. *Our* country. Finally.

Art played an essential role in the construction of this new country. Since before independence, when Mozambique was still considered a property of Portugal, it was through art that collective imaginaries of independence were shaped. After independence, art acquired an even more central role. From day one. To celebrate independence, which was on June 25, 1975, the government organized an art exhibition from June 21 to 29, around the themes of independence, the end of colonialism, the suffering during colonial times, and the new era that was coming. Art and decoloniality at the centre of a celebration of independence—how beautiful is that? The government saw and used art as a powerful tool in constructing the "New Society," a society free from colonial domination. And artists played an active role in the "new Mozambique."

"My father helped build this country," Albino told us with pride. Mankew went from being a gold miner in apartheid South Africa—like many Mozambicans—to one of the country's most renowned painters. How unlikely is it for a miner to become a painter? This does not happen, at least not today. But it could,

AMBRE ALFREDO

WENN EINE BEGEGNUNG MIT DER GESCHICHTE TRÄUME BEHERBERGEN KÖNNTE

PERSÖNLICHE REFLEXIONEN ÜBER DAS INTERVIEW MIT ALBINO MAHUMANA

Ich war immer neugierig auf das Mosambik nach der Unabhängigkeit und fühlte mich davon inspiriert. Selbst habe ich nur das Mosambik kennengelernt, das danach kam – das Mosambik der „freien Wahlen", der „Spendenorganisationen", der Strukturanpassungsprogramme und der Verschuldung der öffentlichen Hand. Das Mosambik des „deixa-andar" (laisser-faire).

Ich kenne das Mosambik nach der Unabhängigkeit nur aus Erzählungen und Anekdoten. Die Leute reden nicht viel darüber. Es war eine schwierige Zeit. Eine Zeit des Krieges und des Hungers, der Einschränkungen und der Unterdrückung. Es gab Umerziehungslager. Aber es war auch eine Zeit der Hoffnung, der Träume und neuen Möglichkeiten. Schließlich bauten wir ein neues Land auf. *Unser* Land. Endlich.

Die Kunst spielte eine wesentliche Rolle beim Aufbau dieses neuen Landes. Schon vor der Unabhängigkeit, als Mosambik noch als Eigentum Portugals galt, erlaubte es die Kunst, kollektive Vorstellungen von Unabhängigkeit zu formen. Nach der Unabhängigkeit nahm sie eine noch zentralere Rolle ein. Und zwar vom ersten Tag an. Zur Feier der Unabhängigkeit, die offiziell am 25. Juni 1975 erfolgte, organisierte die Regierung vom 21. bis 29. Juni eine Kunstausstellung zur Unabhängigkeit, zum Ende des Kolonialismus, dem erlittenen Leid während der Kolonialzeit und dem Aufbruch in eine neue Zeit. Kunst und Dekolonisation im Zentrum einer Feier der Unabhängigkeit – wie schön ist das? Die Regierung sah und nutzte die Kunst als ein mächtiges Instrument beim Aufbau der „neuen Gesellschaft", einer Gesellschaft frei von kolonialer Herrschaft. Und die Künstler·innen spielten eine aktive Rolle im „neuen Mosambik".

1. Ulla Massow, "Gemalte Geschichten über sein afrikanisches Volk," *Neues Deutschland*, April 30, 1984, AdK-O 2385.

at that specific time, when art was "a weapon in the class struggle". It made sense back then for a miner to become a painter. Not anymore.

"The works he did had to do with love and peace. Most of his works had a dove and always a flower, which symbolizes love, symbolizes peace. He dreamed a lot about his own country," as the painter's son, Albino, relates. Dreaming of love and peace in a country that went through ten years of war for independence followed by fifteen years of civil war is quite reasonable. Dreaming of love and peace becomes a necessity, a form of resistance. Mankew himself said, "The images that emerged from such experiences were my weapon against exploitation and, at the same time, my support for the FRELIMO party for liberation from oppression."[1]

The 1980s were Mankew's golden years. He gained great recognition at national and international levels—this alone is already an achievement, as very few Mozambican artists were (or are) known outside of Mozambique. He traveled at a time when being allowed to travel was a privilege of the very few, and he exhibited his work in several countries of the Eastern Bloc. The GDR was probably the country Mankew visited the most. "He felt at home [in the GDR]. It was his second home." Unlike many fellow Mozambicans—including two of his sons—who went to the GDR as "contract workers," Mankew went there to exhibit his work and participate in conferences, workshops, and other events. The GDR was also the country where Mankew was most acclaimed. In 1983, he was appointed a corresponding member of the East German Academy of Arts—another thing that could only have happened then. "One thing that will never fade from memory: he was a member of the East German Academy of Arts. This will never be erased. It's written there. This is the greatest memory," recalls Albino.

It is not written anymore. It was erased. In 1993, following the merger of the Academies of Arts of East and West Germany, Mankew was removed from the corresponding members' list. Together with the Berlin Wall, many things fell apart. "*Foi mágoa* … All that support that used to happen … didn't happen anymore. Nothing happened anymore."

With the 1990s came the IMF and its structural adjustment programs. Art was not a priority anymore—and still isn't. Constructing a "new Mozambique" neither.

„Mein Vater hat mitgeholfen, dieses Land aufzubauen", sagt der Sohn des Malers, Albino. Mankew wurde von einem Arbeiter in den Goldminen im Südafrika der Apartheid – wie es viele Mosambikaner waren – zu einem der bekanntesten Maler des Landes. Wie unwahrscheinlich ist es, dass ein Minenarbeiter zum Maler wird? Das passiert nicht, zumindest nicht heute. Aber zu jener Zeit, als die Kunst „eine Waffe im Klassenkampf" war, war es möglich. Damals sah man einen Sinn darin, dass ein Bergarbeiter Maler wurde. Das ist heute nicht mehr so.

„Seine Arbeit war von seinem Einsatz für Liebe und Frieden geprägt. Auf den meisten seiner Werke gibt es eine Taube und immer eine Blume, die Liebe und Frieden symbolisieren. Er hatte viele Träume für sein Land" – so beschreibt es Albino. Von Liebe und Frieden zu träumen in einem Land, das einen zehnjährigen Unabhängigkeitskrieg und einen 15-jährigen Bürgerkrieg hinter sich hat, ist ziemlich nachvollziehbar. Das Träumen von Liebe und Frieden wird zu einer Notwendigkeit, zu einer Form des Widerstands. Mankew selbst sagte: „Die auf Grund solcher Erlebnisse entstandenen Bilder waren meine Waffe gegen die Ausbeutung und zugleich eine Unterstützung der FRELIMO-Partei zur Befreiung von der Knechtschaft."[1]

Die 1980er waren die goldenen Jahre für Mankew. Ihm wurde große Anerkennung auf nationaler und internationaler Ebene zuteil – das allein ist schon eine Leistung, denn nur sehr wenige mosambikanische Künstler waren (und sind) außerhalb des Landes bekannt. Er unternahm Reisen zu einer Zeit, in der das Reisen ein Privileg der Wenigsten war, und stellte seine Werke in mehreren Ländern des Ostblocks aus. Die DDR war wahrscheinlich das Land, das Mankew am häufigsten besuchte. „Er fühlte sich [in der DDR] zu Hause. Es war seine zweite Heimat." Im Gegensatz zu vielen anderen Mosambikanern – darunter zwei seiner Söhne –, die als „Vertragsarbeiter" in die DDR gingen, war Mankew dort, um seine Arbeiten auszustellen und an Konferenzen, Workshops und anderen Veranstaltungen teilzunehmen. Die DDR war auch das Land, in dem Mankew am meisten Anerkennung erfuhr. Im Jahr 1983 wurde er zum korrespondierenden Mitglied der Akademie der Künste der DDR ernannt – auch das war nur in dieser Zeit möglich. „Das ist das, was ich nie vergessen werde: Er war Mitglied der Akademie der Künste der ehemaligen DDR. Das wird nie gelöscht werden. Es steht dort geschrieben", sagt Albino.

1. Ulla Massow, „Gemalte Geschichten über sein afrikanisches Volk", in: *Neues Deutschland*, 30.4.1984, AdK-O 2385.

Hope gave way to frustration. From the 1980s on, one thing remained: the friendship with Harald Heinke and, with it, the connection to Germany. The friendship, which started in Maputo in 1979, continued through letters after Harald's return to Germany in 1985. In the many letters Mankew wrote to Harald, there is a lot of affection, updates on family and health, requests for painting material, and plans for future exhibitions. There is an urge to make things happen. Some did happen, others never did.

"His dream hasn't materialized yet." The Mozambique Mankew and so many others, myself included, dreamed of things that never happened. I left the country six years ago, frustrated and hopeless—and very privileged, I know. I am not proud of leaving. Albino's words, "Don't abandon your country. No. Help build your country," are still vivid in my mind—the shame I felt listening to them, too. Being part of this project is a sort of reconciliation. Listening to Albino talk about his father Mankew, listening to David Abílio, reading Alda Costa, Luís Bernardo Honwana, and Eduardo Mondlane gives me hope. It makes me dream of a Mozambique that never got the chance to be, but perhaps still can?

Doch es steht da nicht mehr geschrieben. Die Erinnerung wurde ausradiert. 1993, nach der Fusion der Akademien der Künste in Ost- und Westdeutschland, wurde Mankew aus der Liste der korrespondierenden Mitglieder gestrichen. Zusammen mit der Berliner Mauer zerbrach vieles. „Er fühlte sich schrecklich. Auch die gesamte Unterstützung, die es gegeben hatte, endete mit dem Fall der Berliner Mauer. Es geschah einfach nichts mehr."

In den 1990er Jahren kamen der IWF und seine Strukturanpassungsprogramme. Die Kunst hatte keine Priorität mehr – und hat sie auch nicht wiederbekommen. Ein „neues Mosambik" aufzubauen auch nicht.

Die Hoffnung wich der Frustration. Aus den 1980er Jahren blieb eines: die Freundschaft mit Harald Heinke und damit die Verbindung nach Deutschland. Die Freundschaft, die 1979 in Maputo ihren Anfang genommen hatte, wurde nach Heinkes Rückkehr nach Deutschland 1985 mit Briefen fortgesetzt. In den zahlreichen Briefen, die Mankew an Heinke schrieb, findet sich viel Zuneigung, Neuigkeiten über Familie und Gesundheit, Bitten um Malutensilien und Pläne für zukünftige Ausstellungen. Es gibt den Wunsch, Dinge zu verwirklichen. Manches davon ist umgesetzt worden, anderes nie.

„Sein Traum ist noch nicht in Erfüllung gegangen." Der Mosambikaner Mankew und so viele andere, ich eingeschlossen, träumten von Dingen, die nie eingetreten sind. Ich verließ das Land vor sechs Jahren, frustriert und hoffnungslos – und sehr privilegiert, wie ich weiß. Ich bin nicht stolz darauf, es verlassen zu haben. Albinos Worte haben sich mir tief eingeprägt: „Lass dein Land nicht im Stich. Nein. Hilf mit, dein Land aufzubauen" – und auch die Scham, die ich bei diesen Worten empfand. Teil dieses Projekts zu sein, ist ein Versuch der Versöhnung. Wenn ich Albino über seinen Vater Mankew sprechen höre, wenn ich David Abílio zuhöre, wenn ich Alda Costa, Luís Bernardo Honwana und Eduardo Mondlane lese, gibt mir das Hoffnung. Es lässt mich von einem Mosambik träumen, das nie die Chance hatte, zu existieren. Aber was nicht ist, kann vielleicht noch werden?

CULTURE AT THE SERVICE OF THE PEOPLE

A LOOK AT THE CONTEXT AND CULTURAL RELATIONS BETWEEN MOZAMBIQUE AND THE GERMAN DEMOCRATIC REPUBLIC

Alda Costa

KULTUR IM DIENSTE DES VOLKES

EIN BLICK AUF DEN KONTEXT UND DIE KULTURELLEN BEZIEHUNGEN ZWISCHEN MOSAMBIK UND DER DEUTSCHEN DEMOKRATISCHEN REPUBLIK

52

1. Opening speech of the 1st National Meeting of the District Committees, Mocuba, February 16–21, 1975. Joaquim Chissano was then the prime minister of the transitional government.

2. "Os paradoxos da moçambicanidade," *Savana*, November 14, 2003, 10.

3. "A rica nossa cultura," *Savana*, May 15, 2009, 14 & 19.

4. Secretary of State for Culture, Maputo, 1986.

5. Interview with the vice minister of education of the GDR conducted by the Mozambican Ministry of Education and Culture's *Jornal do professor* 7 (March–April 1982): 43–45.

We cannot talk about the consolidation of our independence without talking about the consolidation of Mozambican culture.

Joaquim Chissano (1975)[1]

The most important aspect of the effort towards Mozambicanization consists … in accepting difference as a constitutive element of our nationality.

Elísio Macamo (2003)[2]

The belief that uniformity is an imperative condition for national unity paved the way for the gradual, albeit unconscious, introduction of the fiction of uniformity.

Luís Bernardo Honwana (2009)[3]

This text aims to contribute to the understanding of Mozambique's cultural history, reflecting on the transformations in local artistic and cultural practices, particularly since independence on June 25, 1975. In the context of this development, international cultural exchanges were facilitated "as a means to foster closeness, mutual understanding, friendship, and comprehension among people."[4] The text further explores the relations between Mozambique and the German Democratic Republic—a topic that, despite its significant impact on the history of Mozambique and numerous individuals, remains relatively unknown and has yet to attract the attention it merits.

The liberation struggle for Mozambique's independence occurred in an ideologically divided world, amidst the Cold War, where options and alliances were possible. The decision to fight against oppression and exploitation and for socialism united these two countries from the onset of the national liberation struggle, encompassing the internationalist duty of cooperation. As the Vice Minister of Education of the GDR stated: "We have already progressed on the path to socialism … drawing on the experiences of the Soviet Union. We understand, from our own experiences, the significance of having the support and expertise of other socialist countries."[5]

„Wir können nicht über die Konsolidierung unserer Unabhängigkeit sprechen, ohne über die Konsolidierung der mosambikanischen Kultur zu sprechen."

Joaquim Chissano (1975)[1]

„Der wichtigste Aspekt der Bemühungen um eine Mosambikanisierung […] besteht darin, die Differenz als konstitutives Element unserer Nationalität zu akzeptieren."

Elísio Macamo (2003)[2]

„Die Annahme, dass Uniformität eine unabdingbare Voraussetzung für nationale Einheit ist, ebnete den Weg für die allmähliche, wenn auch unbewusste Einführung einer Fiktion von Einheitlichkeit."

Luís Bernardo Honwana (2009)[3]

Dieser Text soll zum Verständnis der Kulturgeschichte Mosambiks beitragen, indem er die Transformation der lokalen künstlerischen und kulturellen Praktiken, insbesondere seit der Unabhängigkeit am 25. Juni 1975, beleuchtet. Im Zuge dieser Entwicklung wurde der internationale kulturelle Austausch „als Mittel zur Förderung der Nähe, des gegenseitigen Verständnisses, der Freundschaft und des Einvernehmens zwischen den Menschen"[4] etabliert. Der Text untersucht auch die Beziehungen zwischen Mosambik und der Deutschen Demokratischen Republik – ein Thema, das trotz seiner großen Bedeutung für die Geschichte Mosambiks und vieler einzelner Menschen noch weitgehend unerforscht ist und nicht die Aufmerksamkeit erfahren hat, die es verdient.

Der Befreiungskampf Mosambiks fand in der ideologisch gespaltenen Welt des Kalten Krieges statt, in der verschiedene Optionen und Allianzen möglich waren. Die Entscheidung, gegen Unterdrückung und Ausbeutung und für den Sozialismus zu kämpfen, verband die DDR mit Mosambik von Beginn des nationalen Befreiungskampfes an und beinhaltete die internationalistische Verpflichtung zur Zusammenarbeit. So erklärte der stellvertretende Bildungsminister der DDR: „Wir sind auf dem Weg zum Sozialismus bereits fortgeschritten […], weil wir uns auf die Erfahrungen der Sowjetunion stützen konnten. Aus unseren eigenen Erfahrungen wissen wir, wie wichtig es ist, auf

1. Eröffnungsrede der ersten Nationalen Tagung der Bezirksausschüsse, Mocuba, 16. bis 21. Februar 1975. Joaquim Chissano war damals der Premierminister der Übergangsregierung.

2. „Os paradoxos da moçambicanidade", in: *Savana*, 14.11.2003, S. 10.

3. „A rica nossa cultura", in: *Savana*, 15.5.2009, S. 14 und S. 19.

4. Staatssekretariat für Kultur, Maputo, 1986.

6. David Abílio in an interview with Francisco Manjate. *Notícias*, June 29, 2015, 2.

From my own experience, in both education and culture, I lived through a context that extended beyond just the support and presence of individuals from socialist countries, encompassing contributions from people across many other countries and various other forms of support and cooperation—a diverse and rich experience on which, in my view, it is also important to reflect. However, this text specifically addresses the cooperation between Mozambique and the GDR, and the education "of the youth in the spirit of socialist ideals," referred to by the vice minister of education in his interview, was integral to the development of the New Man and the establishment of a new culture, as I will demonstrate later.

Carlos Siliya (b. 1953) and David Abílio Mondlane (b. 1949), the former becoming involved in cultural activities during the liberation struggle and the latter in the capital of the colony, a "divided" city where diverse cultural practices coexisted and interacted, would collaborate in many of the first post-independence initiatives in music, theater, and dance. Both were awarded scholarships for training in the former GDR. Siliya earned his degree in cultural and art sciences from Karl Marx University in Leipzig and returned to the country in the latter half of the 1980s, taking on various roles. David Abílio chose a different direction. Inspired by Bertolt Brecht's theater, he led the National Company of Song and Dance (CNCD) for many years and remains a "militant" of culture today. A man driven by his passions, he believes that dreams guide him—hence his desire for "a prosperous country, where people love and respect each other in their cultural diversity, are in solidarity, and join hands to build a strong country."[6]

There were numerous scholarship recipients, creators on various fronts, young artists, and artists who had begun their careers during the colonial period, sooner or later. This is where I locate some artists who visited or exhibited in the former GDR, including Mankew V. Mahumana (1934–2021), an artist who, as we shall see, occupied a special position in the cultural relations between the two countries.

American historian Edward Alpers contends that they engaged in a struggle over years, both individually and collectively, to define their practice as

die Unterstützung und den Sachverstand anderer sozialistischer Länder zurückgreifen zu können."[5]

Ich habe in den Bereichen Bildung und Kultur eine Breite an Förderung und Zusammenarbeit erlebt, die sich keineswegs auf die von sozialistischen Ländern geleistete Unterstützung und die Präsenz von Menschen aus diesen Ländern beschränkte. Das ist eine vielfältige und reichhaltige Erfahrung, über die es sich meiner Meinung nach nachzudenken lohnt. In diesem Text geht es jedoch speziell um die Zusammenarbeit zwischen Mosambik und der DDR. Die Erziehung „der Jugend im Geiste der sozialistischen Ideale", auf die sich der stellvertretende Bildungsminister in dem zitierten Interview bezieht, war ein wesentlicher Bestandteil der Entwicklung des „Neuen Menschen" und der Schaffung einer neuen Kultur, wie ich im Folgenden zeigen werde.

Direkt nach der Unabhängigkeit entstanden Initiativen in den Bereichen Musik, Theater und Tanz durch die Kollaboration von Carlos Siliya (geb. 1953) und David Abílio Mondlane (geb. 1949). Carlos Siliya war während des Befreiungskampfes kulturell aktiv. David Abílio hatte sich bereits zur Kolonialzeit in der Hauptstadt engagiert, einer „geteilten" Stadt, in der verschiedene kulturelle Praktiken nebeneinander existierten und miteinander interagierten. Beide erhielten Stipendien für eine Ausbildung in der ehemaligen DDR. Siliya schloss sein Studium der Kultur- und Kunstwissenschaften an der Karl-Marx-Universität in Leipzig ab und kehrte in der zweiten Hälfte der 1980er Jahre nach Mosambik zurück, wo er verschiedene Funktionen übernahm. David Abílio wählte eine andere Richtung. Inspiriert von Bertolt Brechts Theater, leitete er viele Jahre lang das Staatliche Gesangs- und Tanzensemble von Mosambik (CNCD) und ist bis heute ein „Kämpfer" für die Kultur. Er ist ein Mann, der von seiner Leidenschaft angetrieben wird und große Träume hat, daher sein Wunsch nach „einem blühenden Land, in dem die Menschen einander in ihrer kulturellen Vielfalt lieben und respektieren, solidarisch sind und sich die Hände reichen, um ein starkes Land aufzubauen".[6]

Es gab zu der Zeit zahlreiche Stipendiat·innen, Schöpfer·innen an verschiedenen Fronten, junge Künstler·innen und solche, die ihre Karriere bereits während der Kolonialzeit begonnen hatten. Einige dieser Künstler·innen besuchten die ehemalige DDR oder stellten dort aus, darunter Mankew

5. Interview mit dem Vizeminister für Bildung der DDR, geführt vom *Jornal do Professor* des Ministeriums für Bildung und Kultur der Volksrepublik Mosambik, Nr. 7, März / April 1982, S. 43–45.

6. David Abílio in einem Interview mit Francisco Manjate, *Notícias*, 29.6.2015, S. 2.

7. Edward A. Alpers, "Representation and historical consciousness in the art of modern Mozambique," *Canadian Journal of African Studies* 22, no. 1 (1988): 73–94.

8. Malangatana Valente Ngwenya, in *Notícias*, March 1, 1961, last page and p. 4.

Mozambican art.[7] The movement for the affirmation and re-evaluation of African/Mozambican culture, which was denied by colonialism and spread across various cultural fronts, took place in a historical context marked by the rise of nationalism, liberation struggles, and African independence. In Mozambique's case, taking into account its history, this included white Mozambicans striving to break free of colonial paradigms and discover or redefine their roles, Black Mozambicans contemplating what it meant to be or become "assimilated," and mixed-race Mozambicans who had lived their lives between two or more cultures. Not all belonged to the small colonial or "assimilated"—or rather urbanized—elite. There were artists from rural backgrounds, newcomers to the city embarking on a deep process of cultural transformation, and other participants from modest social environments who had access to some form of education or sought to acquire it. This emerging generation profoundly influenced the cultural and artistic landscape post independence (1975) and left a mark on subsequent generations. We will discuss this generation next.

1. THE INITIATORS OF THE CULTURAL DIALOGUE: "I WANT TO SHOW THE THINGS OF THE ANCIENTS, FOR WE CAN BE CIVILIZED WITHOUT ABANDONING OUR THINGS."[8]

I start with Malangatana (1936–2011), the artist who, from the 1960s until his death, became most prominent outside of Mozambique. His desire to draw, paint, and become an artist unfolded in parallel with the development of awareness about the colonial reality, when the doors of the Núcleo de Arte da Colónia de Moçambique (Nucleus of Art of the Colony of Mozambique), established in 1936, began to open to Black artists. In the very limited context of access to education, in general, and to artistic education, in particular, attending courses in drawing, easel painting, or sculpture was an opportunity not to be wasted by those who wanted to be artists. For most of the colonized population, the chances for artistic education in its various aspects were nearly non-existent, confined to the efforts of a few religious missions, individual initiatives, occasional specific projects, or the outcomes of momentary political aims.

V. Mahumana (1934–2021), ein Künstler, der eine besondere Stellung in den kulturellen Beziehungen zwischen beiden Ländern einnahm.

Der amerikanische Historiker Edward Alpers schreibt, dass diese Künstler·innen über Jahre hinweg sowohl individuell als auch kollektiv darum rangen, ihr Schaffen als mosambikanische Kunst zu definieren.[7] Die Bewegung für eine Anerkennung und Neubewertung von afrikanischer / mosambikanischer Kultur, die durch den Kolonialismus verleugnet worden war, fand in einem historischen Kontext statt, der durch den Aufstieg des Nationalismus, durch Befreiungskämpfe und Unabhängigkeitserklärungen gekennzeichnet war. Im Falle Mosambiks und unter Berücksichtigung seiner Geschichte gehörten auch Weiße Mosambikaner·innen dazu, die sich von kolonialen Paradigmen befreien und ihre Rolle entdecken oder neu definieren wollten, Schwarze Mosambikaner·innen, die darüber nachdachten, was es bedeutete, „assimiliert" zu sein oder zu werden, und solche mit europäischen und afrikanischen Vorfahren, die sich zwischen zwei oder mehr Kulturen befanden. Nicht alle gehörten zur kleinen kolonialen oder „assimilierten", besser gesagt: urbanisierten Elite. Es gab Künstler·innen aus dem ländlichen Raum, Neuankömmlinge in der Stadt, die sich auf einen tiefgreifenden Prozess der kulturellen Transformation einließen, und andere aus bescheidenen sozialen Verhältnissen, die Zugang zu Bildung bekommen hatten oder sich darum bemühten. Diese aufstrebende Generation hat die kulturelle und künstlerische Landschaft nach der Unabhängigkeit 1975 tiefgreifend beeinflusst und die nachfolgenden Generationen geprägt. Auf diese erste Generation möchte ich nun näher eingehen.

1. DIE INITIATOREN DES KULTURELLEN DIALOGS: „ICH MÖCHTE DIE DINGE UNSERER VORFAHREN AUSSTELLEN, DENN WIR KÖNNEN ZIVILISIERT SEIN, OHNE UNSER EIGENES AUFZUGEBEN."[8]

Ich beginne mit Malangatana (1936–2011), dem Künstler, der von den 1960er Jahren bis zu seinem Tod den größten Bekanntheitsgrad außerhalb Mosambiks genoss. Sein Wunsch, zu zeichnen, zu malen und Künstler zu werden, entfaltete sich parallel zur Entwicklung seines Bewusstseins für die koloniale Realität, als sich nämlich die Türen des 1936 gegründeten Núcleo de Arte da Colónia de Moçambique (Kunstzentrum der Kolonie Mosambik) für Schwarze Künstler zu öffnen begannen. Angesichts des sehr begrenzten Zugangs zu Bildung im Allgemeinen

7. Edward A. Alpers, „Representation and historical consciousness in the art of modern Mozambique", in: *Canadian Journal of African Studies*, 22 (1988), Nr. 1, S. 73–94.

8. Worte von Malangatana Valente Ngwenya, *Notícias*, 1. 3.1961, letzte Seite und S. 4.

9. *A Tribuna*, November 11, 1962, 9.

Malangatana chose, as he personally told me, to take art lessons at the Núcleo de Arte's School of Painting. There, he formed friendships and met the architect Pancho Guedes/Amâncio Alpoim Guedes (1925–2015), who had an interest in all the arts. This encounter changed his life significantly, and much has been written about it. Following the architect's advice, he eventually left the Núcleo de Arte to seek a path as free from external influences as possible. His name became synonymous with a "purely" African form of modern expression. He was hailed as "one of Africa's first painters," described as a "natural, authentic, real, and sincere painter," whose work integrated composition and color harmony as seamlessly as it did stories and visions. Navigating between the "concrete city" and the "suburb," his path to international acclaim continued.

Bertina Lopes (1924–2012) also significantly influenced Malangatana's generation with her compelling paintings, characterized by social and political themes. Her artistic proposals, drawing on themes of the land, its people, and customs, resonated with local realities and her own personal experiences. As José Craveirinha stated at the time, she was "an entirely Mozambican artist from Mozambique" through her work.[9] Prior to leaving Mozambique in 1963 on a scholarship from the Calouste Gulbenkian Foundation, which took her to Portugal and Italy, where she eventually settled, Bertina Lopes was a formidable presence in the local art scene. Thereafter, her subsequent career, though based in Rome, remained deeply connected to Mozambique, adopting various artistic languages while embracing her identity as both European and African and her experiences across different worlds.

Encouraged by the colonial government to take art lessons, learn European techniques, and become artists, the Estêvão brothers, Vasco Campira, and other Black African artists held exhibitions in Mozambique and the metropolis to showcase the "civilizing action" being exercised. Viewed as derivative and imitative, and incapable of rebelling against their masters, their work was never appreciated independently. However, the influence these artists had on the youth of their time was considerable.

Other Black Africans were encouraged by Malangatana's example. Shikhani (1934–2010) was one of the first. "I owe it principally to Malangatana

und zur künstlerischen Ausbildung im Besonderen war die Teilnahme an Kursen im Zeichnen, in der Staffeleimalerei oder Bildhauerei eine Gelegenheit, die sich diejenigen, die Künstler werden wollten, nicht entgehen ließen. Für den größten Teil der kolonisierten Bevölkerung waren die Chancen auf eine künstlerische Ausbildung nahezu inexistent, sie beschränkten sich auf die Bemühungen einiger weniger religiöser Missionen, individuelle Initiativen, gelegentliche spezifische Projekte oder auf die Ergebnisse kurzfristiger politischer Ziele.

Malangatana hatte sich, wie er mir erzählte, dafür entschieden, Unterricht an der Malschule des Núcleo de Arte zu nehmen. Dort schloss er Freundschaften und lernte den Architekten Pancho Guedes (eigentlich: Amâncio Alpoim Guedes, 1925–2015) kennen, der an allen Künsten interessiert war. Diese Begegnung veränderte sein Leben entscheidend, darüber ist viel geschrieben worden. Auf Anraten des Architekten verließ er schließlich den Núcleo de Arte, um einen Weg zu finden, der so frei wie möglich von äußeren Einflüssen war. Sein Name wurde zum Synonym für eine „rein" afrikanische Form des modernen Ausdrucks. Er wurde als „einer der ersten Maler Afrikas" gefeiert und als „natürlicher, authentischer, echter und aufrichtiger Maler" beschrieben, in dessen Werk Komposition und Farbharmonie ebenso nahtlos ineinandergreifen wie Erzählungen und Visionen. Er bewegte sich zwischen „Betonstadt" und „Vorort", während er seinen Weg zu internationaler Anerkennung fortsetzte.

Auch Bertina Lopes (1924–2012) beeinflusste die Generation von Malangatana mit ihren fesselnden, von gesellschaftlichen und politischen Themen bestimmten Bildern maßgeblich. Ihre künstlerischen Entwürfe, die Land, Leute und Bräuche zum Thema haben, spiegeln die lokalen Gegebenheiten und ihre eigenen Erfahrungen wider. Wie José Craveirinha seinerzeit feststellte,[9] war sie in ihrem Werk „eine ganz und gar mosambikanische Künstlerin aus Mosambik". Bis sie Mosambik 1963 mit einem Stipendium der Calouste-Gulbenkian-Stiftung verließ, das sie nach Portugal und Italien führte, wo sie sich schließlich niederließ, war Bertina Lopes eine feste Größe in der lokalen Kunstszene. In ihrer weiteren Laufbahn blieb sie, wenn auch von Rom aus, eng mit Mosambik verbunden. Sie eignete sich verschiedene künstlerische Ausdrucksformen an und hielt an ihrer Identität sowohl als Europäerin als auch als Afrikanerin fest und verband die Erfahrungen aus den verschiedenen Welten miteinander.

9. *A Tribuna*, 11.11.1962, S. 9.

10. *O brado africano,* January 17, 1970, 3.

11. *Tempo* 95, July 9, 1972, 46–53.

12. Text from the *Khani-mambo* exhibition catalog, National Museum of Art, 2007.

that I am what I would call a sculptor today. For it was Malangatana who took me to the Núcleo de Arte," said Shikhani.[10] While Malangatana was an important influence during the early years, the fact that he settled in Beira from 1970 led Shikhani to develop a personal style, his "own path," to which he remained faithful until his death. His work included relief sculptures, large cement murals integrated into various Beira city buildings, and wood sculptures with a distinct style, completely diverging from the sculpture practiced by his contemporaries, who were heavily influenced by the modern sculpture, forms, and symbolism of Alberto Chissano (1935–1994).

Chissano did not arrive at the Núcleo de Arte as a student, like Shikhani, but to work—in the jobs available at the time for most of the colonized: handyman, guard, assistant. With no other training than what he had acquired as a child when he tried to imitate what he saw being done, he began to carve wood and developed his own, innovative language, which he refined over time. His sculpture expressed what he felt, what he saw, what surrounded him, and what he dreamed of. The "peasant world to which he was indissolubly linked and the urban world where he lived" were present in his work and marked his artistic trajectory.[11]

The Aeroporto neighborhood, on the outskirts of the city, became a breeding ground for new aspiring artists looking to follow the examples of Malangatana and Chissano.

Mankew navigated the journey common to many colonized people, moving from the rural area of his birth to the city in pursuit of opportunities, then to the gold mines of South Africa, where he worked for several years. Upon his return, among various occupations, he cultivated an interest in drawing and painting. As an active participant in the cultural movement in Matalana (Marracuene), he took part in several group exhibitions, showcasing his drawings and paintings. As Malangatana noted, Mankew also excelled in singing and dancing and as a promoter of the Ronga language and culture.[12] Mankew's first solo exhibition was in 1973, featuring thirty-four works. It depicted life in the countryside, family, women, activities, beliefs, habits, and dramas, as well as

Von der damaligen Kolonialregierung ermutigt, Kunstunterricht zu nehmen, europäische Techniken zu erlernen und Künstler zu werden, veranstalteten die Brüder Estêvão, Vasco Campira und andere Schwarze afrikanische Künstler·innen Ausstellungen in Mosambik und der Metropole und sollten damit das Ergebnis der „zivilisierenden Maßnahmen" demonstrieren. Da ihre Werke als Nachahmung wahrgenommen wurden und sie nicht in der Lage waren, sich gegen ihre Meister aufzulehnen, wurden sie nie als eigenständige Künstler gewürdigt. Der Einfluss, den diese Künstler auf die Jugend ihrer Zeit hatten, war jedoch beträchtlich.

Andere Schwarze Afrikaner·innen wurden durch Malangatanas Beispiel ermutigt. Shikhani (1934–2010) war einer der ersten. „Ich verdanke es weitgehend Malangatana, dass ich mich heute als Bildhauer bezeichnen kann. Denn es war Malangatana, der mich in den Núcleo de Arte brachte", so Shikhani.[10] Während Malangatana in den ersten Jahren einen wichtigen Einfluss ausübte, führte Shikhanis Entscheidung, sich ab 1970 in Beira niederzulassen, dazu, dass er seinen „eigenen Weg" entwickelte, einen persönlichen Stil, dem er bis zu seinem Tod treu blieb und den er stetig weiterentwickelte. Sein Werk umfasst Reliefskulpturen, große Wandgemälde aus Zement, die in verschiedene Gebäude der Stadt Beira integriert wurden, und Holzskulpturen in einem sehr auffälligen Stil, der sich deutlich von der Bildhauerei seiner Zeitgenossen unterscheidet, die stark von der modernen Bildhauerei sowie von den Formen und dem Symbolismus von Alberto Chissano (1935–1994) beeinflusst waren.

Chissano kam nicht wie Shikhani als Student zum Núcleo de Arte, sondern um dort zu arbeiten, und zwar in jenen Tätigkeitsfeldern, die der einheimischen Bevölkerung üblicherweise offenstanden: Handwerker, Wachmann, Assistent. Ohne eine andere Ausbildung als die, die er sich als Kind selbst angeeignet hatte, indem er versuchte, das Gesehene nachzuahmen, begann er mit Holzschnitzereien und entwickelte seine eigene, innovative Sprache, die er mit der Zeit verfeinerte. Seine Skulpturen drückten aus, was er fühlte, was er sah, was ihn umgab und wovon er träumte. Die „bäuerliche Welt, mit der er untrennbar verbunden war, und die städtische Welt, in der er lebte",[11] sind in seinem Werk beide präsent und prägten seinen künstlerischen Werdegang.

Das Aeroporto-Viertel am Rande der Stadt wurde zu einem Nährboden für aufstrebende Künstler·innen, die dem Beispiel von Malangatana und Chissano folgten.

10. *O Brado Africano,* 17.1.1970, S. 3.

11. *Tempo,* Nr. 95, 9.7.1972, S. 46–53.

miners and healthcare issues. On the occasion of the independence celebrations in 1975, he presented with other artists in a popular art exhibition of painting, sculpture, and drawing. The exhibition included five paintings with themes associated with the occasion and the liberation struggle. He remained active but less visible. Only after more than three decades did he hold his second solo exhibition (2007), critical of himself because "an artist never knows everything and should never say I am fine and ready."[13]

Since its inception, the Coop Gallery / Salon in Maputo, where Mankew had presented, opened up a space for the promotion of new artists, particularly Black Africans. Some of those who were showcased had been seen as talented artisans to whom it was fair to give an opportunity to assert themselves. They usually sold their work on the street. They began to exhibit alongside young, or less young, individuals who wanted to be artists and next to recognized painters and sculptors, with some of them integrating into the artistic circles of the colony. The interest shown by the public encouraged them to continue their work and motivated many young people. It provoked reflections on art and Black African artists, the different artistic traditions present in Mozambique, the relationships between them, and what could become the Mozambican culture.

This movement increased the number of individuals who considered themselves artists, especially in the capital city, where there were opportunities for interaction between artists and some masters to follow. Educational opportunities in art remained limited; there was no art school to nurture the emerging interest and talents.[14] However, the courses offered by the Núcleo de Arte and the regular courses at the Industrial School[15]—where various artists taught and from which new names and proposals emerged[16]—were operational. The art market was in its infancy[17]—as was art criticism—but artists had the opportunity to present diverse proposals and explore what they wished.[18] The individual and collective exhibitions that took place, in various spaces and also outside Mozambique, during the last years of colonial rule, are examples of this.

But the cultural movement, as I have already mentioned, extended to other forms of artistic expression and had various participants and mediators.

---

13. *Domingo*, July 28, 1985.

14. Only after independence (1975) would art schools be established in Mozambique. The General University Studies, created in 1962, did not include courses of this nature.

15. The painting and decorative sculpture courses created at the Industrial School qualified for admission to the painting and sculpture courses of the Higher Schools of Fine Arts.

16. Roberto Chichorro (b. 1941), Inácio Matsinhe (b. 1945), Zito Craveirinha / J. J. Craveirinha Junior / João Craveirinha (b. 1947), just to mention a few.

17. The Texto Art Gallery, attached to the bookstore of the same name, opened in 1972 as the first experiment by a commercial art gallery.

18. João Ayres, Pancho Miranda Guedes, Garizo do Carmo, João Paulo, António Bronze, José Júlio, Álvaro Passos, Dana Michaelles, Augusto Cabral, Maria Alice,

---

Mankew durchlief einen Weg, der typisch für die Zeit war: Er zog aus der ländlichen Gegend, in der er geboren war, in die Stadt, um dort nach Möglichkeiten zu suchen, und ging dann in die Goldminen Südafrikas, wo er mehrere Jahre lang arbeitete. Nach seiner Rückkehr widmete er sich unter anderem dem Zeichnen und Malen. Als aktives Mitglied der kulturellen Bewegung in Matalana (Marracuene) nahm er an mehreren Gruppenausstellungen teil, bei denen er seine Zeichnungen und Gemälde präsentierte. Wie Malangatana betont hat,[12] tat sich Mankew auch als Sänger und Tänzer sowie als Förderer der Ronga-Sprache und Kultur hervor. Mankews erste Einzelausstellung fand 1973 statt und umfasste 34 Werke. Sie zeigte das Leben auf dem Land, Familie, Frauen, Tätigkeiten, Glauben, die Gewohnheiten und die Dramen, aber auch die Bergleute und die Gesundheitsprobleme. Anlässlich der Unabhängigkeitsfeierlichkeiten im Jahr 1975 präsentierte er zusammen mit anderen Künstlern eine „Popular Art Exhibition" mit Malerei, Skulpturen und Zeichnungen. Die Ausstellung umfasste fünf Gemälde mit Themen, die mit der Unabhängigkeit und dem Befreiungskampf verbunden waren. Er blieb aktiv, aber weniger im Rampenlicht. Erst nach mehr als drei Jahrzehnten (2007) veranstaltete er seine zweite Einzelausstellung, in der er sich selbstkritisch äußerte, denn „ein Künstler weiß nie über alles Bescheid und sollte nie sagen, ich bin gut und fertig".[13]

Schon seit ihrer Gründung stellte die Coop-Galerie / Salon in Maputo, in der Mankew ausstellte, einen Raum für die Förderung neuer Künstler·innen, insbesondere Schwarzer Künstler·innen, zur Verfügung. Einige der ausgestellten Künstler·innen wurden als talentierte Kunsthandwerker·innen angesehen, denen man eine faire Chance geben wollte, sich zu behaupten. Sie verkauften ihre Werke meist auf der Straße. Nun fingen sie an, neben jungen oder weniger jungen Menschen, die Künstler·innen werden wollten, und bereits anerkannten Maler·innen und Bildhauer·innen ihre Arbeiten auszustellen, und manche von ihnen schafften es, in die Künstlerkreise der Metropole aufgenommen zu werden. Das Publikum zeigte großes Interesse, was sie dazu ermutigte, ihre Arbeit fortzusetzen, und es motivierte junge Menschen überhaupt. Die Ausstellungen regten dazu an, über Kunst und über afrikanische Künstler·innen nachzudenken, über die verschiedenen künstlerischen Traditionen in Mosambik, die Verbindungen zwischen ihnen und darüber, was die mosambikanische Kultur ausmachen könnte.

---

12. Text aus dem Katalog der Khanimambo-Ausstellung, National Museum of Art, 2007.

13. *Domingo*, 28.7.1985.

António Quadros (who arrived in the colony in 1964), Jorge Mealha, Zeca Mealha, Teresa Roza de Oliveira, Eugénio de Lemos, and José Pádua were among the artists and teachers who promoted the artistic environment of the colony.

19. Title inspired by Frantz Fanon, *Les damnés de la terre* (1961; François Maspero, 1975), 162–63.

20. See *Tempo* 398, May 21, 1978, 27–37. Poet, writer, and politician Sérgio Vieira (1941–2021) was one of the founding members of FRELIMO and held several prominent positions in the government over the course of his life.

2. "TO FIGHT FOR NATIONAL CULTURE AND THE LIBERATION OF THE NATION":[19] CULTURE IN THE CONTEXT OF THE LIBERATION STRUGGLE AND PARALLEL PATHS TOWARD THE INDEPENDENCE OF MOZAMBIQUE

Various currents of thought influenced the different stages of the liberation struggle of colonized peoples and had an impact on the concept of culture that was being constructed and on the cultural policies, more or less formulated, that were being implemented. FRELIMO (Liberation Front of Mozambique), in the case of Mozambique, was no exception. Based on this knowledge, the experiences taking place, the ideological struggle within the movement, and the action of the Department of Education and Culture (DEC), resolutions reflecting the concept of culture in creation were approved. In September 1970, on the occasion of the 2nd DEC Conference, Samora Machel, already president of FRELIMO, used the slogan "Educate the man to win the war, create the New Society and develop the Homeland." It was from then on that, for Sérgio Vieira, the theme of the New Society and the New Man began to be clearly articulated.[20] Developing a new revolutionary and Mozambican culture that arose from the contributions of all, men and women, young and old, from the North and the South, became the objective. Various initiatives taking place in the liberated zones and reflections on what a revolutionary national culture or the role of the creator and artist, among others, would be, were disseminated through publications, participation in continental cultural festivals, and international seminars. It was also possible, during the proclamation of independence and the following period, to showcase the choir and the stage group of the Mozambican Liberation Popular Forces (FPLM). This front, the Cultural Front, has been the subject of dissemination, with various testimonies recorded from those who lived through this time or were actively involved, and, more recently, it has sparked the interest of researchers.

In various ways, the struggle for political independence, which began in 1964, significantly impacted both rural and urban areas of the colony,

Durch diese Bewegung wuchs die Zahl der Menschen, die sich als Künstler·innen betrachteten, vor allem in der Hauptstadt, wo es Möglichkeiten zur Interaktion zwischen Künstler·innen und einigen Meistern gab, denen man folgen konnte. Die Bildungsmöglichkeiten im Bereich der Kunst blieben begrenzt; es gab keine Kunsthochschule, um das aufkommende Interesse und die Talente zu fördern,[14] aber die vom Núcleo de Arte angebotenen Klassen und die regelmäßigen Kurse an der Industrieschule,[15] die von verschiedenen Künstler·innen angeboten wurden und aus denen neue Namen und Initiativen hervorgingen,[16] waren gefragt. Der Kunstmarkt steckte noch in den Kinderschuhen,[17] ebenso wie die Kunstkritik, doch die Künstler·innen hatten nun die Möglichkeit, Vorschläge zu präsentieren und zu erkunden, was ihnen vorschwebte.[18] Die Einzel- und Gruppenausstellungen, die in den letzten Jahren der Kolonialherrschaft in verschiedenen Räumen und auch außerhalb Mosambiks stattfanden, sind Beispiele dafür.

Doch die kulturelle Bewegung erstreckte sich, wie ich bereits erwähnt habe, auch auf andere künstlerische Ausdrucksformen und umfasste ganz unterschiedliche Teilnehmer·innen und Vermittler·innen.

2. „EIN KAMPF FÜR DIE NATIONALE KULTUR UND DIE BEFREIUNG DER NATION":[19] KULTUR IM KONTEXT DES BEFREIUNGSKAMPFES UND WEGE IN DIE UNABHÄNGIGKEIT

Unterschiedliche Denkrichtungen beeinflussten die verschiedenen Phasen des Befreiungskampfes in den Kolonien und hatten Auswirkungen auf das sich entwickelnde Verständnis von Kultur und die mehr oder weniger ausformulierte Kulturpolitik. Die FRELIMO bildete da keine Ausnahme. Auf der Grundlage dieser Kenntnisse, der Erfahrungen, des ideologischen Kampfes innerhalb der Bewegung und der Aktivitäten der Abteilung für Bildung und Kultur (DEC) wurden Beschlüsse verabschiedet, die vom Konzept einer sich neu entwickelnden Kultur ausgehen. Im September 1970, anlässlich der II. DEC-Konferenz, benutzte Samora Machel, bereits Präsident der FRELIMO, den Slogan „Erzieht den Menschen, um den Krieg zu gewinnen, die Neue Gesellschaft zu schaffen und das Heimatland voranzubringen". Nach Einschätzung von Sérgio Vieira[20] wurde das Thema der „Neuen Gesellschaft" und des „Neuen Menschen" ab diesem Zeitpunkt klar formuliert. Das erklärte Ziel war nun die Entwicklung einer neuen revolutionären

14. Erst nach der Unabhängigkeit (1975) wurden in Mosambik Kunstschulen eingerichtet. Das 1962 eingerichtete allgemeine Universitätsstudium umfasste keine Kurse dieser Art.

15. Die an der Industrieschule eingerichteten Kurse für Malerei und dekorative Bildhauerei qualifizierten für die Zulassung zu den Kursen für Malerei und Bildhauerei an den Hochschulen für bildende Künste.

16. Roberto Chichorro (geb. 1941), Inácio Matsinhe (geb. 1945), Zito Craveirinha / J.J. Craveirinha Junior / João Craveirinha (geb. 1947), um nur einige zu nennen.

17. Die Texto Art Gallery, die an die gleichnamige Buchhandlung angeschlossen ist, wurde 1972 als erster Versuch einer kommerziellen Kunstgalerie eröffnet.

18. João Ayres, Pancho Miranda Guedes, Garizo do Carmo, João Paulo, António Bronze, José Júlio, Álvaro Passos, Dana Michaelles, Augusto Cabral, Maria Alice, António Quadros (der 1964 in die Kolonie kam), Jorge Mealha, Zeca

particularly the capital. Colonizer and colonized experienced this period separately, yet not always in opposition. As in previous decades, writers, musicians, visual artists, and intellectuals engaged in culture across diverse professions, students from the only university, and associations voiced their opposition to the humiliation and injustice of their times. The photography of Ricardo Rangel (1924–2009) and other photographers highlighted the colonial reality. Theater, which had seen some development since the latter half of the 1960s despite a limited audience, was rooted in and closely connected to the African reality it depicted and practiced. In addition to interactions with the theater group from the Mozambique Railways (CFM) Social Center, the collaborative work with Lindo Lhongo and his theater group deserves mention, exemplified by *Os noivos ou Conversa dramática sobre o lobolo*, and, by 1974, *As trinta mulheres de Muzeleni* by Lindo Lhongo and Samuel Dabula.

Far from the colonial cities, there was a search for the "new form," understood as the result of combining the old form with new content, seeking a "revolutionary aesthetic." The skilled Makonde sculptors, originating from the north of Mozambique, and the thematic and formal renewal of their sculptural forms, are associated with the emerging national culture, claimed by the liberation movement and, later, by the project to build modern Mozambique. In Tanzania, where they had long migrated, a movement that came to be known as the beginning of modern sculpture was born in the 1960s. To the realistic forms used to depict the human figure, scenes of daily life, and animals were added compositions of small groups that increased in length and volume (*ujamaa*) and sculptures of spirits, good or bad, which took various forms (*shetani*) and are still practiced and developed today. The interest in collecting or even experimenting with the forms or integrating elements of Makonde culture was (is) visible in the work of various artists. The dissemination of this modern sculpture and a large number of hitherto little-known sculptors who practiced it was significant in the years of affirmation and search for a national, Mozambican art. It also interested researchers from various geographies, especially institutions that had long known or possessed examples of this sculpture.

mosambikanischen Kultur, die aus den Beiträgen aller, Männer und Frauen, jung und alt, aus dem Norden und dem Süden, hervorgehen sollte. Verschiedene Initiativen in den bereits befreiten Territorien und Überlegungen darüber, wie eine revolutionäre nationale Kultur oder die Rolle der Kulturschaffenden und Künstler·innen aussehen könnte, wurden unter anderem durch Veröffentlichungen, die Teilnahme an gesamtkontinentalen Kulturfestivals und durch internationale Seminare verbreitet. Während der Proklamation der Unabhängigkeit und in der Folgezeit traten auch der Chor und die Theatergruppe der Mosambikanischen Volksbefreiungskräfte (FPLM) auf. Es war eine andere Art der Front, die Kulturfront, und die Erzählungen davon wurden weitergegeben und verbreitet. Zeugnisse von Menschen, die diese Zeit erlebt oder damals aktiv beteiligt waren, wurden aufgezeichnet und haben in jüngster Zeit das Interesse von Wissenschaftler·innen geweckt.

Der 1964 begonnene Kampf um die politische Unabhängigkeit wirkte sich auf die ländlichen und die städtischen Gebiete der Kolonie, insbesondere die Hauptstadt, ganz unterschiedlich aus. Kolonisatoren und Kolonisierte erlebten diese Zeit zwar getrennt, aber nicht immer in Opposition zueinander. Ähnlich wie in den vorangegangenen Jahrzehnten brachten Schriftsteller·innen, Musiker·innen, bildende Künstler·innen und Intellektuelle aus verschiedenen Berufsgruppen sowie die Studierenden der Universität und Vereine ihren Widerstand gegen die Unterdrückung und Ungerechtigkeit zum Ausdruck. Die Fotografien von Ricardo Rangel (1924–2009) und anderen beleuchteten die koloniale Realität. Das Theater, das sich seit der zweiten Hälfte der 1960er Jahre trotz geringer Besucherzahlen weiterentwickelt hatte, war tief in der afrikanischen Realität, die es darstellte und lebte, verankert. Erwähnenswert sind insbesondere die Theatergruppe des Sozialzentrums der Caminhos de Ferro de Moçambique (CFM) sowie die gemeinschaftlichen Projekte von Lindo Lhongo und seiner Theatergruppe, etwa in der Inszenierung *Os Noivos ou Conversa Dramática sobre o Lobolo* und 1974 bei dem Stück *As Trinta Mulheres de Muzeleni* von Lindo Lhongo und Samuel Dabula.

Auch fernab der kolonialen Städte suchte man nach der „neuen Form", die sich aus der Verbindung alter Formen mit neuen Inhalten ergeben sollte und eine „revolutionäre Ästhetik" anstrebte. Die aus dem Norden Mosambiks stammenden Bildhauer der Makonde und die thematische und formale Erneuerung ihrer skulpturalen Ausdrucksformen wurden mit der entstehenden nationalen Kultur in

Mealha, Teresa Roza de Oliveira, Eugénio de Lemos, José Pádua waren weitere Künstler·innen, Lehrer·innen und Förderer·innen des künstlerischen Umfelds der Kolonie.

19. Titel in Anlehnung an Frantz Fanon, *Les Damnés de la Terre*, Paris: François Maspero 1975 (1961), S. 162–163.

20. *Tempo*, Nr. 398, 21.5.1978, S. 27–37. Der Dichter, Schriftsteller und Politiker Sérgio Vieira (1941–2021) war eines der Gründungsmitglieder der FRELIMO und bekleidete im Laufe seines Lebens mehrere prominente Positionen in der Regierung.

21. "Decreto n.º 1/75 de 27 de Julho," in *Boletim da República*, ser. 1, no. 15, July 29, 1975, 55.

22. Ibid. (art. 19), 58.

3. INDEPENDENT MOZAMBIQUE: DEVELOPING POPULAR CULTURE AND COMBATING BOURGEOIS CULTURE

The coup d'état of April 25, 1974, in Portugal, the colonizing country, initiated in Mozambique, then a colony, a profound change for which many were unprepared, despite the war that had been waged for several years. The transition period that followed was tense, marked not only by distrust and violence but also by enthusiasm and the desire to embrace the revolutionary cause and Mozambique's independence. FRELIMO disseminated its program and the outlines of its cultural policy at the neighborhood level, workplaces, and schools. In this process and in preparation for the grand Independence Day celebration on June 25, 1975, various initiatives took place, including the traveling exhibition *Show the People What the People Do*, organized by the African Association of Mozambique and framed within the official festivities, and many young people began their involvement in the arts during these years. Amidst great enthusiasm and euphoria, the first structures and national state cultural institutions were outlined, proving to be a complex process of advances and setbacks. They would play important roles, despite multiple weaknesses, in the new context being created for the arts, artists, and cultural practice, where there were no parallel or alternative institutions or initiatives.

The new government had defined in its first session that its action should be based on "materializing … the power of the peasant and worker masses, revolutionizing the existing structures to serve the people."[21] For this, it outlined tasks and functions for each ministry, delineated competencies, and established the operation of existing services or new services to be put in place. The Ministry of Education and Culture (MEC) was tasked with creating conditions in which instruction, education, and culture would serve the broad masses: "Fighting … the heavy legacy left by colonialism: illiteracy, ignorance, and obscurantism…. Promoting the valorization of all cultural manifestations of the People of Mozambique, giving them a revolutionary content and disseminating them nationally and internationally, to project the Mozambican personality."[22]

Verbindung gebracht, die von der Befreiungsbewegung und später vom Projekt des Aufbaus eines modernen Mosambik gefordert wurde. In Tansania, wohin sie lange zuvor ausgewandert waren, entstand in den 1960er Jahren eine Bewegung, die als Beginn der modernen Bildhauerei bekannt wurde. Zu den realistischen Formen, mit denen die menschliche Figur, Szenen des täglichen Lebens und Tiere dargestellt wurden, gesellten sich Kompositionen kleiner Gruppen, die an Länge und Volumen zunahmen (*ujamaa*), und Skulpturen guter oder böser Geister, die verschiedene Formen annahmen (*shetani*) und noch heute hergestellt und weiterentwickelt werden. Das Interesse am Sammeln oder sogar Experimentieren mit den Formen oder der Integration von Elementen der Makonde-Kultur war (und ist) in den Werken vieler Künstler·innen sichtbar. Die Verbreitung dieser modernen Bildhauerei und einer großen Zahl bisher wenig bekannter Bildhauer·innen, die sie praktizierten, war in den Jahren der Behauptung und Suche nach einer nationalen, mosambikanischen Kunst von großer Bedeutung. Sie hat auch das Interesse von Wissenschaftler·innen aus verschiedenen Regionen geweckt, insbesondere von Institutionen, die diesen Stil bereits kannten und entsprechende Sammlungen besaßen.

3. UNABHÄNGIGES MOSAMBIK: FÖRDERUNG DER VOLKSKULTUR UND KAMPF GEGEN DIE BÜRGERLICHEN KÜNSTE

Der Sturz der Regierung am 25. April 1974 in Portugal, dem Land der Kolonialherren, leitete in Mosambik einen tiefgreifenden Wandel ein, auf den viele trotz des jahrelangen Krieges nicht vorbereitet waren. Die darauffolgende Übergangszeit war angespannt, geprägt von Misstrauen und Gewalt, aber auch von Enthusiasmus und dem Wunsch, sich die revolutionäre Sache und die Unabhängigkeit Mosambiks zu eigen zu machen. Die FRELIMO verbreitete ihr Programm und die Grundzüge ihrer Kulturpolitik in den Stadtvierteln, an den Arbeitsplätzen und in den Schulen. In diesem Prozess und in Vorbereitung auf die große Unabhängigkeitsfeier am 25. Juni 1975 fanden verschiedene Initiativen statt, zum Beispiel die Wanderausstellung *Zeigt den Menschen, was die Menschen tun*, die von der Afrikanischen Gesellschaft Mosambiks organisiert und in die offiziellen Feierlichkeiten eingebettet wurde. Viele junge Menschen fanden in diesen Jahren ihren Weg in die Kunst. Mit großem Enthusiasmus und Euphorie wurden die ersten staatlichen Strukturen und nationalen Kultureinrichtungen

23. The National Directorate of Culture, established in 1976 within the Ministry of Education and Culture, had the function of guiding, stimulating, and controlling artistic activity (literary, visual arts, theater, and music).

24. "Decreto n.° 39/76 de 14 de Fevereiro," in *Boletim da República*, ser. 1, no. 18, February 14, 1976.

25. The *Jornal do professor*, a publication of the Ministry of Education and Culture, features interviews about the Friendship School in its issues 7 and 9 of 1982. On the experience of Mozambican students at the Friendship School, see Tanja R. Müller. *Legacies of Socialist Solidarity: East Germany in Mozambique*, (Lexington Books, 2014).

26. Graça Simbine, opening speech, UNESCO seminar, Maputo, July 19–22, 1975. See *Tempo* 303, July 25, 1976, 49–53.

27. Second World Festival of Black African Arts and Culture.

In the field of culture, in addition to the inventory of actions already undertaken by FRELIMO, which should serve as a reference point for future actions, there were specific guidelines that the National Directorate of Culture (DNC[23]) tried to implement.[24] Cultural exchange between the various regions of the country and with friendly peoples and countries was also recommended. The German Democratic Republic (GDR) was one of these countries. Just as had happened during the armed struggle after 1975, technicians, the so-called cooperants, from various countries worked in Mozambique in different sectors of activity. Among them were the internationalist cooperants from socialist countries and others from various places, with connections to political parties, solidarity organizations, and political exiles. I worked with several throughout my professional life, which began in 1977, including teachers and educators from the GDR, particularly in the preparation of the National Education System (SNE) introduced in 1983. The cooperation in education with the GDR, which covered secondary and higher education, also included the Friendship School, which received Mozambican students in Staßfurt (in Saxony-Anhalt), within the framework of the Treaty of Friendship and Cooperation between the two countries.[25] Mozambican and German teachers embodied this project and certainly have memories and stories to share. But other technicians, intervening in social and economic sectors, sometimes for a considerable number of years, with more or less interaction with Mozambicans, also have much to share.

Through the DNC, the state assumed broad functions, including executive roles. The concept of culture taking shape rejected the foreign cultural values of the dominant classes of colonialism, capitalism, and imperialism, affirming peasant-worker power.[26] Negritude and African authenticity were considered, in this context, racist, bourgeois, and reactionary theories. In Lagos—at FESTAC '77[27]—Mozambique opposed an identity based on race and the past as the sole source for its construction. The search for and development of a new culture and a New Man were ever-present challenges. In the years that followed, the DNC was responsible for significant achievements, such as the National Festivals of Popular Dance (since 1978), Traditional Song and Music (since 1980),

---

geschaffen, was sich als komplexer Prozess mit Fortschritten und Rückschlägen erwies. Sie spielten – trotz anfänglicher Schwierigkeiten – eine wichtige Rolle in dem neu entstehenden Rahmen, der für die Kunst, die Künstler·innen und die kulturelle Praxis geschaffen wurde und außerhalb dessen es keine parallelen oder alternativen Institutionen oder Initiativen gab.

Die neue Regierung hatte in ihrer ersten Sitzung festgelegt, dass ihr Handeln darauf abzielen solle, „die Macht der Bauern- und Arbeitermassen zu verwirklichen [und] die bestehenden Strukturen im Dienste des Volkes zu revolutionieren".[21] Zu diesem Zweck umriss sie die Aufgaben und Funktionen der einzelnen Ministerien, beschrieb die Zuständigkeiten und legte die Ausführung der bestehenden oder zu schaffenden Dienstleistungen fest. Das Ministerium für Bildung und Kultur (MEC) hatte die Aufgabe, Bedingungen zu schaffen, unter denen Unterricht, Bildung und Kultur den breiten Massen dienen würden. Es sollte „das schwere Erbe, das der Kolonialismus hinterlassen hat – Analphabetismus, Unwissenheit und Obskurantismus – bekämpfen […] und die Wertschätzung aller kulturellen Ausdrucksformen des mosambikanischen Volkes fördern, ihnen einen revolutionären Inhalt geben und sie national und international verbreiten, um die mosambikanische Kultur zu präsentieren".[22]

Im Bereich der Kultur gab es neben der Bestandsaufnahme der von der FRELIMO bereits durchgeführten Maßnahmen, die als Bezugspunkt für künftige Aktionen dienen sollten, spezifische Leitlinien, die die Nationale Kulturdirektion (DNC)[23] umzusetzen versuchte.[24] Auch der kulturelle Austausch zwischen den verschiedenen Regionen des Landes und mit befreundeten Gruppen und Ländern wurde befürwortet. Die Deutsche Demokratische Republik (DDR) war eines dieser Länder. Wie schon während des bewaffneten Kampfes arbeitete auch nach 1975 in Mosambik technisches Fachpersonal, die sogenannten „Kooperanten", aus verschiedenen Ländern in unterschiedlichen Tätigkeitsbereichen. Darunter waren „internationalistische Kooperanten" aus sozialistischen Ländern sowie aus anderen Ländern, die Verbindungen zu politischen Parteien, Solidaritätsorganisationen und politischen Exilant·innen unterhielten. Ich habe während meines gesamten Berufslebens, das 1977 begann, mit solchen „Kooperanten" zusammengearbeitet, unter anderem mit Lehrer·innen und Erzieher·innen aus der DDR, insbesondere bei der Vorbereitung des 1983 eingeführten Nationalen Bildungssystems (SNE).

21. Dekret Nr. 1/75 vom 27. Juli. Staatsanzeiger, Serie I, 29.7.1975.

22. Artikel 19 des Dekrets Nr. 1/75.

23. Die 1976 im Ministerium für Bildung und Kultur eingerichtete Nationale Kulturdirektion hatte die Aufgabe, künstlerische Aktivitäten (Literatur, bildende Kunst, Theater und Musik) zu lenken, zu fördern und zu kontrollieren.

24. Verordnung Nr. 39/76 vom 14. Februar. Staatsanzeiger, Serie I, Nr. 18, 14.2.1976.

28. *Notícias*, Maputo, August 8, 1994, 7.

interventions in the field of cultural heritage, both tangible and intangible, various training actions carried out locally at the newly created Center for Cultural Studies (CEC), and internationally, through internships and the sending of scholarship students, cultural exchange actions, and so on. A considerable number of Mozambicans received scholarships in different areas in various socialist countries, and a smaller number had the opportunity to enter artistic education. It was not easy to continue training in this field and to join the existing courses since training in these areas had been almost nonexistent in colonial Mozambique; many were self-taught or had only attended short courses post independence. I refer, in the case of the GDR, to José Dias Mahlate (b.1958) and Francisco Maria Conde (b.1957), who, in 1984, received scholarships to study at the Dresden Academy of Fine Arts. Upon their return to the country, the results of their training and their contribution to the transforming Mozambican artistic scene were notable. There were comments on the work they presented, but Conde responded in this way: "I am African, and if I learned certain techniques,… to solve certain problems of composition, form, volume, and color, that does not stop me from being what I am."[28]

Both had started very young, in the context of independence, with different experiences but living the same moment of mobilization and broad cultural participation that was happening and eventually "formalized" after the Third Congress of FRELIMO, in 1977. Rui Nogar (1935–1993), a poet and one of the coordinators of the DNC, was one of the advocates for the creation of culture houses, considered an instrument for the popularization and democratization of cultural practice. Since that time, culture houses have been understood as the basic cell of cultural action and they have existed throughout the country, with good and bad times, ever since. Equipping them with resources and trained personnel has never been easy. The experience and support of various countries have always been a resource, through cooperation programs, bilateral conventions, and cultural agreements, as happened with the GDR and other countries like Sweden, which also supported archives, museums, and other cultural institutions and projects. A few years later, cooperations in the context of culture houses, as well as

Die Bildungszusammenarbeit mit der DDR, die sich auf den Sekundar- und Hochschulbereich erstreckte, umfasste auch die sogenannte Schule der Freundschaft. Im Rahmen des Vertrags über Freundschaft und Zusammenarbeit zwischen den beiden Ländern wurden in Staßfurt, in Sachsen-Anhalt, mosambikanische Schülerinnen und Schüler aufgenommen.[25] Mosambikanische und deutsche Lehrkräfte haben dieses Projekt aufgebaut und könnten zweifellos noch von ihren Erinnerungen und Geschichten erzählen. Aber auch andere Berater·innen, die in sozialen und wirtschaftlichen Bereichen tätig waren, oft über viele Jahre, mit unterschiedlich intensivem Kontakt zu Mosambikaner·innen, könnten viel berichten.

Durch den DNC übernahm der Staat weitreichende Funktionen, darunter auch exekutive Aufgaben. Der sich herausbildende Kulturbegriff lehnte die fremden kulturellen Werte der herrschenden Klassen von Kolonialismus, Kapitalismus und Imperialismus ab und bekräftigte die Macht der Bauern und Arbeiter.[26] Negritude und Afrikanische Authentizität wurden unter diesem Blickwinkel als rassistische, bürgerliche und reaktionäre Theorien erachtet. In Lagos, auf dem Festival *FESTAC '77*,[27] wandte sich Mosambik gegen eine Identität, die einzig und allein aus den Quellen von Ethnie und Vergangenheit schöpfen würde. Die Suche nach und die Entwicklung einer neuen Kultur und eines Neuen Menschen waren eine ständige Herausforderung. In den folgenden Jahren war der DNC für bedeutende Errungenschaften verantwortlich, zum Beispiel das Nationale Volkstanzfestival (ab 1978), das Festival für traditionelle Lieder und Musik (ab 1980), Interventionen im Bereich des materiellen und immateriellen Kulturerbes, verschiedene Ausbildungsmaßnahmen, die auf lokaler Ebene im neu gegründeten Centro de Estudos Culturais (CEC) und auf internationaler Ebene durch Praktika und die Entsendung von Stipendiat·innen sowie durch kulturelle Austauschmaßnahmen durchgeführt wurden, und vieles mehr. Eine beträchtliche Anzahl von Mosambikaner·innen erhielt Stipendien in unterschiedlichsten Bereichen in den verschiedenen sozialistischen Ländern, und eine kleinere Anzahl hatte die Möglichkeit, eine künstlerische Ausbildung zu absolvieren. Es war nicht einfach, sich in diesem Bereich weiterzubilden und an den bestehenden Kursen teilzunehmen, da es in der Kolonialzeit in Mosambik so gut wie keine Ausbildung in diesen Bereichen gegeben hatte; viele waren Autodidakten oder hatten nach der Unabhängigkeit nur kurz Kurse besucht. Im Falle der DDR denke ich an José

25. Das *Jornal do Professor*, eine Publikation des Ministeriums für Bildung und Kultur, veröffentlichte in seinen Ausgaben 7 und 9 von 1982 Interviews über die Schule der Freundschaft. Zu den Erfahrungen der mosambikanischen Schüler·innen an der Schule der Freundschaft siehe Tanja R. Müller, *Legacies of Socialist Solidarity: East Germany in Mozambique,* Lanham: Lexington Books 2014.

26. Graça Simbine, Eröffnungsrede. UNESCO-Seminar. Maputo, 19.–22. Juli 1975. *Tempo*, Nr. 303, 25.7.1976, S. 49–53.

27. Zweites Weltfestival für Afrikanische Kunst und Kultur.

cooperations in museology (Leipzig Ethnology Museum – Nampula Museum), were taken as proposals by the delegation from the State Secretariat for Culture (SEC), which I was part of, during the working visit to the GDR in January 1986.[29] From the Schwerin Culture House onward, there was cooperation with the culture houses of Maputo, Beira, and Nampula.

The DNC had already given way to the SEC, which became the central body of the state apparatus for the direction, planning, and control of cultural policy implementation in the People's Republic of Mozambique. The SEC, continuing the path opened by the process of the national liberation armed struggle, also paved the way and space for activities, cultural manifestations, and urban artistic forms. On special occasions, and with the use of existing cultural agreements, it was possible to host and send theater companies, soloists, and music and dance groups, exhibitions, book fairs, and cultural weeks. This was the case with the GDR and other countries.

Culture and its role in the revolutionary process, the cultural directives of the party, popular culture and the experiences from the liberated zones, urban culture—initially seen as the result of cultural depersonalization and bourgeois culture—sparked tensions, contradictions, and reflections. The National Culture Meeting addressed various artistic expressions and cultural domains and produced recommendations.[30] Much was discussed about what it meant to be an artist integrated into a revolutionary process, the function of art, the role and responsibility of the artist, and the formation of associations and organizations that could reflect the achievements of the Mozambican people, a process that encountered some difficulties. It was not until 1982 that the first of these new bodies, the Mozambican Writers' Association (AEMO), was established. Visual artists invited to participate in collective exhibitions, where broad participation was desired, faced many dilemmas and contradictions about the new context they were living in. While some artists paused their journey and dedicated themselves to new tasks, others used the immediate political message as a means of expression. Young and aspiring artists used painting and sculpture to speak of the colonial past that should not be forgotten and repeated the slogans of the

29. The SEC was established by Decree No. 84/83 of December 29, which led, a few years later, to the creation of the Ministry of Culture (Decree No. 11/87 of January 12, in *Boletim da República*, ser. 1, no. 2, January 14, 1987, 6).

30. The National Culture Meeting took place in Maputo from July 25 to 30, 1977.

Dias Mahlate (geb. 1958) und Francisco Maria Conde (geb. 1957), die 1984 Stipendien für ein Studium an der Hochschule für Bildende Künste Dresden erhielten. Nach ihrer Rückkehr ins Land waren ihre Ausbildung und ihr Beitrag zur sich wandelnden Kunstszene Mosambiks bemerkenswert. Es gab auch Kritik an den von ihnen präsentierten Arbeiten, doch Conde antwortete darauf wie folgt: „Ich bin Afrikaner, und wenn ich bestimmte Techniken gelernt habe, […] um bestimmte Probleme der Komposition, der Form, des Volumens und der Farbe zu lösen, so hindert mich das nicht daran, das zu sein, was ich bin."[28]

Beide, Mahlate wie Conde, hatten sehr jung begonnen, im Kontext der Unabhängigkeit. Trotz ihrer unterschiedlichen Erfahrungen erlebten sie jedoch denselben Moment der Mobilisierung und der breiten kulturellen Beteiligung, der schließlich nach dem Dritten Kongress der FRELIMO 1977 „formalisiert" wurde. Rui Nogar (1935–1993), ein Dichter und einer der Koordinatoren des DNC, war ein Befürworter der Gründung von Kulturhäusern, die als Instrument zur Popularisierung und Demokratisierung der kulturellen Praxis angesehen wurden. Diese kulturellen Zentren gibt es bis heute – über die wechselvollen Zeiten hinweg – im ganzen Land. Es war nie einfach, sie mit Ressourcen und geschultem Personal auszustatten. Durch Kooperationsprogramme, bilaterale Abkommen und Kulturabkommen, etwa mit der DDR oder anderen Ländern wie Schweden, das ebenfalls Archive, Museen und andere kulturelle Einrichtungen und Projekte unterstützte, wurden die Erfahrungen und die Unterstützung verschiedener Länder zu einer wertvollen Ressource. Im Januar 1986, während des DDR-Besuchs der Delegation des Staatssekretariats für Kultur (SEK),[29] der ich angehörte, wurden Kooperationen im Rahmen von Kulturhäusern sowie der Museologie (zwischen dem Völkerkundemuseum Leipzig und dem Nampula-Museum) angeregt. Vom Schweriner Kulturhaus aus gab es eine Zusammenarbeit mit den Kulturhäusern von Maputo, Beira und Nampula.

Der DNC war bereits dem SEC gewichen, der zum zentralen Organ des Staatsapparats für die Leitung, Planung und Kontrolle der Umsetzung der Kulturpolitik in der Volksrepublik Mosambik wurde. Der SEC, der den durch den bewaffneten nationalen Befreiungskampf eröffneten Weg fortsetzte, schuf die Voraussetzungen für Aktivitäten, kulturelle Manifestationen und städtische Kultur. Zu besonderen Anlässen und durch die bestehenden Kulturabkommen war es möglich, Theatergruppen, Solist·innen, Musik- und Tanzgruppen und

28. *Notícias*, 8.8.1994, S. 7.

29. Der SEK wurde durch das Dekret Nr. 84/83 vom 29. Dezember eingerichtet, das einige Jahre später zur Schaffung des Kulturministeriums führte (Dekret Nr. 11/87 vom 12. Januar, Amtsblatt, Serie I, Nr. 2, S. 6).

31. See *Notícias*, January 20, 1978, 3.

32. Júlio Carrilho, *Mankew: Trajectory and Inquiries*, catalog of the *Khanimambo* exhibition, National Art Museum, Mozambique, 2007.

33. See *Tempo* 510, July 20, 1980, 49–55.

34. His book *"Nós Matámos o Cão Tinhoso"* [We Killed Mangy Dog and Other Stories] (1964) was translated into German and published by Verlag Philipp Reclam jun. Leipzig.

35. Luís Bernardo Honwana, "A nossa cultura é só a sua metade," *Domingo*, November 18, 1984, 5.

revolution. They started with the Organizational Center of Visual Artists and Artisans (COAPA) with the aim of reaching the public with what they produced.[31] The issues of sales, buyers, prices, and materials that were beginning to become scarce were always a central concern. As is still the case today, there were few Mozambicans who appreciated and bought art. We don't know how many collections were formed during that time and are now in various countries, in multiple hands, without an audience. By 1980, without the artisans, the leadership of the Organizational Center of Visual Artists (COAP) included part of the "first generation of modern Black visual artists"[32]—such as Mankew V. Mahumane, Agostinho Mutemba, Jacob Estevão, Moisés Simbine, and Sansão Cossa—and faced old and new problems.[33]

4. FROM MALANGATANA AND CHISSANO TO A NEW GENERATION SEARCHING FOR ITS "OWN ARTISTIC IDENTITY"

After the initial euphoria caused by the birth of a nation freeing itself from colonization—which was once again experiencing war—had subsided, along with some doubts and tensions, a moment for reflection on cultural policy emerged, voiced by Luís Bernardo Honwana, a writer and then Secretary of State for Culture.[34] What was Mozambican culture? What did it mean to be a Mozambican artist? What was their role? The presence and coexistence of different artistic practices was recognized, including the mutual relationship between contemporary African and Western art. There was a warning against the danger of falling into the trap of cultural nationalism and imposing the values handed down by tradition as limits of creativity. The multiplicity of forms and expressions of Mozambican culture and its interaction with the cultures of other peoples were clearly expressed. "The paintings of a Malangatana, of a Mankew are already and definitively Mozambican paintings in their own right," Honwana declared.[35]

Who were the artists of these years? Beyond the presence of the previously mentioned generation of artists, there was a notable presence of artists from various countries around the world, from Chile to Sweden, from Portugal

---

Ausstellungen zu empfangen oder zu entsenden oder Buchmessen und Wochen der Kultur auszurichten. Das betraf die DDR wie auch andere Länder.

Die Kultur und ihre Rolle im revolutionären Prozess, die kulturellen Richtlinien der Partei, die Populärkultur und die Erfahrungen aus den befreiten Territorien sowie die urbane Kultur – die zunächst als Ergebnis der kulturellen Entfremdung und der bürgerlichen Kultur angesehen wurde – lösten Spannungen und Widersprüche aus. Das Nationale Kulturtreffen[30] befasste sich mit verschiedenen künstlerischen Ausdrucksformen und kulturellen Bereichen und erarbeitete Empfehlungen. Es wurde viel darüber diskutiert, was es bedeutet, ein Künstler zu sein, der in einen revolutionären Prozess integriert ist, welche Funktion Kunst hat, welche Rolle und Verantwortung Künstler·innen tragen, sowie über die Gründung von Verbänden und Organisationen, die die kulturellen Leistungen des mosambikanischen Volkes widerspiegeln könnten – ein Prozess, der auf einige Schwierigkeiten stieß. Erst 1982 wurde die erste dieser neuen Organisationen gegründet, die Vereinigung der mosambikanischen Schriftsteller (AEMO). Bildende Künstler·innen, die zur Teilnahme an Gruppenausstellungen eingeladen wurden, bei denen eine breite Beteiligung erwünscht war, sahen sich unter den drastisch veränderten Umständen mit vielen Dilemmata und Widersprüchen konfrontiert. Während einige Künstler·innen ihre Karriere unterbrachen und sich neuen Aufgaben widmeten, nutzten andere die unmittelbare politische Botschaft als Ausdrucksmittel. Junge und angehende Künstler·innen nutzten Malerei und Bildhauerei, um von der kolonialen Vergangenheit zu sprechen, die nicht unter den Teppich gekehrt werden sollte, und griffen die Parolen der Revolution auf. Sie gründeten das Organisationszentrum der Bildenden Künstler und Handwerker (COAPA)[31] mit dem Ziel, die Öffentlichkeit mit ihren Werken zu erreichen. Die Themen Verkauf, Käufer, Preise und Materialien (die zunehmend knapp wurden) waren stets wichtige Anliegen. Wie heute noch gab es damals nur wenige Mosambikaner·innen, die Kunst schätzten und kauften. Wir wissen nicht, wie viele Sammlungen in dieser Zeit entstanden sind und sich nun in verschiedenen Ländern, in verschiedenen Händen befinden, ohne dort ein Publikum zu haben. Im Jahr 1980 bestand die Leitung des Organisationszentrums für bildende Künstler (COAP – ohne die Kunsthandwerker) aus Mitgliedern der „ersten Generation moderner schwarzer bildender Künstler",[32] darunter Mankew V. Mahumane, Agostinho Mutemba, Jacob

30. Das Nationale Kulturtreffen fand vom 25. bis 30. Juli 1977 in Maputo statt.

31. *Notícias*, 20.1.1978, S. 3.

32. Júlio Carrilho, *Mankew: Trajectory and Inquiries*, Katalog der Khanimambo-Ausstellung, Nationales Kunstmuseum 2007.

to Switzerland, from Cuba to the various Soviet Socialist Republics who had come to work in Mozambique, as well as several young people aspiring to be artists. A significant number of artists were teaching, initially at the Cultural Studies Center (CEC), and later at the School of Visual Arts/ENAV, established in 1983. Battling the scarcity of materials, they made do with what was available, creating what was necessary.[36] This was a period marked by great sharing and creative enthusiasm, in a context that was beginning to diversify in terms of practices and ideas about art and politics, leading to a significant cultural output. So far, I haven't identified any teachers or artists from the former GDR who taught arts in Mozambique, but how many amateur artists lived or worked in the country? How many recorded their impressions of what was happening or changing in the country?

In those years, Malangatana and Chissano were, as Bertina Lopes stated on one of her trips to the country, "the mirror of the plastic arts."[37] Lopes continued to live in Italy, but she always maintained a connection with Mozambique and is one of the most renowned exponents of diaspora art, which was then poorly understood. Other artists, participating in various cultural expressions, embarked on this same journey.

After the initial tensions and the almost exclusive emphasis on collective expression, Malangatana and Chissano gained individual and national recognition. In 1985, President Samora Machel officially visited the residence-gallery of the sculptor Chissano, and Malangatana was honored in 1986 with a retrospective exhibition at the National Museum of Art (which was then in the process of being established).[38] Later that year, the exhibition was displayed at the GRASSI Museum, the museum of ethnography in Leipzig. Selections from this exhibition traveled to other countries, including socialist ones. The prevailing interpretations vis-à-vis Malangatana—one of the pioneers of modern art in Africa—both at the time and in many contexts today, revolved around the paradigm of the "authentic" artist, who, it was argued, should not be exhibited in an art museum.

The National Museum of Art, which organized the retrospective, maintained contacts with researchers and cultural institutions from various countries.

36. See *Tempo,* August 26, 1984, 4–5.

37. *Notícias,* November 23, 1993.

38. The National Museum of Art opened to the public on May 18, 1989, despite having existed as a project since Mozambique's independence.

Estevão, Moisés Simbine und Sansão Cossa, und sie sahen sich sowohl bereits bekannten als auch neuen Problemen gegenüber.[33]

4. VON MALANGATANA UND CHISSANO ZU EINER NEUEN GENERATION AUF DER SUCHE NACH IHRER „EIGENEN KÜNSTLERISCHEN IDENTITÄT"

Nachdem die anfängliche Euphorie über die Geburt einer Nation, die sich vom Kolonialismus befreit hatte – und bereits erneut einen Krieg erlebte –, abgeklungen war und Zweifel und Spannungen aufkamen, wurden kritische Überlegungen zur Kulturpolitik angestellt, die von dem Schriftsteller[34] und damaligen Staatssekretär für Kultur Luís Bernardo Honwana eingeleitet wurden. Was verstand man unter mosambikanischer Kultur? Was bedeutete es, ein mosambikanischer Künstler zu sein? Was war seine oder ihre Rolle? Das Vorhandensein und die Koexistenz verschiedener künstlerischer Praktiken wurde anerkannt, und zwar auch die wechselseitige Beziehung zwischen zeitgenössischer afrikanischer und westlicher Kunst. Honwana warnte davor, in die Falle des kulturellen Nationalismus zu tappen und der Kreativität im Namen traditioneller Werte Grenzen aufzuerlegen. Die Vielfalt der Formen und Ausdrucksweisen der mosambikanischen Kultur und ihre Interaktion mit den Kulturen anderer Regionen kamen deutlich zum Ausdruck. „Die Gemälde eines Malangatana, eines Mankew sind bereits und unwiderruflich eigenständige mosambikanische Werke", erklärte Honwana.[35]

Wer waren die Künstler·innen dieser Jahre? Neben der bereits erwähnten Künstlergeneration gab es eine bemerkenswerte Präsenz von Künstler·innen aus verschiedenen Ländern der Welt, von Chile bis Schweden, von Portugal bis zur Schweiz, von Kuba bis zu den verschiedenen Sowjetrepubliken, die nach Mosambik gekommen waren, um dort zu unterrichten. Zudem kamen junge Menschen ins Land, die Künstler·innen werden wollten. Eine große Zahl von Künstler·innen unterrichtete zunächst am Zentrum für Kulturstudien (CEC) und später an der 1983 gegründeten School of Visual Arts / ENAV. Im Kampf gegen die Materialknappheit begnügten sie sich mit dem, was verfügbar war, oder schufen selbst, was benötigt wurde.[36] Es war eine Zeit intensiven Austauschs und kreativen Enthusiasmus, in einem Kontext, der sich in Bezug auf künstlerische und politische Ideen und Praktiken zu diversifizieren begann, was zu einer bemerkenswerten kulturellen

33. *Tempo,* Nr. 510, 20.7.1980, S. 49–55.

34. Sein Buch *Nós Matámos o Cão Tinhoso* [Wir haben den Räudigen Hund getötet] (1964) wurde ins Deutsche übersetzt und erschien im Verlag Philipp Reclam jun. Leipzig.

35. Luís Bernardo Honwana, „Our culture is only half of it", in: *Weekly Sunday*, 18.11.1984, S. 5.

36. *Tempo*, 26.8.1984, S. 4–5.

39. The work visit to the GDR, following a previous visit by the Secretary of State for Culture, occurred from January 12 to 19, 1986. The museum visit took place all day on January 15. Besides other work meetings and visits, it featured a parallel cultural program (theater, music, dance/ballet) that we greatly appreciated.

40. *Domingo*, June 1, 1986, 3.

41. *Tempo* 809, April 13, 1986, 50–53.

It had previously hosted Giselher Blesse from the GRASSI Museum, the museum of ethnography in Leipzig, who, drawn by his interest in Makonde sculpture, had spent some time in Mozambique. Local researchers who met him were keen to involve him in the emerging project of a Makonde art exhibition, leading to an exchange of bibliographies on the topic. The ongoing museum creation and upgrade program, of which the National Museum of Art was a part, enabled a visit in 1986 to the Leipzig museum and another meeting with Blesse, who was director of the Collections and Archives Department. This visit was brief, but it provided valuable insights and knowledge.[39] At the time, the requalification project of the Nampula Museum and the Makonde art project were priorities. The visit to the museum, which was undergoing renovations and improvements at the time, was significant for Mozambican museologists (I was one of them) and marked the beginning of a path that would lead to the reopening of the Nampula Museum as the National Museum of Ethnology, despite the unrealized proposal for cooperation in museology with the GDR. It also facilitated engagement with Mozambique's collections, especially the Makonde collection, the focal point of our program at the time, and encouraged further efforts to reclaim information on Mozambican cultural heritage abroad. This drive to discover and reclaim, to obtain images and documentation for each object, extended to other museums and collectors. Contacts with the researcher and the Leipzig Museum continued, with Blesse contributing an article to the catalog of the exhibition *Art Makondé / tradition et modernité*, which opened in Paris in 1989.

As I have already mentioned, among the artists of the new generation asserting themselves in the first years post independence were those who had experienced the diversity of means and environments of the colonial context, the young people who had received training in courses at the Industrial School or even from established artists. This was the case, for example, with Ídasse Tembe (b. 1955). He considered himself part of a generation that knew what it wanted—a different generation, "by virtue of being free men."[40] He was not in a hurry; he wanted to get to know more African artists, deepen his understanding of international artists, "discover himself in art and mature with practice."[41]

66

Produktion führte. Bisher habe ich keine Dozent·innen oder Künstler·innen aus der ehemaligen DDR ausfindig machen können, die in Mosambik Kunst unterrichteten, aber wie viele von denjenigen, die hier arbeiteten, waren Hobbykünstler·innen? Wie viele haben ihre Eindrücke von dem Land und seinen Veränderungen festgehalten?

In jenen Jahren waren Malangatana und Chissano zum „Spiegel der bildenden Künste" geworden, wie Bertina Lopes auf einer ihrer Reisen ins Land feststellte.[37] Die Künstlerin lebte weiterhin in Italien, hielt jedoch stets die Verbindung mit Mosambik und steht für eine Form der Diaspora-Kunst, die damals noch wenig verstanden wurde. Auch andere Künstler·innen, die in verschiedenen künstlerischen Genres arbeiteten, gingen später diesen Weg.

Nach den herausfordernden Anfängen und der fast ausschließlichen Betonung des kollektiven Ausdrucks erlangten Malangatana und Chissano individuelle und nationale Anerkennung. 1985 stattete Präsident Samora Machel der Galerie des Bildhauers Chissano einen offiziellen Besuch ab, 1986 wurde Malangatana mit einer Retrospektive im Museu Nacional de Arte (das sich damals im Aufbau befand) geehrt.[38] Noch im selben Jahr wurde die Ausstellung in Leipzig im GRASSI Museum für Völkerkunde gezeigt. Was Malangatana betrifft, einen der Pioniere der modernen Kunst in Afrika, so drehten sich die vorherrschenden Interpretationen sowohl damals als auch heute immer wieder um das Paradigma des „authentischen" Künstlers, der, so wurde argumentiert, nicht in einem Kunstmuseum ausgestellt werden sollte.

Das Nationale Kunstmuseum, das die Retrospektive organisierte, unterhielt Kontakte zu Wissenschaftler·innen und kulturellen Einrichtungen in verschiedenen Ländern. In der Anfangszeit war Giselher Blesse vom GRASSI Museum für Völkerkunde in Leipzig zu Besuch gewesen, der, angetrieben von seinem Interesse an der Makonde-Skulptur, einige Zeit in Mosambik verbrachte. Örtliche Wissenschaftler·innen, die ihn trafen, wollten ihn in das entstehende Projekt einer Makonde-Kunstausstellung einbeziehen, was zu einem Austausch von Bibliografien zu diesem Thema führte. Das laufende Programm zur Schaffung und Modernisierung von Museen, zu dem auch das Nationale Kunstmuseum gehörte, ermöglichte 1986 einen Besuch im Leipziger Museum und ein weiteres Treffen mit Blesse, dem Leiter der Abteilung Sammlungen und Archive. Dieser Besuch war kurz,[39] vermittelte aber wertvolle Einblicke und Erkenntnisse. Zu dieser Zeit

37. *Notícias*, 23.11.1993.

38. Das Nationale Kunstmuseum wurde am 18. Mai 1989 der Öffentlichkeit zugänglich gemacht, existierte allerdings bereits seit der Unabhängigkeit Mosambiks als Projekt.

39. Der Arbeitsbesuch in der DDR, der auf einen früheren Besuch des Staatssekretärs für Kultur folgte, fand vom 12. bis 19. Januar 1986 statt. Der Museumsbesuch fand am 15. Januar ganztägig statt. Neben anderen Arbeitstreffen und Besichtigungen gab es ein paralleles Kulturprogramm (Theater, Musik, Tanz / Ballett), das großen Anklang fand.

42. In addition to the artists referred to in the text, it is also worth mentioning Chiboleca, Dias Mahlate, Fernando Rosa, João Tinga, Neto, Néné, and Nurdino Ubisse.

43. Nurdino Ubisse, presenting Victor Sousa's first solo exhibition in 1982, at the Núcleo de Arte.

44. *Tempo*, June 17, 1984, 45–47.

45. In 2008, the Higher Institute of Arts and Culture (ISArC) was established.

Like Ídasse, other artists of this generation were interested in seeking not only African but also international art references to feed their individualized artistic practices.[42] Victor Sousa (1952–2017), in the words of another artist of his time, "spoke in a different way from the others," experimented with forms and techniques, almost completely forgot the learned norms, and showed "a painting that had nothing to do with what we were used to seeing."[43] Naguib (b. 1955) considered himself a citizen of the world.[44] At this stage of his journey, the expressionist painters were a significant reference for painting what he saw and lived in his country.

This generation of artists, today regarded as figures to measure up to, experienced a very specific historical context: the building of a new country, the outbreak of another war, strong state intervention, and the near absence of other initiatives, with difficulties and many challenges to be faced at every turn. However, this was also a time when cultural endeavors were being professionalized. It was a period that encouraged the emergence of agents and institutions essential for the creation and promotion of the arts and saw the birth of the first cultural associations. In these years, the first students who had received scholarships to study arts or who continued their higher education in various parts of the world (in the former USSR, the former GDR, Cuba, and later Brazil, South Africa, and other places) returned to the country. Higher education in the visual arts within the country only started in 2008.[45] Higher education in music and theater at the School of Communication and Arts (ECA) of Eduardo Mondlane University (UEM) began earlier.

Mankew, from the generation of the older, pioneering artists, advocated unity among artists and was critical, in his own simple and discreet way, of the divide between different generations. With the declaration of independence, he achieved national visibility. As Júlio Carrilho noted, Mankew was one of Samora Machel's preferred visual artists, and his works were given as gifts to foreign dignitaries during official visits. He spoke of and to the people, about peace amidst the ongoing war, and traveled within the scope of existing exchanges to demonstrate that, despite hardships, Mozambique's artists wanted

hatten das Qualifizierungsprojekt des Nampula-Museums und das Makonde-Kunstprojekt Priorität. Der Besuch des Museums, das damals renoviert wurde, war für die mosambikanischen Museolog·innen (zu denen ich gehörte) von großer Bedeutung und stand am Anfang eines Weges, der zur Wiedereröffnung des Nampula-Museums als Nationalmuseum für Ethnologie führen sollte, auch wenn der Vorschlag für eine museologische Zusammenarbeit mit der DDR letztlich nicht umgesetzt wurde. Es erleichterte zudem die Beschäftigung mit den Sammlungen Mosambiks, insbesondere mit der Makonde-Sammlung, die damals im Mittelpunkt unseres Programms stand, und bestärkte uns darin, im Ausland Informationen über das mosambikanische Kulturerbe zu erlangen. Das Bestreben, Objekte zu entdecken und zurückzugewinnen sowie Bilder und eine Dokumentation zu jedem einzelnen Objekt zu erhalten, inspirierte auch andere Museen und Sammler. Der Austausch mit Giselher Blesse und dem GRASSI Museum wurde fortgesetzt, und Blesse steuerte einen Artikel zum Katalog der Ausstellung *Art Makondé / tradition et modernité* bei, die 1989 in Paris eröffnet wurde.

Wie bereits erwähnt, waren unter den Künstler·innen der neuen Generation, die sich in den ersten Jahren nach der Unabhängigkeit etablierten, auch jene, die eine Vielfalt an künstlerischen Mitteln und Räumen im kolonialen Kontext kennengelernt hatten, wie junge Menschen, die in Kursen an der Industrieschule oder sogar von bereits etablierten Künstler·innen ausgebildet worden waren. Dies war zum Beispiel der Fall bei Ídasse Tembe (geb. 1955). Er verstand sich als Teil einer Generation, die wusste, was sie wollte – eine andere Generation, „weil sie freie Menschen waren".[40] Er hatte es nicht eilig; er wollte mehr afrikanische Künstler·innen kennenlernen, sein Wissen über internationale Künstler·innen vertiefen, „sich selbst in der Kunst entdecken und mit der Praxis reifen".[41] Wie Ídasse waren auch andere Künstler·innen dieser Generation auf der Suche nach afrikanischen, aber auch internationalen Kunstreferenzen, um ihre individuelle künstlerische Praxis zu bereichern.[42] Victor Sousa (1952–2017), so ein Künstlerkollege und Zeitgenosse, „sprach anders als die anderen", experimentierte mit Formen und Techniken, vergaß die erlernten Normen fast völlig und zeigte „eine Malerei, die nichts mit dem zu tun hatte, was wir zu sehen gewohnt waren.".[43] Naguib (geb. 1955) sah sich als Weltbürger.[44] In dieser Schaffensphase war der Expressionismus eine wichtige Inspirationsquelle für ihn, um zu malen, was er in seinem Land sah und erlebte.

40. *Domingo*, 1.6.1986, S. 3.

41. *Tempo*, Nr. 809, 13.4.1986, S. 50–53.

42. Neben den im Text genannten Künstler·innen sind unter anderem Chiboleca, Dias Mahlate, Fernando Rosa, João Tinga, Neto, Néné und Nurdino Ubisse zu nennen.

43. Nurdino Ubisse präsentierte die erste Einzelausstellung von Victor Sousa im Jahr 1982 im Núcleo de Arte.

44. *Tempo*, 17.6.1984, S. 45–47.

46. *Tempo*, May 27, 1984, 4–5.

47. *Tempo*, August 30, 1987.

48. On the life and work of Reinata Sadimba, see the book by Gianfranco Gandolfo, *Reinata Sadimba: "Não estamos iguais, estamos diferentes"* (Kapikua, 2012).

to continue their artistry. This period of visibility extended to the international stage. He visited the GDR, engaged with the work of its artists, had opportunities to exhibit there, and worked in Wolfgang Eckardt's studio.[46] Eckardt, a member of the Artists' Association, had previously visited Mozambique and would return in 1987 for the Mozambique Commercial and Industrial Activities Fair (FACIM), displaying twenty-five sculptures, including a bust of Samora Machel now in the National Museum of Art of Maputo's collection.[47] Eckardt also crafted a bust of Mankew. This artist received numerous accolades: the *Nachingweya* medal in Mozambique, medals in Bulgaria, and in the former GDR, where he became a corresponding member of the East German Academy of Arts and was invited, as were other African artists, to become a corresponding member of the Academy of Fine Arts.

During this time, the Store-Gallery company and its various services played a crucial role in the training and promotion of artists and artisans. One such project took place in a village on the Mueda plateau in Cabo Delgado in the early 1980s. Makonde sculptors had the chance to share their experiences and learn woodcutting from Swiss artist Maya Zürcher in 1981 at the sculpture cooperative in the village of Nandimba. The work produced at the sculpture cooperative was exhibited in Maputo in 1982. Matias Ntundu (born in 1948), one of the sculptors Maya worked with, participated in the first commercial artistic-cultural venture (art and handicraft) between Mozambique (Craftsmanship Store-Gallery) and the GDR (Staatlicher Kunsthandel der DDR) in Berlin in 1985. Besides the woodcutting and sculpture by the Makonde, the exhibition featured paintings (by Mankew, Samate, Estevão Mucavele, and Naguib, among others), ivory and semi-precious stone jewelry, basketry, and wood sculpture also known as *Pshikelekedane* from southern Mozambique.

Maya Zürcher also met Reinata Sadimba (b. 1945) during her work in Cabo Delgado. Sadimba was beginning to gain recognition for her skills in pottery, traditionally considered a female craft. She added decorations and sculptural forms to traditional items, like pots. Later, in Maputo, where she moved to live, Sadimba has carved a unique path in the realm of ceramic sculpture.[48]

Diese Generation von Künstler·innen, die heute als Referenzfiguren gelten, entwickelte sich in einem sehr spezifischen historischen Kontext: dem Aufbau eines neuen Staates, dem Ausbruch eines weiteren Krieges, einer starken staatlichen Einflussnahme, einem Mangel an sonstiger Unterstützung sowie zahlreichen Hindernissen und Herausforderungen auf allen Ebenen. Es war aber auch eine Zeit der Professionalisierung der kulturellen Arbeit. Es war eine Zeit, die das Auftreten von Akteur·innen und Institutionen förderte, die für die Schaffung und Förderung der Künste unerlässlich waren, und in der die ersten kulturellen Vereinigungen entstanden. In diesen Jahren kehrten die ersten Studierenden in das Land zurück, die ein Stipendium für ein Kunststudium erhalten hatten oder ihre akademische Ausbildung in verschiedenen Teilen der Welt fortgesetzt hatten (in der UdSSR, der DDR, Kuba, später Brasilien, Südafrika und anderenorts). Ein Hochschulstudium der bildenden Künste wurde im Land selbst erst im Jahr 2008 eingeführt.[45] Die Hochschulausbildung in Musik und Theater an der Schule für Kommunikation und Kunst (ECA) der Eduardo-Mondlane-Universität (UEM) wurde schon früher eingerichtet.

Mankew, selbst Teil der Generation der älteren, wegweisenden Künstler, engagierte sich für den Zusammenhalt unter den Künstler·innen und äußerte auf seine eigene einfache und diskrete Art Kritik an der Kluft zwischen den verschiedenen Generationen. Nach der Unabhängigkeit wurde er landesweit bekannt. Wie Júlio Carrilho bemerkt hat, war Mankew einer der bildenden Künstler, die Samora Machel besonders schätzte, und seine Werke wurden ausländischen Würdenträgern bei offiziellen Besuchen als Geschenk überreicht. Er sprach von und zu den Menschen, er sprach vom Frieden inmitten des andauernden Krieges und unternahm Reisen im Rahmen des bestehenden Austauschs, um zu demonstrieren, dass die Künstler·innen Mosambiks ungeachtet aller Schwierigkeiten ihre künstlerische Arbeit fortsetzen wollten. Diese Periode der Sichtbarkeit erstreckte sich auch auf die internationale Bühne. Mankew besuchte die DDR, setzte sich mit der Arbeit ihrer Künstler·innen auseinander, hatte Gelegenheit, dort auszustellen, und arbeitete im Atelier von Wolfgang Eckardt.[46] Eckardt, Mitglied der Künstlervereinigung, hatte zuvor Mosambik besucht und kehrte 1987 anlässlich der Mosambikanischen Messe für Handel und Industrie (FACIM) zurück, wo er 25 Skulpturen ausstellte, darunter eine Büste von Samora Machel,[47] die sich heute in der Sammlung des Nationalmuseums für Kunst in Maputo befindet. Eckardt fertigte auch eine Büste

45. Im Jahr 2008 wurde die Instituto Superior de Artes e Cultura (ISArC) gegründet.

46. *Tempo*, 27.5.1984, S. 4–5.

47. *Tempo*, 30.8.1987.

49. See Annett Bourquin, *Madgermany* (pub. by author, 2010).

FINAL CONSIDERATIONS

As was the case in the former GDR, deep changes gradually took place in Mozambique, both internally and as a result of the global context. Starting in the 1990s, the conditions of production and the discourse around art saw new developments. A new constitution was enacted in 1990, the General Peace Agreement was signed in 1992, and the first multiparty general elections were held in 1994. After many years of conflict, Mozambique was at peace. Art and culture did not remain untouched by this new scenario established in the country, the region, and globally. However, the growth seen across various cultural sectors has not been met with the level of attention that culture and cultural development deserve. Since then, numerous proposals have been made by various thinkers to address this issue.

The past never truly passes. It has been explored here through the research conducted to date and my personal archives, and it is essential to continue investigating and reflecting upon it. This entails broadening the perspectives of our gaze, without devaluing, diminishing, or forgetting the past. It also seems to me that this should be done collectively, moving beyond simplification, seeking the interactions and cultural exchanges that took place, identifying other yet unknown participants, and reflecting on the personal relationships formed as well as tensions and conflicts. I believe this path has already started, in part with the reflection and documentation on the *Madgermanes / Madjermanes*—the Mozambican contract workers who worked in the GDR, as portrayed in the book by photographer Annett Bourquin.[49] Other examples worth mentioning here are the exhibition *(Re)Lembrar—Mystery of Foreign Affairs*, involving various artists, which took place in several locations in Schwerin, Germany, and in Maputo, Mozambique, between September 2017 and July 2018, and the exhibition *GDR in Mozambique*, showcasing photographs of the daily lives and personal relationships of German citizens who lived in the country, recorded their experiences, and were willing to share them. The curator, Katrin Bahr, who lived in Beira, where her father worked, sought to give a voice to anonymous authors, thus contributing to a narrative beyond the official account propagated in the GDR.

von Mankew an. Der Künstler erhielt zahlreiche Auszeichnungen: die Nachingwea-Medaille in Mosambik, Medaillen in Bulgarien und in der ehemaligen DDR, wo er zu einem korrespondierenden Mitglied der Akademie der Künste ernannt wurde.

In dieser Zeit spielte die Store-Gallery mit ihren unterschiedlichen Projekten eine entscheidende Rolle bei der Ausbildung und Förderung von Künstler·innen und Kunsthandwerker·innen. Ein solches Projekt fand Anfang der 1980er Jahre in einem Dorf auf der Mueda-Hochebene in Cabo Delgado statt. Makonde-Bildhauer hatten 1981 in einer Bildhauer-Kooperative im Dorf Nandimba die Möglichkeit, ihre Erfahrungen auszutauschen und Holzschnitttechniken von der Schweizer Künstlerin Maja Zürcher zu erlernen. Die in der Bildhauerkooperative entstandenen Arbeiten wurden 1982 in Maputo ausgestellt. Matias Ntundu (geb. 1948), einer der Bildhauer, mit denen Maja Zürcher zusammenarbeitete, nahm 1985 am ersten kommerziellen künstlerisch-kulturellen Projekt (Kunst und Kunsthandwerk) zwischen Mosambik (Craftsmanship Store-Gallery) und der DDR (Staatlicher Kunsthandel der DDR) in Berlin teil. Neben den Holzschnitten und Skulpturen der Makonde waren Gemälde (unter anderem von Mankew, Samate, Estevão Mucavele und Naguib), Elfenbein- und Halbedelsteinschmuck, Korbwaren und Holzskulpturen, auch *Psikhelekedana* genannt, aus dem Süden Mosambiks Teil der Verkaufsausstellung.

Maja Zürcher lernte während ihrer Arbeit in Cabo Delgado auch Reinata Sadimba (geb. 1945) kennen. Sadimba erlangte erste Anerkennung für ihre Fertigkeiten in der Keramik, die traditionell als weibliches Handwerk galt. Sie verlieh klassischen Gegenständen wie Töpfen kunstvolle Verzierungen und skulpturale Formen. Später, als sie sich in Maputo niedergelassen hatte, fand Sadimba einzigartige neue Formen im Bereich der keramischen Bildhauerei.[48]

ABSCHLIESSENDE ÜBERLEGUNGEN

Wie in der ehemaligen DDR vollzogen sich auch in Mosambik allmählich tiefgreifende Veränderungen, sowohl im Inneren als auch durch globale Entwicklungen bedingt. Seit den 1990er Jahren veränderten sich die Produktionsbedingungen und der Diskurs über die Kunst. Im Jahr 1990 wurde eine neue Verfassung verabschiedet, 1992 das Allgemeine Friedensabkommen unterzeichnet, 1994 fanden die ersten allgemeinen Wahlen im Mehrparteiensystem statt. Nach vielen Jahren des Konflikts kehrte in Mosambik Frieden ein. Kunst und Kultur

48. Zu Leben und Werk von Reinata Sadimba siehe das Buch von Gianfranco Gandolfo, *Reinata Sadimba: ‚We are not the same, we are different‘*, Maputo: Kapicua 2012.

blieben von dieser neuen Situation im Land, in der Region und weltweit nicht unberührt. Allerdings wurde der Entwicklung, die in den verschiedenen Kulturbereichen zu beobachten war, nicht die Aufmerksamkeit zuteil, die ihr gebührt. Seitdem haben verschiedene Intellektuelle Strategien vorgeschlagen, um das Problem anzugehen.

Die Vergangenheit vergeht nie wirklich. Sie wurde hier im Lichte der bisherigen Forschung und meines persönliches Archivs betrachtet, und es ist unerlässlich, sie weiter zu erforschen und zu reflektieren. Das bedeutet, unsere Perspektive zu weiten, ohne die Vergangenheit abzuwerten, zu schmälern oder zu vergessen. Außerdem scheint es mir wichtig, dies kollektiv zu tun, über verkürzte Darstellungen hinauszugehen, die Interaktionen und kulturellen Austauschprozesse aufzuzeigen, die stattgefunden haben, andere, bisher unbekannte Teilnehmer·innen ausfindig zu machen und die entstandenen persönlichen Beziehungen ebenso wie Spannungen und Konflikte zu reflektieren. Ich glaube, dass sich dieser Weg bereits abzeichnet, zum Teil mit der Reflexion und Dokumentation über die *Madgermanes / Madjermanes*, die mosambikanischen Vertragsarbeiter·innen, die in der DDR arbeiteten, wofür das Buch der Fotografin Annett Bourquin nur ein Beispiel ist.[49] Zu nennen ist auch die Ausstellung *(Re)Lembrar — Mystery of Foreign Affairs*, an der verschiedene Künstler·innen beteiligt waren und die zwischen September 2017 und Juli 2018 in Schwerin und Maputo stattfand, oder die Ausstellung *DDR in Mosambik*, die Fotografien aus dem Alltag und von den persönlichen Beziehungen deutscher Bürger·innen zeigt, die im Land lebten, ihre Erlebnisse festhielten und bereit waren, diese zu teilen. Die Kuratorin Katrin Bahr, die in Beira lebte, als ihr Vater dort arbeitete, bemühte sich darum, bisher unbekannten Autor·innen eine Stimme zu geben und so zu einer Erzählung beizutragen, die über die offizielle, in der DDR propagierte hinausgeht.

49. Annett Bourquin, *Madgermany*, Maputo (Selbstverlag) 2010.

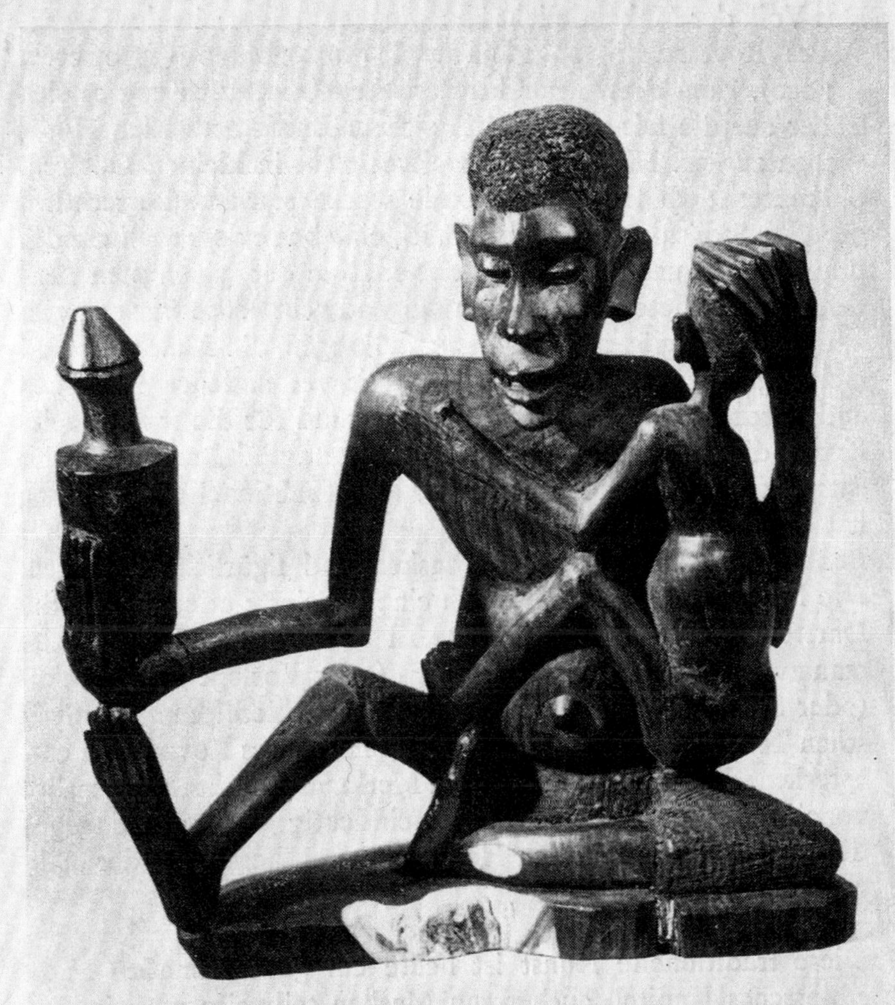

Fig. 30: Leaflet of the exhibition *Moderne Makonde Plastik: Kunst aus Ostafrika* at the GRASSI Museum für Völkerkunde zu Leipzig and the Mölkau House of Culture in 1984, published by Kulturbund der DDR

Abb. 30: Faltblatt zur Ausstellung *Moderne Makonde-Plastik. Kunst aus Ostafrika* im GRASSI Museum für Völkerkunde Leipzig und Kulturhaus Mölkau, 1984, herausgegeben vom Kulturbund der DDR

ON THE EDUCATIONAL FRONT
A TEACHER, A MATH TEXTBOOK, AND THE STRUGGLE

Peter Stobinski

AN DER BILDUNGSFRONT
EIN LEHRER, EIN MATHE-LEHRBUCH UND DER KAMPF

Peter Stobinski was born in 1941 in Halle an der Saale. He studied history and journalism at Leipzig University and worked for the East German Solidarity Committee for over seventeen years, first as secretary, then going on to become deputy secretary general. The Solidarity Committee was a nongovernmental organization (NGO) financed by popular donations. In the late 1970s, Stobinski established relations with the Sandinista National Liberation Front in Nicaragua and coordinated numerous aid shipments to the country. In his text, he tells the story of a math textbook, one of the many projects that the committee implemented in Mozambique in collaboration with FRELIMO. In 1992, he became managing director of the successor organization of the Solidarity Committee, the NGO SODI – Solidaritätsdienst International e.V., and from 2000 he was on the board of the Stiftung Nord-Süd-Brücken (North-South Bridges Foundation).

For many years, my bookshelf has contained two slim, plain-looking first- and second-grade mathematics textbooks in Portuguese. They may be the last remaining copies of a large print run that helped tens of thousands of schoolchildren in villages in Mozambique, Angola, and Guinea-Bissau learn how to count and do arithmetic during the liberation struggle in Africa. They were the start of an extensive aid, development, and trade program that the GDR launched in the 1970s and 1980s to express solidarity with FRELIMO. Unfortunately, it was encumbered to some extent by errors of judgment, paternalistic attitudes, and wishful thinking.

The East German state took an early stand in support of the struggle of Africans against imperialism, colonialism, and racism. Its fundamental conception of internationalism involved giving assistance to liberation movements and organizations such as SWAPO in Namibia, the ANC in South Africa, the MPLA in Angola, ZAPU in Zimbabwe, the PAIGC in Guinea-Bissau, and FRELIMO in Mozambique in their struggle for national independence and political self-determination.

East Germany was one of the countries that FRELIMO president Dr. Eduardo Mondlane visited in 1966 in search of international support. In talks with the East German Solidarity Committee, he spoke about the great poverty his country

Peter Stobinski wurde 1941 in Halle an der Saale geboren. Er hat Geschichte und Journalistik an der Universität Leipzig studiert und arbeitete über 17 Jahre für das Solidaritätskomitee der DDR, erst als Sekretär, zuletzt als stellvertretender Generalsekretär. Das Solidaritätskomitee war eine nichtstaatliche Organisation, die sich aus Spenden der Bevölkerung finanzierte. Ende der 1970er Jahre baute er Beziehungen zur Sandinistischen Befreiungsfront in Nicaragua auf und koordinierte zahlreiche Hilfslieferungen in das Land. In seinem Text berichtet er von einem der vielen Projekte, die das Solidaritätskomitee in Zusammenarbeit mit der FRELIMO in Mosambik realisierte – ein Lehrbuch für Mathematik. Ab 1992 war Peter Stobinski Geschäftsführer der Nachfolgeorganisation des Solidaritätskomitees, der NGO Solidaritätsdienst international (SODI) e.V., und ab 2000 im Vorstand der Stiftung Nord-Süd-Brücken tätig.

Seit vielen Jahren bewahre ich in meinem Bücherregal zwei schmale, unscheinbar wirkende Mathematik-Schulbücher für die 1. und 2. Klasse in portugiesischer Sprache auf. Es sind vielleicht die letzten Exemplare einer großen Auflage, die während des Befreiungskampfes in Afrika halfen, Zehntausenden von Schülern in den Dörfern Mosambiks, Angolas und Guinea-Bissaus das Zählen und Rechnen zu vermitteln. Sie stehen am Anfang eines umfangreichen Hilfs-, Entwicklungs- und Handelsprogramms, das die DDR in solidarischer Zusammenarbeit mit der FRELIMO im Laufe der 1970er und 1980er Jahre auf den Weg brachte. Leider war es nicht frei von Fehleinschätzungen, paternalistischen Haltungen und Wunschdenken.

Die DDR unterstützte schon früh den Kampf der Völker Afrikas gegen Imperialismus, Kolonialismus und Rassismus. Es gehörte zu ihrem internationalistischen Grundverständnis, den Befreiungsbewegungen und -organisationen wie dem SWAPO in Namibia, dem ANC in Südafrika, der MPLA in Angola, der ZAPU in Simbabwe, der PAIGC in Guinea-Bissau und der FRELIMO in Mosambik in deren Ringen um nationale Unabhängigkeit und politische Selbstbestimmung beizustehen.

Auf der Suche nach internationaler Unterstützung besuchte der Präsident der FRELIMO Dr. Eduardo Mondlane 1966 auch die DDR. In Gesprächen mit dem Solidaritätskomitee der DDR sprach er über die große Armut, koloniale

was experiencing, colonial exploitation, and the terror wrought by the Portuguese colonial army as well as the tremendous challenge involved in establishing the underground organization. With the country hampered by an illiteracy rate of over 95 percent, it was first necessary for FRELIMO's own members, functionaries, and fighters to get an education. Instructors were needed to teach a range of different subjects, and they in turn could train others to do their job. To this end, Mondlane asked the GDR to send out a teacher specializing in the natural sciences. Joachim Kindler, a specialist teacher of physics and "polytechnics" from Magdeburg, was selected for the task. He had prior experience in this area having being deployed in Ghana and Tanzania. A few months later, he traveled to Dar es Salaam, where he started work at the Mozambique Institute.

The Mozambique Institute (Instituto Moçambicano) had originally been established with funding from the American Ford Foundation to cater to young Mozambican refugees who were simply striving for a higher level of education, which was denied them in their own country. It had developed over the years into a FRELIMO planning center for primary and secondary education as well as for technical education and healthcare. Janet Rae Mondlane, the president's wife, had become head of the institute.

More and more new students were coming to the institute who were illiterate and only spoke the language of their particular tribe. They had fled the

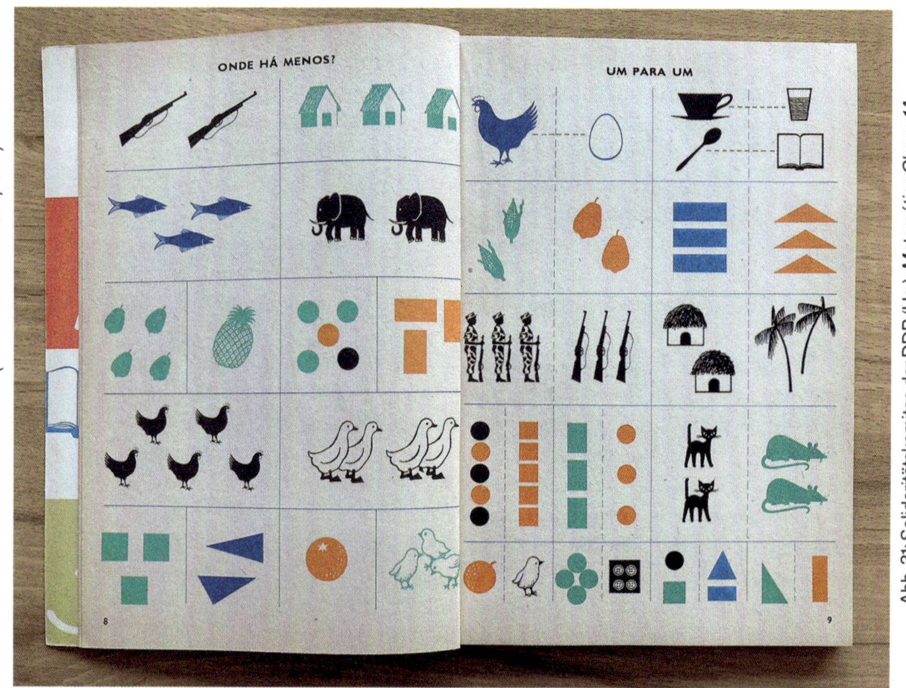

Fig. 31: Solidaritätskomitee der DDR, ed., *Matemática Classe 1A* (Nationales Druckhaus, 1972)

Abb. 31: Solidaritätskomitee der DDR (Hg.), *Matemática Classe 1A*, Nationales Druckhaus, 1972

Ausbeutung und den Terror der portugiesischen Kolonialarmee sowie über die gewaltige Herausforderung beim Aufbau der Untergrundorganisation. Angesichts einer Analphabetenrate von über 95% im Lande sei es zunächst nötig, die eigenen Mitglieder, Funktionäre und Kämpfer zu qualifizieren. Es brauche Ausbilder auf den verschiedensten Gebieten, die wiederum andere beschulen könnten. Eduardo Mondlane bat deshalb die DDR um die Entsendung eines Fachlehrers für die naturwissenschaftlichen Fächer. Joachim Kindler, ein Fachlehrer für Physik und Polytechnik aus Magdeburg, wurde für die Aufgabe ausgewählt. Kindler hatte schon Erfahrungen bei Einsätzen in Ghana und Tansania gesammelt. Wenige Monate später reiste er nach Daressalam, wo er am Mosambik-Institut seine Arbeit aufnahm.

Das Mosambik-Institut (Instituto Moçambicano), einst gegründet mit Mitteln der amerikanischen Ford Foundation für jugendliche Flüchtlinge aus Mosambik, die einen höheren Bildungsweg anstrebten, der ihnen im eigenen Land verwehrt war, hatte sich im Laufe der Jahre zu einem Planungszentrum der FRELIMO für Ober- und Grundschulbildung sowie für technische Bildung und Gesundheitsfürsorge entwickelt. Janet Rae Mondlane, die Frau des Präsidenten, hatte die Leitung übernommen.

Es kamen zunehmend neue Schüler ins Institut, die Analphabeten waren und nur ihre jeweilige Stammessprache beherrschten. Sie waren vor dem Terror geflohen und wollten gegen die portugiesische Kolonialarmee kämpfen. Nun mussten sie erfahren, dass sie zuerst Grundwissen erlernen sollten. Und so absolvierten 10-, 12-, oder 14-Jährige die ersten vier Klassen. Da waren Joachim

Portuguese reign of terror and wanted to fight against the colonial army. They now discovered perforce that they first needed to acquire a basic level of education. As a result, children aged between ten and fourteen were completing the first four grades. Kindler was called upon to apply all his pedagogical expertise, his knowledge of chemistry and physics, and his empathy for a foreign culture. With the help of teaching materials that he had sent to him from the Solidarity Committee in Berlin, he managed to set up a small lab for chemistry and physics.

The lessons took place against a background of internal political disputes about the teaching style and questions about how the struggle would proceed. Some of the students were unhappy about having Portuguese as the language of instruction. Their experience of colonialism had made them wary of white teachers. As Kindler stated in a subsequent interview, "The conflict evolved into a boycott. They were unhappy with the medical care they received, they were unhappy with how strictly regimented things were, they were unhappy with being used in the liberation struggle, [because] they saw themselves as an elite."[1]

The eruption of violence caused the institute to close for a while in 1968. Kindler made use of the difficult period before the institute reopened in late 1969. From the start, he had been exasperated with the poor quality of the Portuguese teaching materials. As a result, he decided to produce a math book for first-grade students. "So I started, using the most primitive of means; the illustrations were potato prints. My little daughter helped with the potatoes and colored paper. A colleague of mine, Fernandes, who was from Goa, was good at drawing and made stencils for me."[2]

Kindler gave the manuscript to Eduardo Mondlane, commenting: "This is my idea for the first grade; I want to try to get the East German government to print it. It was clear to me that in doing arithmetic the children learn Portuguese by necessity, and in learning Portuguese, they are obliged to internalize life under the conditions of armed struggle."[3] FRELIMO accepted Kindler's proposal, and the manuscript was sent to the Solidarity Committee in Berlin, where it was translated, reviewed, and approved for publication.

1. "Um de nós – einer von uns! Gespräch mit Achim Kindler, der als Lehrer im Auftrag des Solidaritätskomitees der DDR als erster DDR-Bürger bei der FRELIMO arbeitete," in *Wir haben Spuren hinterlassen! Die DDR in Mosambik: Erlebnisse, Erfahrungen und Erkenntnisse aus drei Jahrzehnten*, ed. Matthias Voß (LIT Verlag, 2005), 34–46, here: 37.

2. Ibid., 43.

3. Ibid.

Kindlers ganzes pädagogisches Wissen, seine chemischen und physikalischen Kenntnisse und sein Einfühlungsvermögen in eine fremde Kultur gefragt. Mithilfe von Lehrmaterialien, die er vom Solidaritätskomitee aus Berlin geschickt bekam, gelang es ihm, ein kleines chemisch-physikalisches Labor aufzubauen.

Interne politische Auseinandersetzungen über die Art des Unterrichts bis hin zu Fragen des weiteren Kampfes begleiteten den Unterricht. Ein Teil der Schüler war unzufrieden mit der Unterrichtssprache Portugiesisch. Aufgrund ihrer kolonialen Erfahrungen waren sie misstrauisch gegenüber weißen Lehrern. „Der Konflikt entwickelte sich bis zum Boykott", berichtete Joachim Kindler in einem späteren Interview. „Sie waren unzufrieden mit der medizinischen Betreuung, sie waren mit der strengen Reglementierung unzufrieden, sie waren unzufrieden mit dem Einsatz im Befreiungskampf, [denn] sie fühlten sich als Elite."[1]

Aufgrund der ausbrechenden Gewalt wurde 1968 die vorübergehende Schließung des Instituts veranlasst. Joachim Kindler nutzte die schwierige Zeit bis zur Wiedereröffnung des Instituts Ende 1969. Er hatte sich von Anfang an über das schlechte portugiesische Lehrmaterial geärgert. Deshalb nahm er sich vor, ein Mathematik-Buch für die Schüler der 1. Klasse zu erstellen. „Da habe ich angefangen, mit den primitivsten Mitteln, die Abbildungen sind entstanden als Kartoffeldruck. Meine kleine Tochter hat mit Kartoffeln und Buntpapier mitgeholfen. Kollege Fernandes, ein Mann aus Goa, konnte gut zeichnen und stellte mir Schablonen her."[2]

Das Manuskript übergab Joachim Kindler Eduardo Mondlane mit der Bemerkung: „Das ist die Idee für die erste Klasse und ich würde gerne versuchen, dass die DDR das druckt. Für mich war klar, das Kind muss mit dem Rechnen die portugiesische Sprache erlernen und muss mit dem Erlernen der portugiesischen Sprache das Leben unter den Bedingungen des bewaffneten Kampfes verinnerlichen."[3] Die FRELIMO akzeptierte Kindlers Vorschlag und das Manuskript wurde nach Berlin an das Solidaritätskomitee geschickt. Dort wurde es übersetzt, begutachtet und für druckwürdig befunden.

Die Abteilung Internationale Verbindungen des Zentralkomitees der SED schaltete sich noch mit dem Vorschlag ein, die Befreiungsorganisationen MPLA und PAIGC in Angola und in Guinea-Bissau zu befragen, ob auch sie ein solches Schulbuch benötigen würden. Nachdem endlich Anfang 1971 die Drucklegung

1. „Um de nós – einer von uns! Gespräch mit Achim Kindler, der als Lehrer im Auftrag des Solidaritätskomitees der DDR als erster DDR-Bürger bei der FRELIMO arbeitete", in: Matthias Voß (Hg.), *Wir haben Spuren hinterlassen! Die DDR in Mosambik. Erlebnisse, Erfahrungen und Erkenntnisse aus drei Jahrzehnten*, Münster: LIT Verlag 2005, S. 34–46, hier S. 37.

2. Ebd., S. 43.

3. Ebd.

The International Relations Section of the Central Committee of the SED weighed in with the idea of asking the liberation organizations MPLA in Angola and PAIGC in Guinea-Bissau whether they also needed a textbook of this kind. After the printing finally took place in early 1971, the first copies of 75,000 math textbooks for first graders were presented to FRELIMO president Samora Machel at a formal event in May. A little later, the MPLA likewise received 75,000 copies, with 50,000 being issued to the PAIGC. In the meantime, Kindler had finished his math book for second grade.

During this time, the World Council of Churches (WCC)'s program to combat racism also ruled that the churches had participated in racial discrimination and bore some of the blame for institutionalized racism. The WCC called on the churches to go beyond the performance of charitable works and contribute to a radical restructuring of society. There were intense discussions among Protestant Christians within the ecumenical movement about the options for championing the liberation movements in an appropriate way, without supporting the armed struggle and East German foreign policy. During this period, the idea was put forward of co-financing the math book for FRELIMO. The East German Protestant churches covered half of the printing costs through donations and collections. The book thus prompted an ongoing collaboration between two very different institutions. Further joint aid and solidarity projects were realized in the years that followed. These included the co-financing in 1985 of seven different schoolbooks with a print run of 3.5 million copies for use in Nicaragua, in support of the Sandinista National Liberation Front (FSLN)'s large-scale educational campaign.

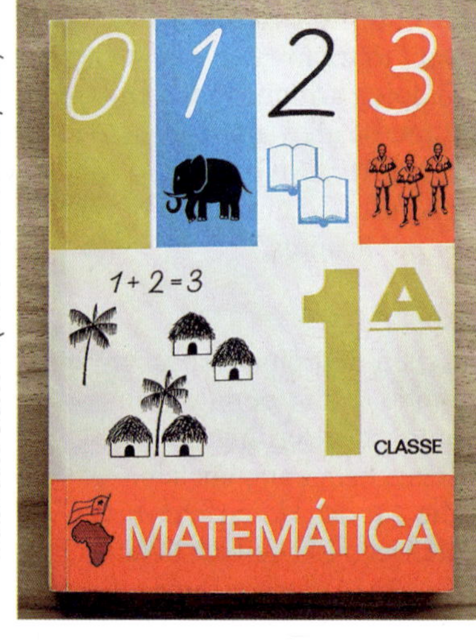

Figs. 32–33: Solidaritätskomitee der DDR, ed., *Matemática Classe 1A* (Nationales Druckhaus, 1972)

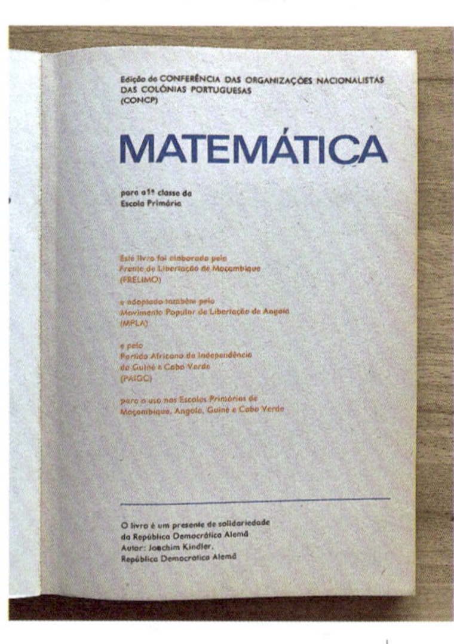

Abb. 32–33: Solidaritätskomitee der DDR (Hg.), *Matemática Classe 1A*, Nationales Druckhaus, 1972

erfolgt war, konnten im Mai im Rahmen einer feierlichen Veranstaltung die ersten Exemplare von 75.000 Mathe-Lehrbüchern für die 1. Klasse an den Präsidenten der FRELIMO Samora Machel übergeben werden. Die MPLA erhielt wenig später ebenfalls 75.000 Stück und die PAIGC 50.000 Stück. Joachim Kindler hatte unterdessen das Mathe-Buch für die 2. Klasse beendet.

In diese Zeit fiel auch der Beschluss des Anti-Rassismusprogramms des Weltkirchenrates. Dort hieß es, dass sich die Kirchen an der „Rassendiskriminierung" beteiligt hätten und eine Mitschuld am institutionalisierten Rassismus trügen. Der Weltkirchenrat rief die Kirchen auf, über Wohltätigkeit hinaus an einem radikalen Neuaufbau der Gesellschaft mitzuwirken. Die evangelischen Christen in der DDR diskutierten innerhalb der ökumenischen Bewegung heftig über die Möglichkeiten eines geeigneten Engagements für die Befreiungsbewegungen, ohne damit den bewaffneten Kampf und die Außenpolitik der DDR unterstützen zu wollen. Da bot sich zu dieser Zeit die Mitfinanzierung des Mathe-Buches für die FRELIMO an. Über Spenden und Kollekten übernahmen die evangelischen Kirchen der DDR die Hälfte der Druckkosten. So wurde das Mathe-Buch der Ausgangspunkt für eine andauernde Zusammenarbeit zwischen zwei sehr unterschiedlichen Institutionen. In den Folgejahren wurden noch weitere gemeinsame Hilfs- und Solidaritätsprojekte realisiert. Dazu zählte unter anderem 1985 die Mitfinanzierung von sieben verschiedenen Schulbüchern mit einer Auflage von 3,5 Millionen Exemplaren für den Unterricht in Nicaragua, um die breit angelegte Bildungskampagne der Sandinistschen Befreiungsfront (FSLN) zu unterstützen.

Under the leadership of Eduardo Mondlane, FRELIMO received financial support from all three power blocs. In the early 1960s, China was still the Mozambique independence movement's closest ally within the Communist world. Under the presidency of John F. Kennedy, the United States also began to provide Mondlane with covert support. The Mozambique Institute, where Kindler worked for the GDR and taught fledgling members of FRELIMO, was started with funding from the CIA and the Ford Foundation. In the mid-1960s, however, FRELIMO intensified its ties with the Soviet Union, Czechoslovakia, and East Germany, increasingly turning its back on Beijing. For some FRELIMO members, however, the movement's most important goal was to end all forms of White supremacy in Mozambique. Mondlane's wife, the American Janet Mondlane, and his inner circle were accused of cultivating ties with and accepting support from the US. In 1968, a year before Eduardo Mondlane was assassinated in Dar es Salaam, unrest broke out in the FRELIMO camp. The students called for the institute's White teachers to be dismissed. The question of how close the independence movement could get to the socialist or Western camp in seeking support was just one of the fault lines causing conflict within FRELIMO. The Mozambique Institute in Dar es Salaam was grappling with how to design the future social order and put an end to dependent relationships of all kinds.

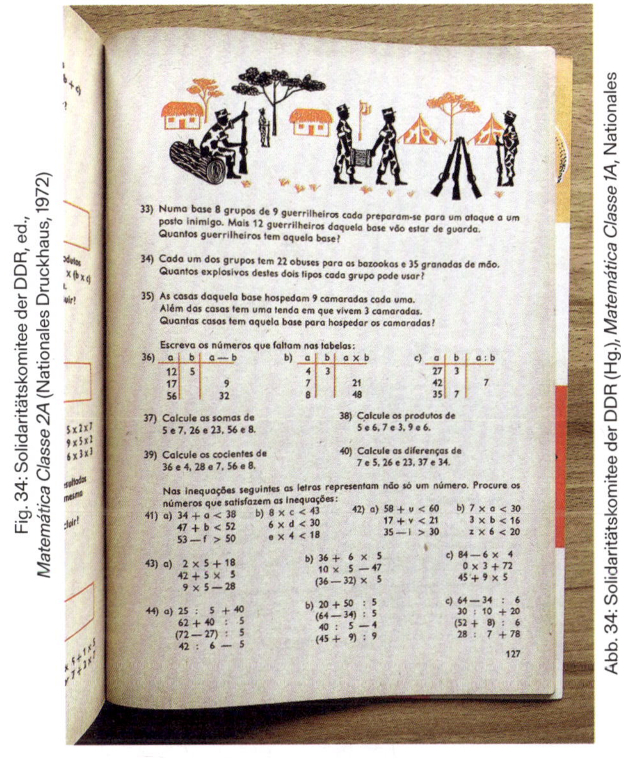

33) Numa base 8 grupos de 9 guerrilheiros cada preparam-se para um ataque a um posto inimigo. Mais 12 guerrilheiros daquela base vão estar de guarda. Quantos guerrilheiros tem aquela base?

34) Cada um dos grupos tem 22 obuses para as bazookas e 35 granadas de mão. Quantos explosivos destes dois tipos cada grupo pode usar?

35) As casas daquela base hospedam 9 camaradas cada uma. Além das casas tem uma tenda em que vivem 3 camaradas. Quantas casas tem aquela base para hospedar os camaradas?

Escreva os números que faltam nas tabelas:

36)

a	b	a — b
12	5	
17		9
56		32

b)

a	b	a × b
4	3	
7		21
8		48

c)

a	b	a : b
27	3	
42		7
35	7	

37) Calcule as somas de
5 e 7, 26 e 23, 56 e 8.

38) Calcule os produtos de
5 e 6, 7 e 3, 9 e 6.

39) Calcule os cocientes de
36 e 4, 28 e 7, 56 e 8.

40) Calcule as diferenças de
7 e 5, 26 e 23, 37 e 34.

Nas inequações seguintes as letras representam não só um número. Procure os números que satisfazem as inequações:

41) a) $34 + a < 38$
$47 + b < 52$
$53 — f > 50$

b) $8 × c < 43$
$6 × d < 30$
$e × 4 < 18$

42) a) $58 + u < 60$
$17 + v < 21$
$35 — i > 30$

b) $7 × a < 30$
$3 × b < 16$
$z × 6 < 20$

43) a) $2 × 5 + 18$
$42 + 5 × 5$
$9 × 5 — 28$

b) $36 + 6 × 5$
$10 × 5 — 47$
$(36 — 32) × 5$

c) $84 — 6 × 4$
$0 × 3 + 72$
$45 + 9 × 5$

44) a) $25 : 5 + 40$
$62 + 40 : 5$
$(72 — 27) : 5$
$42 : 6 — 5$

b) $20 + 50 : 5$
$(64 — 34) : 5$
$40 : 5 — 4$
$(45 + 9) : 9$

c) $64 — 34 : 6$
$30 : 10 + 20$
$(52 + 8) : 6$
$28 : 7 + 78$

127

Fig. 34: Solidaritätskomitee der DDR, ed., *Matemática Classe 2A* (Nationales Druckhaus, 1972)

Abb. 34: Solidaritätskomitee der DDR (Hg.), *Matemática Classe 1A*, Nationales Druckhaus, 1972

Unter der Leitung von Eduardo Mondlane erhielt die FRELIMO finanzielle Unterstützung von allen drei Blockmächten. Noch zu Beginn der 1960er Jahre war China der engste Verbündete der mosambikanischen Unabhängigkeitsbewegung, innerhalb der kommunistischen Welt. Unter der Präsidentschaft von John F. Kennedy begannen auch die Vereinigten Staaten, Eduardo Mondlane verdeckt zu unterstützen. Das Mosambik-Institut, in dem Joachim Kindler für die DDR arbeitete und den Nachwuchs der FRELIMO unterrichtete, wurde mit Geldern der CIA und der Ford Foundation gegründet. Mitte der 1960er Jahre hingegen intensivierte die FRELIMO ihre Verbindungen zur Sowjetunion, der Tschechoslowakei und der DDR und wandte sich vermehrt von Peking ab. Für einige Mitglieder der FRELIMO war jedoch das Ende der weißen Vorherrschaft in Mosambik das wichtigste Ziel der Bewegung. Eduardo Mondlanes Frau, die Amerikanerin Janet Mondlane, sowie seine Vertrauten, wurden beschuldigt, Verbindungen zu den USA zu pflegen und Unterstützung anzunehmen. Im Jahr 1968, ein Jahr vor der Ermordung von Eduardo Mondlane in Daressalam, brachen Unruhen im Lager der FRELIMO aus. Die Studenten forderten die Entlassung der weißen Lehrer des Instituts. Die Frage, wie stark sich die Unabhängigkeitsbewegung auf der Suche nach Unterstützung dem sozialistischen oder dem westlichen Lager annähern dürfe, war nur eine der Konfliktlinien innerhalb der FRELIMO. In Mosambik-Institut in Daressalam wurde um die Gestaltung der zukünftigen Gesellschaftsordnung und das Ende aller Abhängigkeitsverhältnisse gerungen.

DAVID ABÍLIO

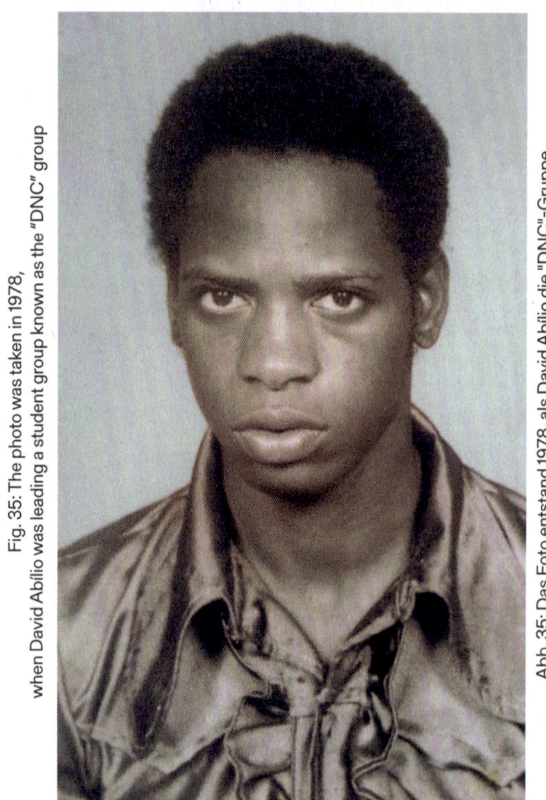

Fig. 35: The photo was taken in 1978, when David Abílio was leading a student group known as the "DNC" group

Abb. 35: Das Foto entstand 1978, als David Abílio die "DNC"-Gruppe, eine Gruppe von Studierenden, leitete.

MONDLANE

1. See BArch DR1/11646.

AMBRE ALFREDO AND LEA MARIE NIENHOFF IN CONVERSATION
WITH DAVID ABÍLIO MONDLANE

WHY THE THEATER OF THE REVOLUTION NEEDS TO BE UNDISCIPLINED

David Abílio Mondlane, theater director, playwright and choreographer, was born in Chibuto, in the south of Mozambique, in 1949. For more than thirty years, he directed the Companhia Nacional de Canto de Dança (CNCD, National Song and Dance Company of Mozambique), a renowned cultural institution in the country. In addition to his work with the CNCD, for which he has received several national and international awards, David Abílio was an advisor to the Minister of Culture and a theater professor. For his significant contribution to the arts and culture, he was recently awarded the Medal of Merit for Arts and Letters by the Mozambican government.

In March 1982, David Abílio Mondlane arrived in East Berlin for an internship in theater directing. Before arriving, the *Zentrum für kulturelle Auslandsarbeit*, a department of the Ministry of Culture, had prepared a meticulous program for his stay. On a "development sheet," they specified the schedules and locations of the training: three months of German classes in Wilsdruff and nine months of internship at the Mecklenburg State Theater in Schwerin. By arranging the internship, the Mozambican and East German governments fulfilled Article 30 of the Cultural Work Plan 1981–1982.[1]

Before starting his internship in the GDR, David Abílio had built an extensive career in Mozambique. A self-taught theater director and an advocate of "Teatro Popular," he had already directed several plays, given classes in theater practice, and been appointed head of the theater department in Mozambique's

AMBRE ALFREDO UND LEA MARIE NIENHOFF
IM GESPRÄCH MIT DAVID ABÍLIO MONDLANE

WARUM DAS THEATER DER REVOLUTION UNDISZIPLINIERT SEIN MUSS

David Abílio Mondlane, Theaterregisseur, Dramatiker und Choreograf, wurde 1949 in Chibuto im Süden Mosambiks geboren. Mehr als 30 Jahre lang leitete er die Companhia Nacional de Canto de Dança (CNCD, Nationale Gesangs- und Tanzkompanie von Mosambik), eine renommierte Kulturinstitution des Landes. Neben seiner Arbeit mit der CNCD, für die er mehrere nationale und internationale Auszeichnungen erhielt, war David Abílio Mondlane Berater des Kulturministers und Lehrbeauftragter für Theater. Für seinen bedeutenden Beitrag zu Kunst und Kultur wurde er kürzlich von der mosambikanischen Regierung mit dem Verdienstorden für Kunst und Literatur ausgezeichnet.

Im März 1982 traf David Abílio Mondlane in Ost-Berlin ein, um ein Praktikum im Bereich Theaterregie zu absolvieren. Vor seiner Ankunft hatte das Zentrum für kulturelle Auslandsarbeit, eine Abteilung des Kulturministeriums, einen detaillierten Zeitplan für seinen Aufenthalt erstellt. Auf einem „Entwicklungsbogen" waren Ablauf und Orte der Ausbildung festgelegt: drei Monate Deutschunterricht in Wilsdruff und neun Monate Praktikum am Mecklenburgischen Staatstheater in Schwerin. Mit der Vermittlung des Praktikums erfüllten die mosambikanische und die ostdeutsche Regierung Artikel 30 des Kulturarbeitsplans 1981/82.[1]

Bevor er sein Praktikum in der DDR antrat, hatte David Abílio in Mosambik bereits Karriere gemacht. Als autodidaktischer Theaterregisseur und Pionier des „Teatro Popular" hatte er zu diesem Zeitpunkt schon mehrere Theaterstücke inszeniert, Unterricht in Theaterpraxis gegeben und war zum Leiter der Theaterabteilung der Nationalen Kulturdirektion Mosambiks ernannt worden. Als großer Verehrer von Bertolt Brecht war David Abílio fest entschlossen, am Berliner Ensemble Erfahrungen zu sammeln. „Wie Sie sich vorstellen können, war das das Mekka für mich", sagt er in unserem Gespräch und lächelt bei der Erinnerung

1. BArch DR1/11646.

2. Ibid.

National Directorate of Culture. As a firm admirer of Bertolt Brecht, David Abílio was determined to study at the Berliner Ensemble. "As you can imagine, for me, it meant getting to Mecca," he says in our interview, smiling at the memory of his younger self. David Abílio contacted the theater directors he wanted to learn from and single-handedly renegotiated the terms of his internship in the GDR with the Ministries of Culture of both countries. The autonomy he seized to shape his education upset "the program" drawn up for foreign interns.

Skimming through the GDR's Ministry of Culture archives, the name David Abílio Mondlane stood out. In letters and reports, David Abílio is described as someone who "is not convinced of the usefulness of the internship in Schwerin" and "is of the opinion that he can choose his own internship location and that his place of residence is none of the center's business."[2] Intrigued and impressed by this young Mozambican student who wanted to do things his own way rather than follow the plans the GDR had for him at a time when many things could not be said or done, we searched for a way to contact him. After several exchanges and attempts to meet, the following interview took place in May 2023, online via video call, with each of us in a different country. Lea joined from Basel, Ambre from Cotonou, and together we connected with David Abílio in Maputo for a conversation about an internship that started in 1982 and ended four months ahead of schedule.

After the independence of Mozambique in 1975, you began to do community theater, showed theater pieces in schools and factories, and were promoted to the national director of theater in the Ministry of Culture of the People's Republic of Mozambique. At the time, culture was understood as one of the main pillars needed to build the new society—freed from the shackles of colonialism. How did you experience this time, and how did you understand your own role as a theater practitioner in this moment of transformation?

In the 1970s, shortly after independence, I was young and deeply passionate about the arts, particularly dance and theater. It was a time of revolution, and there was a strong push for pamphleteering-style theater. The main goal was to make the people realize that the situation had changed; we were now

an die Vergangenheit. David Abílio nahm Kontakt zu den Theaterdirektoren auf, von denen er lernen wollte, und verhandelte eigenständig die Bedingungen seines Praktikums in der DDR mit den Kulturministerien beider Länder neu. Die Autonomie, die er zur Gestaltung seiner Ausbildung nutzte, brachte das Programm, das für ausländische Praktikanten vorgesehen war, ordentlich durcheinander.

Der Name David Abílio Mondlane fiel uns bei der Durchsicht der Archivdokumente des Kulturministeriums auf. In Briefen und Berichten wird David Abílio als jemand beschrieben, der „von der Zweckmäßigkeit des Praktikums in Schwerin nicht überzeugt ist" und „der Meinung ist, dass er sich seinen Praktikumsort selbst aussuchen kann und dass sein Wohnort das Zentrum nichts angeht".[2] Fasziniert und beeindruckt von diesem jungen mosambikanischen Studenten, der die Dinge selbst in die Hand nehmen wollte, anstatt den Plänen zu folgen, die die DDR für ihn hatte, suchten wir nach einer Möglichkeit, mit ihm in Kontakt zu treten. Nach mehreren Gesprächen und Versuchen, sich zu treffen, fand das folgende Interview im Mai 2023 statt, online per Videoanruf, wobei sich jeder von uns aus einem anderen Land zuschaltete. Lea Marie Nienhoff meldete sich aus Basel, Ambre Alfredo aus Cotonou. Gemeinsam führten wir ein Gespräch mit David Abílio in Maputo über ein Praktikum, das 1982 begann und vier Monate früher als geplant endete.

Nach der Unabhängigkeit Mosambiks im Jahr 1975 begannen Sie, Community-Theater zu machen, führten Theaterstücke in Schulen und Fabriken auf und wurden dann zum Nationaldirektor für Theater im Kulturministerium der Volksrepublik Mosambik ernannt. Damals galt die Kultur als eine der wichtigsten Säulen für den Aufbau einer neuen Gesellschaft – befreit von den Fesseln des Kolonialismus. Wie haben Sie diese Zeit erlebt und wie haben Sie Ihre eigene Rolle als Theatermacher in diesem Transformationsprozess verstanden?

In den 1970er Jahren, kurz nach der Unabhängigkeit, war ich jung und ganz versessen auf Kunst, insbesondere Tanz und Theater. Es war eine Zeit der Revolution, und es gab einen starken Drang nach politischem, propagandistischem Theater. Das Hauptziel bestand darin, den Menschen klarzumachen, dass sich die Situation geändert hatte; wir waren nun unabhängig, wir mussten ein neues Mosambik aufbauen und uns lösen von den Problemen und

2. Ebd.

independent and needed to build a new Mozambique, free from the problems and traumas of colonial times. Popular theater aimed to communicate this message of a new world being constructed in Mozambique.

I began my journey in theater as a self-taught individual, without any formal training. I explored various theater theories, focusing especially on popular and avant-garde theater, which was trendy at the time. This exploration included Latin American experiences of collective creation theater, as well as the work of avant-garde authors like Konstantin Stanislavski, Vsevolod Meyerhold, and Antonin Artaud. My significant influence was the Theater of the Oppressed movement by the Brazilian Augusto Boal. The Theater of the Oppressed is a form of liberation theater. The theory behind the Theater of the Oppressed incorporates all Brechtian theater concepts. Understanding Brecht through Augusto Boal's Theater of the Oppressed was instrumental for me.

In my quest for innovative theatrical forms, I entered the theater scene in a revolutionary and challenging manner. During this time, I wrote and staged several plays in Mozambique. These plays were not performed in traditional theaters but in neighborhoods, camps, and schools. I also engaged in what Augusto Boal called Invisible Theater, which involved performing in buses. It wasn't clear who the author or actors were, and it wasn't even apparent that we were performing theater. It involved creating a stir on the bus by starting a discussion on a topic that the audience, the non-actors, would also engage in. This method aimed to awaken people's consciousness and get them involved in solving their issues, doing so without realizing they were participating in theater. This was one of the experiences.

You wrote several theater pieces; you hold various positions in important cultural institutions in Mozambique. The time you spent in the GDR was very short when seen in relation to this. Yet, we would be curious to hear what you remember most about your experiences in the GDR. In what ways did it shape your work?

Traumata der Kolonialzeit. Das Teatro Popular sollte diese Botschaft von einer neuen Welt, die in Mosambik aufgebaut werden sollte, vermitteln.

Ich begann meine Beschäftigung mit dem Theater als Autodidakt, ohne jede formale Ausbildung. Ich machte mich mit verschiedenen Theatertheorien vertraut und konzentrierte mich dabei vor allem auf das populäre und avantgardistische Theater, das zu dieser Zeit in Mode war. Dazu gehörten die lateinamerikanischen Erfahrungen mit dem kollektiven Theater sowie die Werke von Avantgarde-Autoren wie Konstantin Stanislawski, Wsewolod Meyerhold und Antonin Artaud. Ein wichtiger Einfluss war für mich die Bewegung um das „Theater der Unterdrückten" des Brasilianers Augusto Boal. Das Theater der Unterdrückten ist eine Art Theater der Emanzipation. Die Theorie des Theaters der Unterdrückten hat alle Brecht'schen Theaterkonzepte in sich aufgenommen. Der beste Zugang zum Verständnis von Brecht war für mich Augusto Boals Theater der Unterdrückten.

Auf meiner Suche nach innovativen Theaterformen trat ich mit sicherlich revolutionären und herausfordernden Gesten in der Theaterwelt auf. Während dieser Zeit schrieb und inszenierte ich mehrere Stücke in Mosambik. Diese Stücke wurden nicht in traditionellen Theatern aufgeführt, sondern in Wohnvierteln, Lagern und Schulen. Ich habe auch das praktiziert, was Augusto Boal als „Unsichtbares Theater" bezeichnet, indem ich zum Beispiel in Bussen aufgeführt habe. Dabei war nicht offensichtlich, wer der Autor oder wer die Schauspieler waren, es war nicht einmal offensichtlich, dass wir überhaupt Theater spielten. Es ging darum, in einem Linienbus Aufsehen zu erregen, indem wir eine Diskussion über ein Thema anstießen, an der sich auch das Publikum, die Nicht-Schauspieler, beteiligen sollten. Diese Methode zielte darauf ab, ihr Bewusstsein dafür zu wecken, dass sie sich an der Lösung ihrer Probleme selbst beteiligen können, ohne dass ihnen dabei bewusst war, dass sie Teil eines Theaterstücks waren. Das war eine dieser Erfahrungen.

Sie haben diverse Theaterstücke geschrieben; Sie bekleiden verschiedene Positionen in wichtigen kulturellen Einrichtungen in Mosambik. Die Zeit, die Sie in der DDR verbracht haben, erscheint im Verhältnis dazu

In the early 1980s, due to my profound passion for theater, the government awarded me a scholarship to go to East Germany, the GDR. It was a significant dream of mine to visit Brecht's homeland. I had extensively read and studied Brecht's methodologies and philosophies, which I utilized in creating my plays. My entire theatrical mindset was dominated by Bertolt Brecht. Upon my arrival, they took me to see the Berliner Ensemble, Brecht's theater company. As you might imagine, for me, it was akin to reaching Mecca. When the actors of the Berliner Ensemble saw a Black man arriving, and the translator with me explained that I was a Brecht enthusiast eager to study Brecht, their initial question was: "Brecht in Africa? Do you know about Brecht? How did you come to know Brecht?" They truly hadn't considered that Brecht was a worldwide figure, one who had crossed beyond Europe's barriers and borders and was studied in every country experiencing this kind of revolutionary movement.

You had read the writings of Bertolt Brecht, you were inspired by his theater—theater understood as a form of liberation and emancipation, epic theater as a liberation of the actor, in a way, as political commentary. When you arrived in the GDR, you encountered a theater quite different from the community theater you had been doing. What did you think of it?

When I arrived in Germany, despite my deep passion for Brecht, the Germans didn't want to send me to the Berliner Ensemble. They intended to place me in smaller theaters, which they believed would be more fitting for someone from a developing country. To them, it didn't seem worthwhile for me to go to the Berliner Ensemble. Initially, they enrolled me in a language school and then directed me to small theaters. However, I didn't appreciate those small theater companies. Many practiced forms of theater that Brecht opposed, what he termed "Aristotelian theater." Brecht's theater was the antithesis of this. He developed his Organon, a theater with a new philosophy, a new vision. Being young and full of ideas, I regarded the theater produced by those small companies as

sehr kurz. Dennoch würden wir gerne wissen, woran Sie sich am meisten erinnern, wenn Sie an Ihre Erfahrungen in der DDR denken. Inwiefern haben diese Ihre Arbeit geprägt?

Anfang der 1980er Jahre erhielt ich aufgrund meiner großen Leidenschaft für das Theater ein Stipendium der Regierung, um nach Ostdeutschland, in die DDR, zu gehen. Es war ein großer Traum von mir, das Heimatland von Brecht zu sehen. Ich hatte Brechts Methoden und Theorien ausgiebig gelesen und studiert und nutzte das auch bei der Entwicklung meiner Stücke. Mein Verständnis von Theater war komplett von Bertolt Brecht geprägt. Bei meiner Ankunft nahm man mich mit zum Berliner Ensemble, dem Theater von Brecht. Wie Sie sich vorstellen können, war das das Mekka für mich. Als die Schauspieler des Berliner Ensembles einen Schwarzen ankommen sahen und der Übersetzer, der mich begleitete, erklärte, dass ich ein Brecht-Enthusiast sei, der sich eingehender mit Brecht beschäftigen wolle, kam als Erstes: „Brecht in Afrika? Sie kennen Brecht? Woher kennen Sie Brecht?" Sie hatten wirklich nicht begriffen, dass Brecht eine weltweit bekannte Figur war, die die Grenzen Europas überschritten hatte und in jedem Land diskutiert wurde, das diese Art von revolutionärer Bewegung erlebte.

Sie hatten Schriften von Bertolt Brecht gelesen, Sie waren inspiriert von seinem Theater – einem Theater, das als Mittel der Befreiung und Emanzipation verstanden wurde, episches Theater als Befreiung des Schauspielers, gewissermaßen als politischer Kommentar. Als Sie in der DDR ankamen, trafen Sie auf ein ganz anderes Theater als das Community-Theater, das Sie gemacht hatten. Wie dachten Sie darüber?

Als ich in Deutschland ankam, wollten mich die Deutschen trotz meiner großen Leidenschaft für Brecht nicht ans Berliner Ensemble schicken. Sie wollten mich an kleineren Theatern unterbringen, von denen sie glaubten, dass sie für jemanden aus einem Entwicklungsland besser geeignet wären. Es schien ihnen nicht lohnend, mich ans Berliner Ensemble zu schicken. Sie meldeten mich zunächst in einer Sprachschule an und verwiesen mich dann an kleine Bühnen. Doch diese kleinen Theaterkompanien brachten

reactionary. Imagine, in Socialist Germany, accusing them of producing reactionary theater? It was utterly misplaced.

You found a theater that was reactionary from your standpoint? That was hierarchical? Like a bourgeois theater of the past?
In Brecht's view, it was a theater of the bourgeoisie. But they didn't want to hear that, especially from an African, coming from a semi-independent country. And, in their words, we didn't even have the tools to consider ourselves socialists. But as a young person, I'd already had a Marxist training and was aligned with the far left. I wasn't an orthodox Marxist, no, I criticized many socialist theories that I considered a bit orthodox. Even in Mozambique, shortly after independence, I always adhered to ultra-left currents.

So, some things that the Germans tried to impart to me as essential for my education I rejected very vehemently, saying, "This is bourgeois

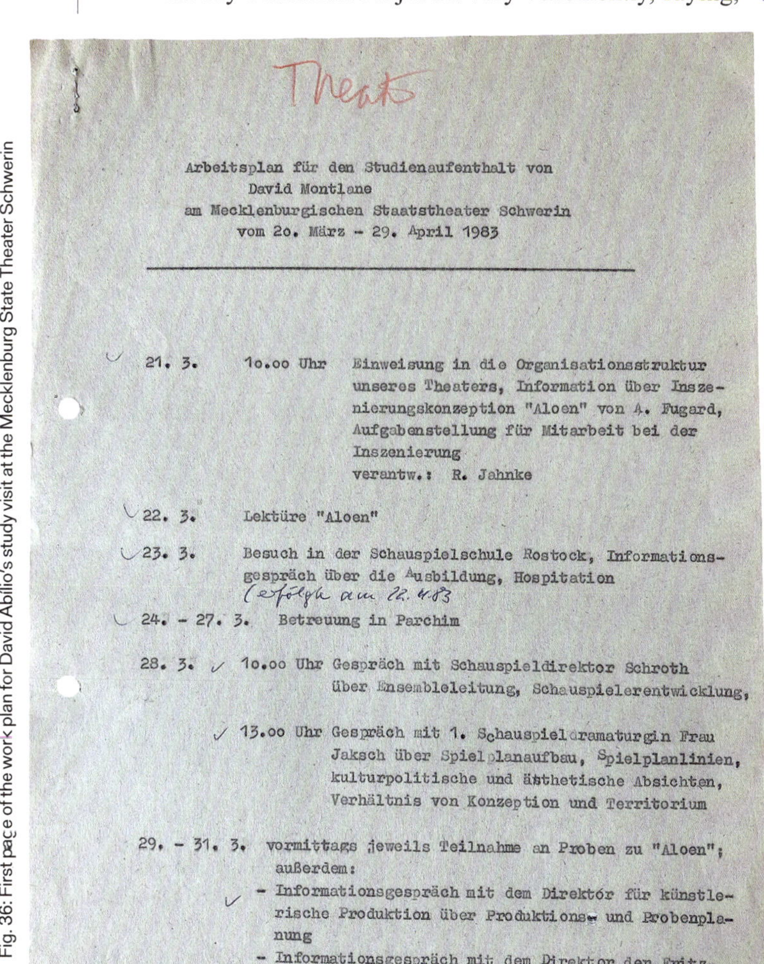

Fig. 36: First page of the work plan for David Abílio's study visit at the Mecklenburg State Theater Schwerin

Abb. 36: Erste Seite des Arbeitsplans für David Abílios Studienaufenthalt am Mecklenburgischen Staatstheater Schwerin

mir nichts. Viele von ihnen praktizierten Formen des Theaters, die Brecht ablehnte, nämlich das, was er „aristotelisches Theater" nannte. Brechts Theater war die Antithese dazu. Deshalb entwickelte er sein Organon, ein Theater mit einer neuen Philosophie, einer neuen Vision. Ich war jung und voller Ideen und hielt das Theater, das diese kleinen Ensembles machten, für reaktionär. Stellen Sie sich nun aber vor, jemand kommt daher und wirft den Leuten im sozialistischen Deutschland vor, sie würden reaktionäres Theater machen. Das war völlig unangebracht.

Sie fanden ein Theater vor, das aus Ihrer Sicht reaktionär war? Das hierarchisch war? Wie das bürgerliche Theater der Vergangenheit?
Mit dem Blick von Brecht betrachtet war es ein Theater der Bourgeoisie. Aber das wollten sie nicht hören, vor allem nicht von einem Afrikaner, der aus einem erst halb unabhängigen Land kam. In ihren Worten verfügten wir nicht einmal über die Mittel, uns als Sozialisten zu bezeichnen. Aber ich hatte als junger Mensch bereits eine marxistische

theater. This is reactionary." This, in a way, helped because it piqued their curiosity, and that's when they finally took me to the Berliner Ensemble. There, I had an interview with Manfred Wekwerth, who was Brecht's assistant and one of the foremost scholars on Brecht. I also came into contact with Ekkehard Schall, who was the lead actor, a model of Brechtian theater. I impressed them with the stories I told, with my passion for Brecht. This led to a very warm reception at the Berliner Ensemble, where they took me under their wing. They arranged an apartment for me that no one else had. Right on Unter den Linden, which is one of the main avenues in Berlin, close to the wall. I had no contact there with Mozambicans.

How did you get to know Manfred Wekwerth?
I became acquainted with him through readings. Wekwerth wrote several books on staging and theatrical direction. So, already being familiar with his work, it was very beneficial. Wekwerth arranged for me to have a director to work with as an assistant and to closely follow the entire process of staging a play at the Berliner Ensemble. I also assisted Christoph Schroth on the play *Drums in the Night* by Bertolt Brecht.

After some time, they sent me to Schwerin, where Christoph Schroth was the director. He was one of the great theater directors and used Bertolt Brecht's method to stage classical plays, such as the "Antike" (Classics) project, on which I was an assistant. It was a super production of stories from ancient Greece and particularly the Trojan War. This was exactly what I wanted, not only to work on Brecht's plays but especially to use Brecht's method in Mozambican plays or those written by me.

Were your East German colleagues curious to learn from you and hear more about Mozambican theater practices and the community theater you had experimented with? Could you speak to your German colleagues about your interpretation of Brecht? You also spoke out, expressed your opinion in public, I imagine. Were you aware of being controlled by the authorities during that time?

Ausbildung und stand zudem der radikalen Linken nahe. Ich war kein orthodoxer Marxist, ich hatte einiges auszusetzen an diversen sozialistischen Theorien, die mir etwas zu orthodox vorkamen. Selbst in Mosambik, kurz nach der Unabhängigkeit, hatte ich mich den ultralinken Strömungen angeschlossen.

Deshalb habe ich einige Dinge, die mir die Deutschen als wesentliche Bestandteile meiner Ausbildung vermitteln wollten, sehr vehement abgelehnt und gesagt: „Das ist bürgerliches Theater. Das ist reaktionär." In gewisser Weise war das sogar hilfreich, denn es hat sie neugierig gemacht, und so haben sie mich schließlich doch ans Berliner Ensemble geholt. Dort hatte ich ein Gespräch mit Manfred Wekwerth, der Brechts Assistent gewesen war und zu den führenden Brecht-Experten zählte. Ich kam auch in Kontakt mit Ekkehard Schall, dem bedeutendsten Schauspieler dort und einem Vorbild im Brecht'schen Spiel. Ich beeindruckte sie mit dem, was ich zu erzählen hatte, mit meiner Leidenschaft für Brecht. Das führte zu einer sehr herzlichen Aufnahme, und in gewisser Weise protegierten sie mich am Berliner Ensemble. Sie vermittelten mir eine Wohnung, wie kein anderer sie hatte. Direkt Unter den Linden, einer der Hauptstraßen von Berlin, in der Nähe der Mauer. Dort gab es sonst keine Mosambikaner.

Wie haben Sie Manfred Wekwerth kennengelernt?
Ich habe ihn über das Lesen kennengelernt. Manfred Wekwerth hatte mehrere Bücher über das Inszenieren und Theaterregie verfasst. Dass ich mit seiner Arbeit bereits vertraut war, war sehr günstig. Manfred Wekwerth vermittelte mich an einen Regisseur, mit dem ich als Assistent den gesamten Prozess der Inszenierung eines Stückes am Berliner Ensemble hautnah miterleben konnte. Dort assistierte ich auch Christoph Schroth bei dem Brecht-Stück *Trommeln in der Nacht*.

Nach einiger Zeit schickten sie mich nach Schwerin, wo Christoph Schroth Regisseur war. Er war einer der großen Theaterregisseure und inszenierte nach der Methode von Bertolt Brecht klassische Stücke wie zum Beispiel das Projekt „Antike", bei dem ich Assistent war. Das war eine großartige Inszenierung von Geschichten aus dem antiken Griechenland

Firstly, I must say that, deep down, the Germans are also conservative. And they suffer from a superiority complex. They know a lot, don't they? They can teach, they can transmit, and whoever wants can learn. But they weren't very open to learning from me, especially in a formal way. Conversations in a bar, on a street corner … there, people were more open to hearing my opinions. But during specific and official work, I just had to listen, watch, and ask about what I didn't understand to have it explained to me. Even at the Berliner Ensemble, the hierarchy was very clear. When I started to actually work, I no longer had much access to Wekwerth or the big names at the Berliner Ensemble. In official work, I was involved with people at a lower level; contacts at a higher level were very, very limited.

Outside the official context, I made various friends and began to connect with some more controversial, more revolutionary artists. And as some of these people had somewhat dissenting ideas, I can say that I started to be monitored. My advantage was that I wasn't a sympathizer of bourgeois Western ideas, of capitalism. I was a Marxist but from the far-left, which they saw in a negative light. They didn't want that kind of leftist, they wanted people very much in line with pre-established standards. So, on the one hand, it was an advantage because they weren't worried that I might be linked to the CIA, for example, because I was against imperialist policies. But, on the other, it was a disadvantage because I also wasn't pro-Soviet, and wasn't pro-system.

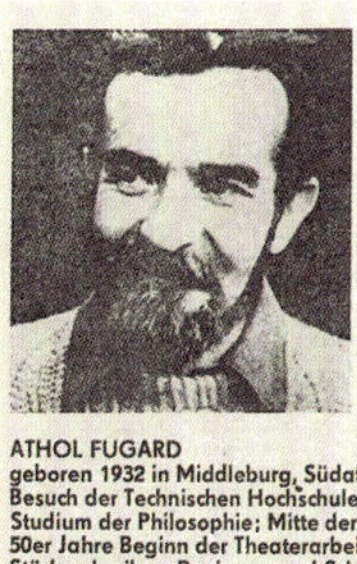

ATHOL FUGARD
geboren 1932 in Middleburg, Südafrika; Besuch der Technischen Hochschule und Studium der Philosophie; Mitte der 50er Jahre Beginn der Theaterarbeit als Stückeschreiber; Regisseur und Schauspieler. Lebt jetzt in Port Elizabeth, einem Industriehafen am Indischen Ozean.

„Ich finde es außerordentlich schwierig, mir über die schöpferische Energie klar zu werden, die mich zum Schreiben veranlaßt. Eines weiß ich: Ich habe das starke Bedürfnis, Zeuge zu sein, die Wahrheit zu sagen … Eine der wesentlichsten Funktionen von Theater in jeder Gesellschaft, von Euripides bis heute, ist sein starker politischer Effekt. Das Theater kann das politische Bewußtsein sensibilisieren …" Athol Fugard

Stücke: DER BÖSE FREITAG (1958), NONGOGO (1959), BLUTSBAND (1961), DA LEBEN LEUTE (1963), HALLO UND ADIEU (1965/66), BUSCHMANN UND LENA (1969), DIE INSEL (1972), SIZWE BANSI IST TOT (1973), AUSSAGEN NACH EINER VERHAFTUNG AUF GRUND DES GESETZES GEGEN UNSITTLICHKEIT (1972), DIMETOS (1974), ALOEN (1980) und MASTER HAROLD AND HIS BOYS (1982).

Aloe (a:loe: ; (griech.)) artenreiche Gattung der Liliengewächse, von krautigem bis baumförmigem Wuchs, mit dicht stehenden bedornten fleischigen Blättern und meist roten Blüten in traubigen Blütenständen; in Trockengebieten Afrikas verbreitet. Die enthaltenen Anthrachinonderivate und Harze finden als Droge Verwendung (Abführmittel). Einige A.-Arten sind bekannte Zimmerpflanzen, die im Sommer im Freien stehen können.

SUDAFRIKA hat fünf große Bevölkerungsgruppen. Das Land wird von Weißen regiert; die Afrikaaner – das sind 2,25 Mill. Nachkommen der Buren, deren Vorfahren sich seit 1651 hier niederließen – haben alle wichtigen Funktionen im politischen Apparat, in der Polizei und bei den Streitkräften inne; Engländer sowie andere Europäer – rund 1,5 Mill. – spielen im Wirtschaftsleben (Großindustrie, Handel) die dominierende Rolle. Mischlinge (2,1 Mill.) und „Asiaten" (0,9 Mill., vor allem Inder) haben gewisse Bürgerrechte, können jedoch nie vollberechtigte Staatsbürger werden. Die eigentlichen Afrikaner – in der offiziellen Terminologie Südafrikas „Bantu" genannt – machen 16 Mill. aus, die sich in verschiedene ethnische Gruppen aufgliedern. Sie werden stufenweise aus den ausschließlich weißen Gebieten entfernt und in für sie bestimmten Homelands, den „Bantustans", angesiedelt. Aus ihren Reihen werden die für die Wirtschaft der Weißen benötigten Arbeitskräfte rekrutiert.

APARTHEID (afrikaans, „Absonderung", „getrennte Existenz"): offizielle Bezeichnung der reaktionären Doktrin der Rassentrennung in der Republik Südafrika. Die A. wird durch eine rassistische Interpretation der Bibel motiviert und geht im Interesse einer „weißen Herrenrasse" davon aus, daß jeder Rasse eine „besondere Lebensart" und ein „beson-derer Entwicklungsweg" vorgezeichnet sei. Die A. soll die Rassendiskriminierung, die ökonomische Ausbeutung und die politische Unterdrückung der nichtweißen Bevölkerung rechtfertigen. Zur Durchsetzung der A. verabschiedete das Parlament zahlreiche Rassengesetze.

Der BANN, in der Regel für 3 oder 5 Jahre ausgesprochen, ist ein Mittel, um politische Aktivitäten bestimmter Personen oder Organisationen zu unterbinden. Gebannte Personen haben einen umfangreichen Katalog von Auflagen zu beachten: Aufenthaltsbeschränkung auf einen Ort oder Stadtbezirk, Hausarrest von 18 bis 6 Uhr, an Wochenenden 14 bis 6 Uhr; Besuchsverbot, außer für nächste Angehörige und einen Arzt; sie dürfen Fabriken, Druckereien, Verlage nicht betreten; dürfen nicht publizieren und nicht von anderen zitiert werden. Jeder Verstoß gegen Bannverfügungen wird mit Haft bis zu drei Jahren bestraft.

Der BOYKOTT ist eine der Formen des südafrikanischen Widerstands. In der Tradition des gewaltlosen Protests beteiligten sich immer wieder Hunderttausende schwarze und farbige Südafrikaner an derartigen Aktivitäten: Schüler, die über Monate hinweg den Besuch ihrer Schulen verweigern und eigene Unterrichtsformen organisieren; Arbeiter, die erhöhte Autobuspreise nicht zahlen und statt dessen in Fahrtgemeinschaften oder zu Fuß ihre Arbeitsplätze erreichen. „Azikwelwa" ist seit dem legendären Busboykott in Alexandra 1957 die Losung solcher Aktionen: „Wir fahren nicht!"

„Dieses Stück handelt vom Überleben: Vom Überleben in Südafrika – und von der Entscheidung, hierzubleiben oder fortzugehen. … Piet und Steve sind Opfer eines Systems, einer sozialen und politischen Ordnung, der sie sich widersetzen wollten. Sie sind Opfer von Menschen." Athol Fugard

Athol Fugard
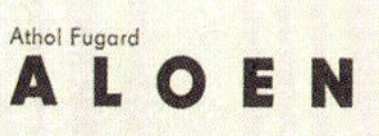

(A Lesson from Aloes)
Deutsch von Jörn van Dyck
Aufführungsrechte: S. Fischer Verlag Frankfurt am Main vertreten durch den Henschelverlag Berlin

Piet Bezuidenhout — Horst Rehberg
ein Weißer burischer Abstammung

Gladys, — Bärbel Röhl
seine Frau

Steve Daniels, — Heinz Kamm
sein Freund, ein Mischling

Regie — Reiner Flath
Ausstattung — Lutz Kreisel
Dramaturgie — Rainer Jahnke
Regieassistenz — Lutz Hollburg

Inspizienz: Lothar Böger, Souffleuse: Karin Bölke, Technische Leitung: Klaus Keller, Bühnenmeister: Gerhard Fritsch, Masken und Haartrachten: Dieter Fischer, Monika Freudenreich, Beleuchtung: Jürgen Rickmann, Kostümanfertigung unter der Leitung von Editha Gutschmidt und Gerhard Rouvel, Werkstätten: Tischlerei: Dieter Lemm, Schlosserei: Carl Frahm, Malsaal: Günter Kypke

Herausgegeben vom Mecklenburgischen Staatstheater Schwerin, amt. Generalintendant: Franz Tichatschke, Redaktion: Rainer Jahnke, Gestaltung: Uwe Sinnecker, Quellen: T. Wojcik/ Z. Domaranczyk, Vorhof der Hölle, Leipzig 1976, Meyers Neues Lexikon, Leipzig 1976, Gedichte aus Südafrika, Berlin 1975, B. Brecht, Gedichte IV, Berlin 1961. Satz und Druck: Druckerei Schweriner Volkszeitung II-16-8 DmG 112-38-83 1 000 (638) Spielzeit: 1982/83, Preis: 0,30 M

Fig. 37: Leaflet from the theater production *Aloen* (Mecklenburgisches Staatstheater Schwerin, 1983). David Abílio participated in the rehearsals

Abb. 37: Programmzettel der Theaterproduktion *Aloen* (Mecklenburgisches Staatstheater Schwerin, 1983). David Abílio nahm an den Proben teil

und insbesondere dem Trojanischen Krieg. Das entsprach dem, was ich wollte: nicht nur an Brechts Stücken arbeiten, sondern vor allem Brechts Methoden auf mosambikanische Stücke anwenden oder auf solche, die ich selbst geschrieben habe.

Waren Ihre deutschen Kollegen neugierig, von Ihnen zu lernen und mehr über die mosambikanische Theaterpraxis und das Community-Theater zu erfahren, mit dem Sie experimentiert hatten? Konnten Sie mit Ihnen über Ihre Interpretation von Brecht sprechen? Zudem haben Sie sich vermutlich offen geäußert und Ihre Meinung gesagt. Hatten Sie in dieser Zeit das Gefühl, bei den Behörden unter Beobachtung zu stehen?

Erstens muss ich sagen, dass die Deutschen tief im Inneren ziemlich konservativ sind. Und sie leiden unter einem Überlegenheitskomplex. Sie wissen viel, nicht wahr? Sie können lehren, sie können ihr Wissen vermitteln, und wer immer will, darf von ihnen lernen. Aber sie waren nicht sehr offen dafür, auch etwas von mir zu lernen, vor allem nicht in einem formellen Rahmen. Gespräche in einer Bar, an einer Straßenecke, in solchen Situationen waren die Leute offener, meine Meinung zu hören. Aber bei der konkreten und offiziellen Arbeit durfte ich nur zuhören, zuschauen und nachfragen, wenn ich etwas nicht verstanden hatte. Auch am Berliner Ensemble war die Hierarchie sehr klar. Sobald ich tatsächlich anfing zu arbeiten, hatte ich keinen wirklichen Zugang mehr zu Manfred Wekwerth oder den anderen großen Namen des Berliner Ensembles. In der offiziellen Arbeit habe

I didn't follow what everyone else was following. I wanted other things, new things. And this was somewhat detrimental because it shortened my stay in the GDR. I had to return to Mozambique a bit earlier than I should have because, in a way, I represented a threat. And my leftism was often grounded in the theories of Brecht. Brecht was not a rigid person. He was constantly seeking methods to fight against ideas that try to put people in the same box.

So, you're saying in the GDR Brecht's theater was understood much more as an acting method, very technical, and less as a political endeavor and a means to liberate?

Exactly. In Germany, what they tried most to convey to me were the technical aspects of Brecht and not the political side. Moreover, Brecht's political aspect was manipulated. But there were also people who had a different way of thinking, especially at the international conferences on Brecht that I participated in, where thinkers from other countries, such as Poland, Italy, etc., attended.

From the East and the West?

Yes. And they had a freer way of thinking about Brecht. Going further than the idea of Brecht within the GDR, where people were trying to position Brecht as a museum figure, static … For example, the first play Brecht wrote was *Baal*. And it was also the last play that he was still trying to

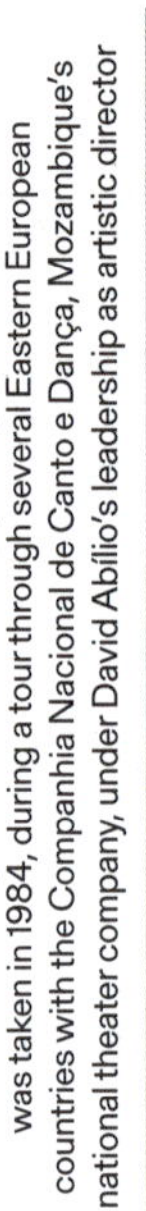

Fig. 38: On the road. This photograph was taken in 1984, during a tour through several Eastern European countries with the Companhia Nacional de Canto e Dança, Mozambique's national theater company, under David Abílio's leadership as artistic director

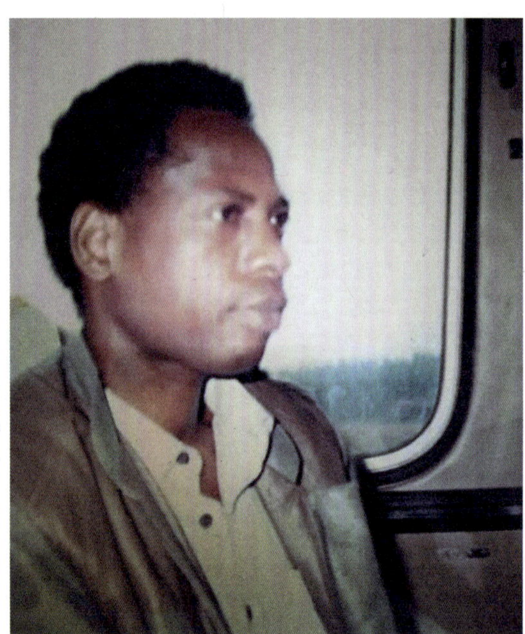

Abb. 38: Auf Reisen: Dieses Foto entstand 1984 während einer Tournee durch mehrere osteuropäische Länder mit der Companhia Nacional de Canto e Dança, der nationalen Theatergruppe von Mosambik, unter künstlerischer Leitung von David Abílio

ich mit Leuten auf einer niedrigeren Ebene zusammengearbeitet, und die Kontakte zur höheren Ebene waren sehr, sehr begrenzt.

Außerhalb des offiziellen Rahmens schloss ich Freundschaften und knüpfte Kontakte mit einigen Künstlern, die als unangepasst und revolutionär galten. Und da einige dieser Leute eher oppositionelle Ideen hatten, kann ich mir vorstellen, dass man anfing, mich zu überwachen. Mir kam aber wohl zugute, dass ich kein Sympathisant von bürgerlichwestlichen Ideen und dem kapitalistischen System gewesen bin. Ich war ganz klar Marxist, aber aus der ganz linken Ecke, das war für sie etwas Negatives. Diese Art von Linken wollten sie nicht, sie wollten Leute, die sich an die bereits etablierten Normen hielten. Einerseits war das ein Vorteil, weil sie keine Angst hatten, dass ich zum Beispiel mit der CIA in Verbindung stehen könnte, denn ich war gegen die imperialistische Politik. Andererseits war es aber auch von Nachteil für mich, weil ich nicht prosowjetisch war und nicht systemtreu. Ich bin gegen den Strom geschwommen. Ich träumte von anderen Dingen, neuen Dingen. Und das war in dem Sinne verhängnisvoll, dass es meinen Aufenthalt in der DDR verkürzt hat. Ich musste etwas früher als nötig nach Mosambik zurückkehren, weil ich in gewisser Weise bedrohlich wirkte. Häufig gründete sich mein linker Standpunkt auf Brechts Theorien. Brecht war kein dogmatischer Mensch. Er suchte fortlaufend nach Methoden, um gegen Denkweisen anzukämpfen, die darauf hinauslaufen, Menschen in eine bestimmte Schublade zu stecken.

modify when he died. This shows what true Brechtian idea is. It's not a static idea. It's a dynamic idea, one that evolves.

I found a document in the archive of the ministry of culture that records that you participated in an international Brecht seminar without the consent of the ministry. The GDR authorities did not seem to be happy about your participation. What happened at the seminar? Did the authorities try to exclude you from it? And, did your situation in the GDR change after you took part in the seminar?

I participated in that seminar and fought for the opportunity to do so. It was where I met other Brecht theorists from different countries and could follow the various debates on the conception each one had and defended about Brecht. For me, this was a confirmation that much more could be done with Brecht's work and methodology. My ambitions were growing; I wanted to learn much more about Brecht. Much more than was being shown to me.

And, as I said, at work, I wasn't there to come up with ideas or make contributions, all I could do was ask questions and get some answers. I didn't have any active participation in the plays. There was a Chilean director, whom I assisted in staging some plays like Brecht's *The Days of the Commune*. I had the opportunity to interact with him in a more free and friendly manner. Speaking Spanish helped, but this exchange happened in private, outside rehearsals.

I also grew fond of the actors. Outside the theater, we would talk, I would give my contributions, even about acting, the way I thought it could be. And, indeed, not being European, I brought a different cultural background, which could be quite new to them. That was how I contributed. But this wasn't something I did during rehearsals or on stage; these were things I did outside of the theater.

For example, actors would come to my house. In this respect, I was always privileged in Germany. They always gave me good apartments. Even in Schwerin, I had a large apartment, and actors and theater

Sie sagen also, in der DDR wurde Brechts Theater eher als eine Schauspielmethode verstanden, sehr technisch, weniger als ein politisches Unterfangen und ein Mittel zur Befreiung?

Ganz genau. In Deutschland hat man vor allem versucht, mir die technischen Aspekte von Brecht zu vermitteln und nicht den politischen Teil. Außerdem wurde der politische Aspekt von Brecht manipuliert. Aber ich traf auch Leute, die anders dachten, vor allem auf den internationalen Konferenzen zu Brecht, an denen ich teilnahm und bei denen Denker aus anderen Ländern wie Polen, Italien und so weiter zusammenkamen.

Aus dem Osten und aus dem Westen?

Ja. Und da gab es einen freieren geistigen Umgang mit Bertolt Brecht. Das ging weit über den DDR-Umgang mit Brecht hinaus, der immer nur darauf abzielte, Brecht zu musealisieren, als statisch zu betrachten … Das erste Stück, das Brecht geschrieben hat, war zum Beispiel *Baal*. Und es war auch das letzte Stück, an dem Brecht kurz vor seinem Tod noch Änderungen vornahm. Das zeigt, was wahres Brecht'sches Denken ist. Es ist kein statisches Gedankengebäude. Es ist ein dynamisches Denken, ein sich weiterentwickelndes Denken.

Ich habe im Archiv des Ministeriums für Kultur ein Dokument gefunden, das festhält, dass Sie ohne Zustimmung des Ministeriums an einem internationalen Brecht-Seminar teilgenommen haben. Die DDR-Behörden scheinen nicht glücklich über Ihre Teilnahme gewesen zu sein. Was ist bei dem Seminar passiert? Haben die Behörden versucht, Sie von der Teilnahme abzubringen? Und hat sich Ihre Situation in der DDR nach dem Seminar verändert?

Ich nahm an diesem Seminar teil und habe sehr dafür gekämpft, diese Gelegenheit wahrzunehmen. Dort traf ich andere Brecht-Theoretiker aus verschiedenen Ländern und verfolgte die Debatten über die unterschiedlichen Auffassungen, die sie jeweils über Brecht hatten und verteidigten. Für mich war das eine Bestätigung, dass man mit Brechts Werk und seiner Methode noch viel mehr anfangen kann. Mein Ehrgeiz wuchs; ich

colleagues would always come to my place to talk. And that's where I took the opportunity to give my contributions to the fullest.

But, to return to your question, I think my participation in that international seminar might have contributed to my premature return to Mozambique. I say "might" because the things done by the secret police are never fully known, what they know about us, what they don't.

How did this come about? How did they tell you to leave? Did you have contact with someone from the Stasi?

The Germans are very intelligent. They did not make it seem like my return was problematic. They praised my work a lot, said that I learned very quickly and had a lot of knowledge, and that I could, with what I learned, contribute to my country, which was in need of people like me. But for myself, I wanted to stay longer in Germany.

Some of my colleagues in Mozambique told me that there were very negative reports about me, and that I needed to be careful because I could be taken straight to jail upon arriving at the airport. In Germany, I was not aware that I was being pursued. If I was, they did it so discreetly that I didn't notice, or perhaps the infiltration was among the Germans who were my friends.

You also spent time at the university in Rostock? What was the experience there like? Were the relations to students and professors similar to what you described at the theater, or were the students more open to hearing your stories of how to work with community?

Yes, thanks to the opportunity given to me by Christoph Schroth, who was a theater professor at the Staatliche Schauspielschule Rostock, I was able to attend theater classes, although not in a formal way.

Schools, by nature, are very formal institutions, and for [theater] professionals, it ends up being what in German is called *langweilig* (boring). It's tedious, isn't it? Because it's too formal. It wasn't really for me. I felt more advanced than those students.

wollte noch viel mehr über Brecht lernen. Viel mehr als das, was mir gezeigt wurde.

Und, wie gesagt, während der Arbeit am Theater waren meine Ideen oder Beiträge nicht gefragt; das Einzige, was meine Rolle mir erlaubte, war Fragen zu stellen und Antworten zu bekommen. Ich konnte mich nicht aktiv bei den Stücken einbringen. Allerdings gab es einen chilenischen Regisseur, dem ich bei der Inszenierung einiger Stücke wie *Die Tage der Commune* von Brecht assistierte und mit dem ich die Möglichkeit hatte, mich auf eine freiere und freundschaftlichere Weise auszutauschen. Es war hilfreich, dass ich Spanisch sprechen konnte, aber dieser Austausch fand unter vier Augen statt, außerhalb der Proben.

Auch die Schauspieler wuchsen mir ans Herz. Außerhalb des Theaters unterhielten wir uns, ich brachte meine Ideen ein, sogar in Bezug auf die schauspielerische Darstellung und meine Vorstellungen davon. Und da ich kein Europäer bin, brachte ich einen anderen kulturellen Hintergrund mit, der für sie durchaus neu sein konnte. Aber das hatte keinen Raum während der Proben oder auf der Bühne, das passierte außerhalb des Theaters.

Schauspieler kamen zum Beispiel auch zu mir nach Hause. In dieser Hinsicht war ich in Deutschland immer privilegiert. Ich bekam gute Wohnungen. Selbst in Schwerin hatte ich eine große Wohnung, in die Schauspieler und Theaterkollegen kamen, um sich auszutauschen. Dort nutzte ich die Gelegenheit, meine Ideen mit ihnen zu teilen.

Aber um auf Ihre Frage zurückzukommen, ich denke, dass meine Teilnahme an diesem internationalen Seminar zu meiner vorzeitigen Rückkehr nach Mosambik beigetragen haben könnte. Ich sage „könnte", weil man nie genau weiß, was die Geheimpolizei macht, was sie über uns weiß und was nicht.

Wie ist es dazu gekommen? Auf welchem Weg hat man Ihnen die Rückkehr angeordnet? Hatten Sie Kontakt zu jemandem von der Stasi?

Die Deutschen sind sehr clever. Sie haben sich nicht die Blöße gegeben, meine Rückkehr wie die Lösung für ein Problem aussehen zu lassen. Stattdessen lobten sie meine Arbeit übermäßig, sagten, dass ich sehr schnell

And, besides Brecht, general theater was taught. And my interest was not so much in theater in general, but in the theater of Bertolt Brecht. But it was very good to have been in a theater academy, especially later, when I became a theater professor in Mozambique. When you leave a developing country to go to countries like this, when you return, you also have the task of passing on this knowledge to others.

Yes, there were students who were very curious. Just the fact of being Black and African, that alone, created a lot of curiosity among people. They wanted to know who I am, what I think … Even physically, some people wanted to touch me, wanted to touch my hair. At the time I had very long, frizzy hair. I mean, their curiosity ranged from physical to emotional aspects, and sometimes it was a bit annoying for me.

So, it was not so much a curiosity about your thinking and methods?
Exactly. I had my self-esteem and was under the impression that I was equal to those people, despite our different colors. But people didn't accept that, they didn't accept me as an equal. Although they liked me, they liked me for being different, not for being the same. These things sometimes bothered me.

But there are always very interesting and genuinely interested people. With them, I shared a lot. I learned from them, and they learned from me. That's why I say, even among them, there were many who were dissenters. My friendships were formed, and my learning was completed outside the walls of schools, especially as an artist. An artist learns on the street, learns from things.

Did you ever come back to Germany with one of your shows?
Yes, I performed in several cities, in Hamburg, Munich, and even Berlin. It was truly spectacular. Spectacular. I said that I was contributing to Germany, "with what I have learned from you, see." It was indeed a memorable show. Memorable.

lernen würde und über viel Wissen verfügte und dass ich mit dem, was ich gelernt hatte, bereits einen Beitrag für mein Land leisten könne, das Leute wie mich schließlich dringend brauche. Aber ich selbst hatte eigentlich durchaus den Wunsch, noch länger in Deutschland zu bleiben.

Einige meiner Kollegen in Mosambik sagten mir, dass es sehr negative Berichte über mich gebe und dass ich vorsichtig sein müsse, weil ich bei meiner Ankunft am Flughafen direkt ins Gefängnis kommen könnte. In Deutschland war mir nicht bewusst gewesen, dass ich beschattet wurde. Falls dem so war, geschah es so diskret, dass ich es nicht bemerkte, oder vielleicht fand die Bespitzelung durch die Deutschen statt, die meine Freunde waren.

Sie haben auch einige Zeit an der Universität Rostock verbracht. Wie war die Erfahrung dort? Waren die Beziehungen zu den Studierenden und Professor·innen ähnlich wie die am Theater oder waren die Studierenden offener für Ihre Erfahrungen mit dem Community-Theater?
Ja, dank Christoph Schroth, der als Dozent an der Staatlichen Schauspielschule Rostock tätig war, konnte ich an Theaterkursen teilnehmen, aber das war nicht offiziell.

Schulen sind von Natur aus hochoffizielle Institutionen, und für einen Theaterprofi ist es am Ende das, was man auf Deutsch „langweilig" nennt. Es ist ermüdend, oder? Es ist zu formal. Das war nichts für mich. Ich hatte das Gefühl, viel weiter zu sein als diese Studierenden. Neben Brecht wurden auch allgemeine Theaterkonzepte gelehrt. Und ich interessierte mich halt nicht so sehr für das Theater im Allgemeinen, sondern für das Theater von Bertolt Brecht. Es war gut, an einer Theaterakademie gewesen zu sein, besonders rückblickend, als ich später Dozent in Mosambik wurde, war das hilfreich. Wenn man aus einem Entwicklungsland in ein Land wie Deutschland geht, hat man nach der Rückkehr auch die Aufgabe, dieses Wissen an andere weiterzugeben.

Ja, es gab auch Studierende dort, die sehr neugierig waren. Allein die Tatsache, dass ich Schwarz und afrikanisch bin, hat eine Menge Neugierde bei den Leuten geweckt. Sie wollten wissen, wer ich bin, was ich denke … Das ging sogar bis ins Körperliche, manche wollten mich anfassen, mein Haar berühren. Damals hatte ich ziemlich langes, krauses

While you were in East Germany, FRELIMO transformed more and more from a resistance movement into a political party running the government and institutions. How did you perceive this change? And, how did your life continue when you returned? Which role did you take on?

Despite the threat that I would probably be arrested upon arrival, fortunately, that did not happen. When I arrived, I began working with small groups, in Maputo and also outside the city. And I was very successful. I was recommended by top-level people, including President Samora Machel. This led me to return to the National Company of Song and Dance, which is one of Mozambique's largest dance companies. It was in this company that I made extensive use of the technical knowledge learned in Germany, including the experience of Bertolt Brecht's method, for which I needed space to experiment with. I wrote major pieces. Shows like *N'tsai*, which is now considered almost a classic work of African choreography. All based on the philosophy of Bertolt Brecht.

First, studying our African reality, where Portuguese, the official language, is not spoken by the majority of the people. People speak in their own languages, and we have many languages. It was necessary to find a way to overcome these barriers, using theater. From there, I deepened my studies in choreography. That is, doing theater using the body, using gestural language, music, dance. I began to do what they call "theatrical storytelling," but in the form of ballets. I introduced the concept of "dancing storytelling," meaning using dance to tell stories, choreography to do theater.

I tried various things. Gradually, I introduced Brecht's methodology, including this idea of doing theater to provoke people to think. One of the great pieces I did, *The Bride of Nha-Kebera*, had a terrible ending. People left the show completely disappointed, not expecting that kind of ending. That's when I felt that I was achieving what I wanted, to make people leave the theater thinking, commenting on it, with others getting angry … It was no longer a show for people to just go and have fun.

Haar. Ich meine, die Neugier reichte von physischen bis hin zu emotionalen Aspekten, und manchmal war es für mich ein bisschen lästig.

Es war also nicht so sehr eine Wissbegierde auf Ihre Gedanken und Ihre Methoden?

Ganz genau. Ich hatte ein gesundes Selbstwertgefühl und die Überzeugung, dass ich diesen Menschen trotz unserer unterschiedlichen Hautfarben gleichgestellt war. Aber die Leute haben das nicht akzeptiert, sie haben mich nicht als gleichwertig akzeptiert. Sie mochten mich zwar, aber sie mochten mich, weil ich anders war, nicht weil ich war wie sie. Diese Dinge haben mich manchmal gestört.

Doch es gibt immer ein paar sehr interessante und wirklich interessierte Menschen. Mit denen gab es echten Austausch. Ich lernte von ihnen, und sie lernten von mir. Deshalb sage ich, dass es auch dort viele gab, die gegen den Strom schwammen. Ich habe Freundschaften geschlossen und außerhalb der Schule viel gelernt, vor allem als Künstler. Ein Künstler lernt auf der Straße, lernt aus den Dingen.

Sind Sie jemals mit einem Ihrer Stücke nach Deutschland zurückgekommen?

Ja, ich habe Stücke in verschiedenen Städten aufgeführt, zum Beispiel in Hamburg, München und sogar in Berlin. Es war wirklich eindrücklich. Spektakulär. Ich habe gesagt, dass ich einen Beitrag für Deutschland leiste: „Mit dem, was ich von euch gelernt habe, seht ihr!" Es war in der Tat eine denkwürdige Show. Unvergesslich.

Während Sie in der DDR waren, wandelte sich die FRELIMO zunehmend von einer Widerstandsbewegung zu einer politischen Partei, die die Regierung stellt und die Institutionen leitet. Wie haben Sie diesen Wandel wahrgenommen? Und wie ging Ihr Leben nach Ihrer Rückkehr weiter? Welche Rolle haben Sie eingenommen?

Entgegen der Warnung, dass man mich wahrscheinlich gleich bei meiner Ankunft verhaften würde, geschah glücklicherweise gar nichts. Als ich da war, begann ich mit kleinen Gruppen in Maputo und auch außerhalb der Stadt zu arbeiten. Und ich war sehr erfolgreich damit. Ich wurde von hochrangigen

Gradually, I introduced Brecht's methodology in this way, but I believe not everything was understood. But my contribution is there, in those works.

I turned the National Company of Song and Dance into one of the best companies on the African continent, which toured the entire world. And the works were well received, both by critics and by the public. So, today I am a significant national point of reference.

Leuten empfohlen, unter anderem von Präsident Samora Machel. Das führte dazu, dass ich zur Nationalen Gesangs- und Tanzkompanie zurückkehrte, einer der größten Tanzkompanien Mosambiks. In dieser Kompanie konnte ich meine in Deutschland erworbenen technischen Kenntnisse ausgiebig nutzen, auch die Erfahrungen mit der Methode von Bertolt Brecht, für die ich Raum zum Experimentieren brauchte. Ich schrieb nun große Stücke. *N'tsai* zum Beispiel gilt heute fast als Klassiker der afrikanischen Choreografie. Alles auf der Grundlage der Philosophie von Bertolt Brecht.

Als Erstes galt es, unsere afrikanische Wirklichkeit zu erfassen, in der die offizielle Sprache – Portugiesisch – nicht von der Mehrheit der Menschen gesprochen wird. Die Menschen sprechen ihre eigenen Sprachen, sehr viele verschiedene. Man musste also einen Weg finden, diese Barrieren zu überwinden, und zwar mithilfe des Theaters. Deshalb vertiefte ich meine Beschäftigung mit Choreografie. Choreografie heißt, mit dem Körper Theater zu machen, mit gestischer Sprache, Musik, Tanz. Ich fing an, sogenanntes „szenisches Storytelling" zu machen, allerdings in Form von Ballett. Ich führte den Begriff „tänzerisches Storytelling" ein, das heißt ich benutzte Tanz, um Geschichten zu erzählen, und Choreografie, um Theater zu machen.

Ich habe verschiedene Dinge ausprobiert. Nach und nach führte ich Brechts Methoden ein, vor allem die Idee, Theater zu machen, um die Menschen zum Nachdenken anzuregen. Eines meiner bekanntesten Stücke, *Die Braut von Nha-Kebera*, hatte ein schreckliches Ende. Die Leute verließen die Vorstellung völlig enttäuscht, weil sie ein solches Ende nicht erwartet hatten. Ich hatte erreicht, was ich wollte: dass die Leute das Theater nachdenklich, kommentierend oder wütend verließen … Es war keine Show mehr, in die man einfach nur geht, um sich zu amüsieren. Nach und nach habe ich Brechts Methode auf diese Weise eingeführt, ich glaube, nicht alles wurde verstanden. Aber mein Beitrag ist da, in diesen Werken.

Ich habe die Nationale Gesangs- und Tanzkompanie zu einer der besten Kompanien des afrikanischen Kontinents gemacht, die in der ganzen Welt auf Tournee war. Die Werke wurden sowohl von Kritikern als auch vom Publikum gut aufgenommen, und so gelte ich heute als ein wichtiges nationales Beispiel.

3. Further research is necessary to explore the involvement of the MfS in monitoring foreign students. For more context, we print here the full response from the Stasi Records Archive: "Files were indeed created for foreign students. However, the person had to be of particular interest to the MfS. If that was not the case, the person from abroad was usually only registered. However, there are no index cards for the individuals you inquired about. It's possible that the MfS destroyed them before 1989 because they were no longer needed. That cannot be said for sure." Stasi-Unterlagen-Archiv, email, October 10, 2023.

David Abílio's internship ended abruptly and he was forced to leave the GDR. Forty years later, we sought to investigate the circumstances behind this decision. Together with David Abílio, we requested a search of the Ministry for State Security (MfS) files. The Stasi Records Archive thoroughly examined files of both the MfS headquarters and all the former branch offices. Yet, no index card was found for David Abílio Mondlane.[3] Why the East German authorities ordered the hasty return of the Mozambican theater director remains unclear. We can only assume that the autonomy with which he negotiated his educational path through East German institutions, his friendship with dissenting artists in the GDR, and his firm stance as a Marxist who speaks his mind constituted an evasion of state control at various levels.

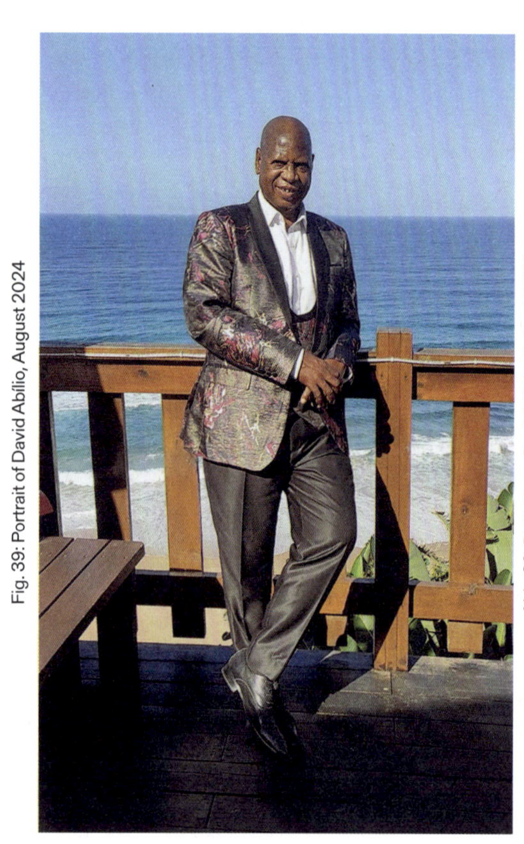

Fig. 39: Portrait of David Abílio, August 2024

Abb. 39: Porträt von David Abílio, August 2024

Das Praktikum von David Abílio endete abrupt und er war gezwungen, die DDR zu verlassen. 40 Jahre später wollten wir die Hintergründe dieser Entscheidung untersuchen. Gemeinsam mit David Abílio beantragten wir eine Recherche in den Akten des Ministeriums für Staatssicherheit (MfS). Das Stasi-Unterlagen-Archiv hat sowohl die Akten der MfS-Zentrale als auch aller ehemaligen Außenstellen gründlich geprüft. Für David Abílio Mondlane wurde jedoch keine Karteikarte gefunden.[3] Warum die DDR-Behörden die überstürzte Rückführung des mosambikanischen Theaterregisseurs anordneten, bleibt unklar. Wir können nur vermuten, dass die eigenständige Art, seinen Bildungsweg zu gestalten, seine Nähe zu oppositionellen Künstler·innen in der DDR und seine marxistischen Überzeugungen, die er offen aussprach, als Umstände gesehen wurden, durch die er sich auf mehreren Ebenen der staatlichen Kontrolle entzog.

3. Weitere Forschung ist notwendig, um die Beteiligung des MfS an der Überwachung ausländischer Studierender zu untersuchen. Zur Kontextualisierung drucken wir hier die vollständige Auskunft des Stasi-Unterlagen-Archivs ab: „Es wurden durchaus Unterlagen zu Studierenden aus dem Ausland angelegt. Die Person musste aber für das MfS von besonderem Interesse sein. Wenn das nicht der Fall war, wurde die Person aus dem Ausland in der Regel nur registriert. Doch für die von Ihnen angefragten Personen gibt es auch keine Karteikarten. Vielleicht hat das MfS sie schon vor 1989 vernichtet, weil sie nicht mehr gebraucht wurden. Dazu lässt sich keine sichere Aussage treffen." Stasi-Unterlagen-Archiv, E-Mail vom 10.10.2023.

1. Joachim Fiebach, "Brecht im Subsaharischen Afrika," in *Brecht in Afrika, Asien und Lateinamerika: Protokoll der Brecht-Tage 1980, 8.–11. Februar*, ed. Brecht-Zentrum der DDR (Henschelverlag Kunst und Gesellschaft, 1980), 70.

LEA MARIE NIENHOFF AND AMBRE ALFREDO

WHAT DOES A LIBERATED THEATER LOOK LIKE?

THE ECHO OF BERTOLT BRECHT

The Kamiriithu Theater of Kenya, the Samaru Community Theater Movement of Nigeria, and the Travelling Theater in Tanzania may be the most famous experiments in developing a postcolonial theatrical form and language. Each developed their own performance style, yet they shared an interest in Latin American models. David Abílio, too, has drawn inspiration from Latin American authors, especially Augusto Boal, to develop his theater practice. He started community theater, involving people in debates on the streets and in buses, and did away with the separation between actors and audience. David Abílio describes in the interview that his theater aimed to create greater awareness, "despertar neles a consciência," and emancipate the audience by encouraging people to develop their own solutions to the problems they faced. The "popular theater" that David Abílio and many of his contemporaries in countries of the "Third World" sought broke away from the fixation on European texts and styles, rediscovered its own traditions and languages, and took a stand against the exploitation through colonial domination and capitalism. Bertolt Brecht was a reference point for David Abílio and for the movement of revolutionary theater practices worldwide.

In his theater, Brecht documented the conditions of exploitation and claimed the humanity of the oppressed while exposing the tools of the powerful. By the 1980s, Brecht's conception of theater had been taken up and transformed by artists like Augusto Boal, Athol Fugard, and Wole Soyinka. Soyinka himself said that Bertolt Brecht influenced his artistic practice, as he demonstrated "complete freedom in dealing with the medium of theater."[1] When David Abílio expresses his connection to Brecht, he binds it to the struggle for decolonization and adds: "For me, the best way to understand Brecht was Augusto Boal's Theater of the Oppressed."

LEA MARIE NIENHOFF UND AMBRE ALFREDO

EIN BEFREITES THEATER?

DAS ECHO VON BERTOLT BRECHT

Das Kamiriithu-Theater in Kenia, die Samaru-Community-Theaterbewegung in Nigeria und das Travelling Theater in Tansania sind vielleicht die bekanntesten Experimente in der Entwicklung einer postkolonialen Theaterform und -sprache. Sie alle bildeten ihren ganz eigenen Aufführungsstil aus, doch verbindet sie ein gemeinsames Interesse an lateinamerikanischen Vorbildern. Auch David Abílio hat sich bei der Entwicklung seiner Theaterpraxis von lateinamerikanischen Autoren, insbesondere Augusto Boal, inspirieren lassen. Er begann mit Community-Theater, das die Menschen in Debatten auf der Straße und in Bussen einbezog und die Trennung zwischen Schauspieler·innen und Publikum aufhob. Im Interview beschreibt David Abílio, dass sein Theater darauf abzielte, ein größeres Bewusstsein zu schaffen, „despertar neles a consciência", und das Publikum zu emanzipieren, indem es die Menschen ermutigte, eigene Lösungen für die Probleme zu entwickeln, mit denen sie konfrontiert waren. Das „Teatro Popular", das David Abílio und viele seiner Zeitgenossen in den Ländern der „Dritten Welt" entwickelten, löste sich von der Fixierung auf europäische Texte und Stile. Es entdeckte seine eigenen Traditionen und Ausdrucksformen neu und bezog Stellung gegen die Ausbeutung durch Kolonialherrschaft und Kapitalismus. Bertolt Brecht war ein Bezugspunkt für David Abílio und für die Bewegung des revolutionären Theaters weltweit.

In seinen Theaterstücken dokumentierte Brecht ausbeuterische Zustände, zeigte die Unterdrückten in ihrer Menschlichkeit und entlarvte die Methoden der Mächtigen. In den 1980er Jahren wurde Brechts Konzeption von Theatermachern wie Augusto Boal, Athol Fugard und Wole Soyinka aufgegriffen und umgestaltet. Soyinka sagte einmal, dass Bertolt Brecht seine künstlerische Praxis beeinflusst habe, weil er „vollkommene Freiheit im Umgang mit dem Medium Theater" demonstrierte.[1] Wenn David Abílio über sein Verhältnis zu Brecht spricht, verbindet er es mit dem Kampf um Dekolonialisierung und fügt hinzu: „Der beste Zugang zum Verständnis von Brecht war für mich Augusto Boals Theater der Unterdrückten."

1. Joachim Fiebach, „Brecht im subsaharischen Afrika", in: *Brecht in Afrika, Asien und Lateinamerika: Protokoll der Brecht-Tage 1980, 8.–11. Februar*, hg. vom Brecht-Zentrum der DDR, Ostberlin: Henschelverlag 1980, S. 67–78, hier S. 70.

The GDR often used Brecht as a figurehead to address artists from the "Third World." In the conferences organized by the Brecht Center or by the East German ITI Center (International Theater Institute), the GDR presented itself as open to different interpretations of Brecht, attempting to create a cosmopolitan atmosphere in which scholars and artists from East Germany would discuss ideas with their partners on an equal footing. However, the views and understandings of Brecht differed widely. "Third World" artists "were not as interested in the predominantly aesthetic issues as their European colleagues. To them, working with Brecht was about changing social conditions," noted Werner Hecht, director of the Brecht Center.[2] In an account of the first international conference of theater professionals at the Berliner Ensemble in 1968, Hecht recounts his surprise when participants from developing nations expressed the need for a session dedicated to internal discussions among themselves, without the presence of East German "experts." Despite this reflection, East German cultural institutions continued claiming interpretative sovereignty over Brecht's work. And, as Manfred Wekwerth ironically commented, "The Berliner Ensemble considered itself the world."[3]

Theater in East Germany frequently served as a platform and a tool for engaging in Cultural Cold War politics. The history of a socialist "cultural revolution," connected to the name of Bertolt Brecht, was used to gain the sympathy of young nations. In March 1978, the Mozambican national newspaper *Notícias* published a feature on Bertolt Brecht—a tribute to the revolutionary German artist. The articles resulted from the lobbying activities of the German embassy in Mozambique.[4] When presented outside East Germany, Brecht's work was brought into alignment with the state's diplomatic interests. The message was as follows: Brecht's work was helpful in the process of rediscovering a national culture characterized by the fight against imperialism.[5] The foremost task for the institutions involved in this foreign cultural diplomacy was not to create a space for mutual inspiration in the arts but to help enforce the recognition of the GDR as a state and to "pass on our experience to the young nation states."[6]

Within the GDR, a prescribed formalism often reduced Brecht to an acting method. When David Abílio entered the Berliner Ensemble, internal disputes over

2. Werner Hecht, "Brecht – Werk und Wirkung," in Brecht-Zentrum der DDR, *Brecht in Afrika*, 7.

3. Manfred Wekwerth, *Erinnern ist Leben: Eine dramatische Autobiographie* (Faber und Faber, 2000), 298.

4. The publication was based on texts that had been sent by the East German Ministry of Culture. See BArch DR1/17805.

5. See Rebecca Sturm, "Brecht as a Model for Cultural Development: East German ITI Events for Theater Artists from the 'Third World,'" in *Performing the Cold War in the Postcolonial World*, ed. Christopher B. Balme (Routledge, 2024), 170.

6. "Rechenschaftsbericht für die ITI-Generalversammlung am 26. Januar 1984," Archiv des Internationalen Theaterinstituts Deutschlands (ITI), Berlin.

Die DDR nutzte Brecht oft als Galionsfigur, um Künstler·innen aus der „Dritten Welt" anzusprechen. In den vom Brecht-Zentrum oder vom ostdeutschen ITI-Zentrum (Internationales Theaterinstitut) organisierten Konferenzen präsentierte sich die DDR als offen für unterschiedliche Brecht-Interpretationen und war bemüht, eine kosmopolitische Atmosphäre zu schaffen, in der Wissenschaftler·innen und Künstler·innen aus der DDR mit eingeladenen Gästen auf Augenhöhe diskutieren konnten. Die Ansichten und Auffassungen über Brecht gingen jedoch weit auseinander. Die Künstler·innen der „Dritten Welt" „waren nicht so sehr an den vorwiegend ästhetischen Fragen interessiert wie ihre europäischen Kollegen. Für sie ging es bei der Arbeit mit Brecht um die Veränderung der gesellschaftlichen Verhältnisse", so Werner Hecht, Direktor des Brecht-Zentrums.[2] In einem Bericht über die erste internationale Konferenz von Theaterfachleuten am Berliner Ensemble im Jahr 1968 berichtet Hecht von seiner Überraschung, als die Teilnehmer·innen aus den Entwicklungsländern das Bedürfnis äußerten, einen Raum für Gespräche untereinander zu haben, ohne die Anwesenheit von ostdeutschen „Experten". Abgesehen von solchen veröffentlichten Reflexionen beanspruchten die ostdeutschen Kultureinrichtungen weiterhin die Deutungshoheit über Brechts Werk. Wie Manfred Wekwerth ironisch bemerkte, „hielt sich das Berliner Ensemble für die Welt".[3]

Das Theater in der DDR diente nicht selten als Plattform und Instrument für Auseinandersetzungen im Kalten Kulturkrieg. Die Geschichte einer sozialistischen „Kulturrevolution", die mit dem Namen Bertolt Brecht verbunden war, wurde genutzt, um die Sympathie junger Nationen zu gewinnen. Im März 1978 veröffentlichte die überregionale mosambikanische Zeitung *Notícias* eine Sonderausgabe zu Bertolt Brecht – eine Hommage an den revolutionären deutschen Künstler. Die Sonderausgabe war ein Ergebnis der Lobbyarbeit der deutschen Botschaft in Mosambik.[4] Wenn Brechts Arbeiten außerhalb der DDR präsentiert wurden, wurden sie mit den diplomatischen Interessen des Staats in Einklang gebracht. Die Kernbotschaft lautete: Brechts Werk sei hilfreich im Prozess des Aufbaus einer nationalen Kultur, die vom Kampf gegen den Imperialismus geprägt ist.[5] Oberste Aufgabe der an dieser auswärtigen Kulturdiplomatie beteiligten Institutionen war weniger, einen Raum der gegenseitigen künstlerischen Inspiration zu schaffen, sondern die Anerkennung der DDR als Staat durchzusetzen und „unsere Erfahrungen an die jungen Nationalstaaten weiterzugeben".[6]

2. Werner Hecht, „Brecht – Werk und Wirkung", in: *Brecht in Afrika*, S. 7.

3. Manfred Wekwerth, *Erinnern ist Leben. Eine dramatische Autobiographie*, Leipzig: Faber & Faber 2000, S. 298.

4. Die Veröffentlichung basierte auf Texten, die vom ostdeutschen Kulturministerium übermittelt worden waren. Siehe BArch DR1/17805.

5. Siehe Rebecca Sturm, „Brecht as a Model for Cultural Development: East German ITI Events for Theater Artists from the 'Third World'", in: Christopher B. Balme (Hg.), *Performing the Cold War in the Postcolonial World*, London: Routledge 2024, S. 152–175, hier S. 170.

6. Archiv des Internationalen Theaterinstituts Deutschlands (ITI), Berlin. „Rechenschaftsbericht für die ITI-Generalversammlung am 26. Januar 1984".

7. See Brecht-Zentrum der DDR, "Umfrage zum 85. Geburtstag Bertolt Brechts", *Notate* 1 (February 1983); Werner Hecht, "Brecht – Werk und Wirkung," in Brecht-Zentrum der DDR, *Brecht in Afrika*, 11.

8. BArch DR 1/11646

9. Ibid.

Brecht's legacy had been going on for years. Even in East German publications, theater scholars openly addressed the problem of "Brecht dogmatism" and "Brecht fatigue."[7] In February 1983, while David Abílio was residing in East Germany, the Brecht Center published a magazine titled "Do We Need Brecht Today?" Merely to pose the question would have amounted to defamation in earlier years. Now, tentative criticism could be leveled at stage productions that made Brecht's plays seem "dead" (Heiner Müller), devoid of meaning, or formalistic. However, David Abílio's clear and sharp critique of East German adaptations of Brecht's works as "reactionary theater" could not be voiced without repercussions.

"He sees himself as a Brecht expert … he wants to direct [a play by] Brecht at the Berliner Ensemble," was noted in a document that described the nonconformist behavior of David Abílio in the framework of the internship.[8] David Abílio's confident claim to be a Brecht expert, his determination to organize his internship, his "unauthorized" participation in the 1983 Brecht seminar, and his independently built network—are formulated as a reproach, something that cannot be.

David Abílio's memories of his time in East Germany have many different colors to them. There is this space of opportunity that he seizes on to develop his practice and his enthusiasm for working at the Berliner Ensemble, as well as his disappointment at the restrictions and the questionable approach to Brecht. Rereading the letters and reports from the archive, we find that the attitude and perception of East German officials toward David Abílio also changed over the months. Initially, the East German embassy in Mozambique presented David Abílio to the Ministry of Culture as "the leading Mozambican theater practitioner and specialist for African popular theater" and therefore the ideal candidate for the internship.[9] He got the position, and the Staatstheater Schwerin was determined to be his "training supervisor." Shortly after arriving in the GDR, David Abílio sent a direct request to the Ministry of Culture to do his internship in Berlin instead. His requests to study elsewhere were initially met with a positive response. His internship began at the Berliner Ensemble. While residing in Berlin, he also attended the rehearsals of the Staatliche Tanzensemble. After submitting a request to the Ministry, he was granted the right to attend classes at the Hochschule

In der DDR reduzierte ein von oben verordneter Formalismus Brecht oft auf eine Schauspielmethode. Als David Abílio ans Berliner Ensemble kam, waren die internen Auseinandersetzungen um das Erbe Brechts schon seit Jahren im Gange. Auch in ostdeutschen Publikationen wurde das Problem des „Brecht-Dogmatismus" und der „Brecht-Müdigkeit" von Theaterwissenschaftler·innen offen angesprochen.[7] Im Februar 1983, als David Abílio in der DDR war, veröffentlichte das Brecht-Zentrum eine Ausgabe seiner Zeitschrift mit dem Titel „Brauchen wir heute Brecht?" Allein die Frage aufzuwerfen wäre in früheren Jahren einer Diffamierung gleichgekommen. Nun konnte zaghafte Kritik an Inszenierungen geäußert werden, die Brechts Stücke „tot" (Heiner Müller), sinnentleert oder formalistisch wirken ließen. Die deutliche und scharfe Kritik von David Abílio an Brecht-Adaptionen als „reaktionäres Theater" blieb dennoch nicht ohne Auswirkungen.

„Er sieht sich als Brecht-Experte […] er will am Berliner Ensemble [ein Stück von] Brecht inszenieren",[8] heißt es in einem Dokument, das über das nonkonforme Verhalten von David Abílio im Rahmen des Praktikums Bericht erstattet. David Abílios selbstbewusster Anspruch, Brecht-Experte zu sein, seine Entschlossenheit, das Praktikum eigenständig zu organisieren, seine „unautorisierte" Teilnahme am Brecht-Seminar 1983 und sein selbstständig aufgebautes Netzwerk wurden ihm angelastet.

Die Erinnerungen von David Abílio an seine Zeit in der DDR haben unterschiedliche Facetten. Da ist der Raum der Möglichkeiten, den er nutzt, um seinen Stil weiterzuentwickeln, seine Begeisterung für die Arbeit am Berliner Ensemble, aber auch seine Enttäuschung über die Einschränkungen und den fragwürdigen Umgang mit Brecht. Bei der Lektüre der Briefe und Berichte aus dem Archiv wird deutlich, dass sich auch die Haltung und Wahrnehmung der Verantwortlichen in der DDR gegenüber David Abílio im Laufe der Monate veränderte. Zunächst stellte die Botschaft der DDR in Mosambik David Abílio dem Kulturministerium als „den führenden mosambikanischen Theatermacher und Experten für afrikanisches Volkstheater"[9] und damit als idealen Kandidaten für das Praktikum vor. Er erhielt die Stelle, und das Staatstheater Schwerin wurde zu seinem „Qualifizierungsbeauftragten" ernannt. Kurz nach seiner Ankunft in der DDR wandte sich David Abílio persönlich an das Ministerium für Kultur mit der Bitte, sein Praktikum stattdessen in Berlin absolvieren zu dürfen. Seine

7. Siehe Brecht-Zentrum der DDR, „Umfrage zum 85. Geburtstag Bertolt Brechts", in: *Notate*, 1, Februar 1983; Werner Hecht, „Brecht – Werk und Wirkung. Zu Fragen der internationalen Brecht-Hezeption", in: *Brecht in Afrika*, S. 7–15, hier S. 11.

8. BArch DR 1/11646.

9. Ebd.

10. Ibid.

11. Ibid.

12. Homi K. Bhabha, *The Location of Culture* (Routledge, 2004), 95.

13. See BArch DR 1/11646

für Schauspielkunst Berlin and later at the Staatliche Schauspielschule Rostock. Before he was forced to finally move to Schwerin, almost a year after his arrival, he had arranged to continue working at the Berliner Ensemble. Recognition was quickly followed by devaluation.

"It was only possible to get him to return to Schwerin by making him choose between this alternative and abandoning the internship altogether.… Through coordination between the Ministry of Culture and the Schwerin District Council, greater discipline was achieved for the remainder of the internship."[10] The time of his internship was shortened, and the participation in the international theater congress that David Abílio had fought for was considered "no longer useful." The letter goes on to say that "Mondlane concentrated exclusively on Brecht in his own practice and would not accept any other theater.… In view of the problems to be overcome in this field in his country, such an attitude seems incomprehensible to us."[11]

David Abílio officially arrived in East Germany as an "intern" and was expected to fit into this "fixed," predetermined role as the recipient of European "higher knowledge." Exploring this history through the eyes of David Abílio reveals the continuities of colonial discourse and cultural imperialism involved in the politics and practices of East German international artistic exchange. As Homi Bhaba said, "An important feature of colonial discourse is its dependence on the notion of "'fixity' in the ideological construction of otherness."[12]

The plays David Abílio had directed in Mozambique addressed the rural population, factory workers, and children. In various provinces of the country, he initiated collective theater creations with titles such as *Forced Labor: Why Does the Enemy Attack Us?* (1979) or *The Fruit of Wealth* (1981).[13] In an article from 1979, David Abílio defines his theater as a form of activism "to advance the revolution." Central to this struggle was the emancipation of all artistic creation from the norms of European bourgeois theater:

> There is a permanent conflict between popular art and bourgeois
> art, which wants to be defined as universally valid, just as there is a

Anfragen, anderswo hospitieren zu dürfen, wurden zunächst positiv beschieden. Er begann sein Praktikum am Berliner Ensemble. Während seines Aufenthaltes in Berlin besuchte er auch die Proben des Staatlichen Tanzensembles. Nach einem Antrag an das Ministerium erhielt er die Berechtigung, an der Hochschule für Schauspielkunst Berlin und später an der Staatlichen Schauspielschule Rostock Kurse zu belegen. Er hatte darüber hinaus eine Weiterbeschäftigung am Berliner Ensemble vereinbart. Doch fast ein Jahr nach seiner Ankunft wurde er gezwungen, endgültig nach Schwerin zu ziehen. Auf die Anerkennung, die er zuerst erfuhr, folgte die Abwertung.

„Seine Rückkehr nach Schwerin konnte nur erreicht werden, indem man ihn vor die Wahl stellte, das Praktikum andernfalls abzubrechen. […] Durch die Koordination zwischen dem Kulturministerium und der Schweriner Bezirksregierung wurde eine größere Disziplin für die restliche Zeit des Praktikums erreicht."[10] Die Praktikumszeit wurde verkürzt, und die Teilnahme am internationalen Theaterkongress, für die David Abílio gekämpft hatte, wurde als „nicht mehr sinnvoll" erachtet. In dem Brief heißt es weiter: „Mondlane konzentrierte sich in seiner eigenen Praxis ausschließlich auf Brecht und wollte kein anderes Theater akzeptieren […]. Angesichts der Probleme, die auf diesem Gebiet in seinem Land zu bewältigen sind, erscheint uns eine solche Haltung unverständlich."[11]

David Abílio kam offiziell als „Praktikant" in die DDR und sollte sich in diese „feste", vorbestimmte Rolle als Empfänger europäischen „höheren Wissens" einfügen. Die Erforschung dieser Geschichte durch die Augen von David Abílio zeigt die Kontinuitäten eines kulturellen Imperialismus und die Diskurse, die sich durch die Politik und die Praktiken des internationalen Künstleraustauschs der DDR zogen. Homi Bhaba formuliert es so: „Ein wichtiges Merkmal des kolonialen Diskurses besteht in seiner Abhängigkeit vom Konzept der ‚Festgestelltheit' in der ideologischen Konstruktion des Andersseins."[12]

Die Theaterstücke, die David Abílio in Mosambik inszenierte, richteten sich an die Landbevölkerung, an Fabrikarbeiter·innen und Kinder. In verschiedenen Provinzen des Landes initiierte er kollektive Theaterproduktionen mit Titeln wie *Zwangsarbeit. Warum greift der Feind uns an?* (1979) oder *Die Frucht des Reichtums* (1981).[13] In einem Artikel von 1979 definiert David Abílio sein Theater als eine Form des Aktivismus mit dem Ziel, „die Revolution

10. Ebd.

11. Ebd.

12. Homi K. Bhabha, *Die Verortung der Kultur*, deutsch von Michael Schiffmann und Jürgen Freudl, Tübingen: Stauffenburg Verlag 2000, S. 97.

13. BArch DR 1/11646.

14. David Abílio Mondlane, "Arte popular: Texto de apoio aos animadores de teatro" (1979), BArch DR 1/11646.

permanent conflict between the forces of revolution and those of conservatism, both on a material and spiritual level.... Art must respond to and participate in the advance of the Revolution, it must be an instrument for uniting and educating the People, attacking and destroying the enemy, it must be an instrument of criticism and self-criticism. Art, as an integral part of the class struggle, must not only reflect the contradictions at a given stage, but also point the way to better orientation, to the dissemination of the correct line, to the rejection and combat of what is wrong, of what is old, and this process is permanent in a revolution.[14]

voranzutreiben". Im Mittelpunkt dieses Kampfes stand für ihn die Emanzipation des gesamten künstlerischen Schaffens von den Normen des europäischen bürgerlichen Theaters:

> „Es gibt einen permanenten Konflikt zwischen populärer Kunst und bürgerlicher Kunst, die als allgemeingültig angesehen werden will, so wie es einen permanenten Konflikt zwischen den Kräften der Revolution und denen des Konservatismus gibt, sowohl auf materieller als auch auf geistiger Ebene. […] Die Kunst muss auf den Vormarsch der Revolution reagieren und sich am Vormarsch beteiligen, sie muss ein Instrument zur Vereinigung und Erziehung des Volkes, zum Angriff und zur Vernichtung des Feindes sein, sie muss ein Instrument der Kritik und der Selbstkritik sein. Die Kunst, als integraler Bestandteil des Klassenkampfes, muss nicht nur die Widersprüche einer bestimmten Entwicklungsstufe widerspiegeln, sondern auch den Weg weisen für eine bessere Orientierung, zur Verbreitung der richtigen Linie, zur Ablehnung und Bekämpfung des Falschen, des Alten, und dieser Prozess ist in einer Revolution permanent."[14]

14. Zitat aus einem Text von David Abílio Mondlane mit dem Titel „Arte Popular. Texto De Apoio Aos Animadores De Teatro" (1979), in BArch DR 1/11646.

"IT SHOULD HAVE BEEN DONE DIFFERENTLY"

LEA MARIE NIENHOFF IN CONVERSATION
WITH GINGA EICHLER

LEA MARIE NIENHOFF
IM GESPRÄCH MIT GINGA EICHLER

„DAS HÄTTE MAN ANDERS MACHEN MÜSSEN"

Ginga Eichler did a degree in African Studies at Leipzig University. In 1968, she read W. E. B. Du Bois's autobiography, which had been published in East Germany with the title Mein Weg, meine Welt. *When we spoke in October 2023, she said: "It made a deep impression on me and validated everything I believe in and wanted to commit myself to. My life in Leipzig played out in the boarding school for foreigners. A lot of my friends were from South Africa and talked to me about their lives under apartheid." Her roommate and best friend in the dormitory was Carol Pitman, an African American woman who was studying in East Germany. American labor organizer and feminist Elizabeth Gurley Flynn became her role model.*

During the 1973 World Festival of Youth and Students in Berlin, Eichler looked after the interpreters translating for the African guests of honor. In the years that followed, she worked for the East German Peace Council and the International Friendship League of the German Democratic Republic. She took part in international peace conferences and took care of countless African guests visiting East Germany. In 1984, she was a member of a delegation from the International Friendship League and the Peace Council that marked the thirty-fifth anniversary of the GDR by visiting their partner organizations in various African countries, including Mozambique.

"It was not until the early 1980s, when more and more contract workers arrived, that I became aware of the problems and racism that people from African countries in particular had to contend with in their day-to-day lives—even from the authorities." After the fall of the Berlin Wall, when there was a wave of racist violence, later referred to in the eastern federal states as "the baseball bat years," she banded together with West Berliners to found the "SOS Racism" association, modeled on its French precursor. She became a member of the Berlin Refugee Council and campaigned for East German contract workers to be accorded the same legal status as West German Gastarbeiter. Most recently, Eichler has worked in the office of the Federal Government Commissioner for Foreigners' Affairs.

Ginga Eichler studierte Afrikanistik an der Universität Leipzig. 1968 las sie die Autobiografie von W. E. B. Du Bois, die in der DDR unter dem Titel Mein Weg, meine Welt *veröffentlicht worden war. „Das hat mich tief beeindruckt und alles bestätigt, woran ich glaube und wofür ich mich engagieren wollte", erzählt sie in unserem Gespräch im Oktober 2023. „Mein Leben in Leipzig spielte sich im Ausländerinternat ab. Viele meiner Freunde kamen aus Südafrika und berichteten mir von ihrem Leben unter der Apartheid." Ihre Zimmernachbarin und beste Freundin im Wohnheim war Carol Pitman, eine Afroamerikanerin, die in der DDR studierte. Ihr Vorbild wurde Elizabeth Gurley Flynn, eine amerikanische Gewerkschaftsführerin und Feministin.*

Während der Weltfestspiele der Jugend und Studenten 1973 in Berlin betreute Ginga Eichler die Dolmetscher·innen der afrikanischen Ehrengäste. In den darauffolgenden Jahren arbeitete sie für den Friedensrat der DDR sowie für die Liga für Völkerfreundschaft. Sie nahm an internationalen Friedenskonferenzen teil und betreute unzählige afrikanische Gäste, die in die DDR kamen. 1984 war sie Mitglied einer Delegation der Liga für Völkerfreundschaft und des Friedensrates, die aus Anlass des 35. Jahrestages der DDR ihre Partnerorganisationen in verschiedenen afrikanischen Ländern besuchte, so auch in Mosambik.

„Erst Anfang der 1980er Jahre, als mehr und mehr Vertragsarbeitende kamen, habe ich gemerkt, mit welchen Problemen und welchem Rassismus im Alltag besonders die Menschen aus afrikanischen Ländern zu kämpfen hatten – sogar seitens staatlicher Stellen." Nach dem Fall der Mauer, als eine Welle rassistischer Gewalttaten aufkam, die später als „die Baseballschläger-Jahre" in den östlichen Bundesländern bezeichnet wurden, gründete sie zusammen mit Westberlinern nach französischem Vorbild den Verein „SOS Rassismus". Sie wurde Mitglied des Berliner Flüchtlingsrates und setzte sich für die rechtliche Gleichstellung der DDR-Vertragsarbeiter mit den Gastarbeitern in der BRD ein. Zuletzt arbeitete Ginga Eichler im Büro des Ausländerbeauftragten für die Bundesregierung.

1. Klaus Willerding, "Grundlagen und Inhalt der Beziehungen der DDR zu den befreiten Staaten Asiens und Afrikas," *Deutsche Außenpolitik* 21, no. 11 (1976): 1615–28, here: 1615.

2. An *Amerikaner* is a pastry topped with lemon icing. It's not altogether clear why it was given this name, but its flat surface is supposedly reminiscent of the helmets of American soldiers.

"Based on the Leninist principle that the national liberation movement is a natural and objective ally of world socialism and the international labor movement in the struggle against imperialism and in support of social progress, it is one of the key elements of socialist foreign policy to stand in solidarity with the just struggle of those who are oppressed and exploited under colonialist and racist systems."[1]

Klaus Willerding

It's taken me a year to track Ginga Eichler down. We've made a date, and she wants to meet at the "old Brecht cemetery," where there's a small café. Bertolt Brecht's grave lies in the Dorotheenstadt Cemetery in Berlin-Mitte. It's a rainy October day. The cemetery gardener tells me the café has been closed for two days. Then I hear someone calling my name. Eichler comes jauntily toward me. Wearing pink boots and a pink beret, she adds a splash of color to the day. We find somewhere to sit in the supermarket café around the corner. "When I was a kid in Leipzig, we had a saying," she says: "Do something to fight imperialism, eat an 'American.'"[2] She can't help laughing and shakes her head as she does. Eichler told me about her parents and grandparents, about her father's career as a scientist, their move to the Soviet occupation zone, and her mother's admiration for Josephine Baker and Paul Robeson. "My mother had been through the Nazi era. She wanted to root out the evils of fascism. We were very political. We felt responsible for making sure that fascism and racism would never again hold sway in Germany."

Ginga Eichler traveled to the People's Republic of Mozambique in 1984 as part of a delegation from the GDR. In our conversation, she speaks about the general framework of the trip and her impressions on the ground:

When I joined the league in 1983, I already knew a lot of the people who were active in the movement abroad. I became executive secretary of the East German Ethiopia Friendship Society.

The thirty-fifth anniversary of the East German state was approaching in 1984. The GDR's partner countries and organizations wanted to

„Ausgehend von dem Leninschen Grundsatz, daß die nationale Befreiungsbewegung natürlicher und objektiver Bündnispartner des Weltsozialismus und der internationalen Arbeiterbewegung im Kampf gegen Imperialismus und für sozialen Fortschritt ist, gehört es zu den Wesenszügen sozialistischer Außenpolitik, dem gerechten Kampf der kolonial und rassistisch unterdrückten und ausgebeuteten Völker solidarische Hilfe zu erweisen."[1]

Klaus Willerding

Ein Jahr hat es gedauert, bis ich Ginga Eichler ausfindig machen konnte. Wir sind verabredet und sie will mich „auf dem alten Brecht-Friedhof" treffen, dort gebe es ein kleines Café. Das Grab von Bertolt Brecht liegt auf dem Dorotheenstädtischen Friedhof in Berlin-Mitte. Es ist ein regnerischer Tag im Oktober. Der Friedhofsgärtner erklärt mir, dass das Café seit zwei Tagen geschlossen hat. Dann höre ich jemanden meinen Namen rufen. Ginga Eichler läuft fröhlich auf mich zu. Mit pinken Stiefeln und einer pinken Baskenmütze bringt sie Farbe in den Tag. Wir finden Platz im Café des Supermarktes um die Ecke. „In meinen Kinderjahren in Leipzig hatten wir einen Spruch", erzählt sie: „Tu was gegen den Imperialismus, friss 'nen Amerikaner."[2] Sie muss lachen und schüttelt den Kopf dabei. Ginga Eichler erzählt mir von ihren Großeltern und ihren Eltern, der wissenschaftlichen Karriere ihres Vaters, dem Umzug in die sowjetische Besatzungszone, und der Bewunderung ihrer Mutter für Josephine Baker und Paul Robeson. „Meine Mutter hatte die Nazi-Zeit selbst erlebt. Sie wollte das faschistische Übel ausreißen. Wir waren sehr politisch. Wir fühlten uns zuständig dafür, dass in Deutschland nie wieder Faschismus und Rassismus regieren würde."

Ginga Eichler reiste 1984 mit einer Delegation der DDR in die Volksrepublik Mosambik. Im Gespräch berichtete sie von den Rahmenbedingungen der Reise und ihren Eindrücken vor Ort:

Als ich 1983 zur Liga kam, kannte ich schon viele der handelnden Personen im Ausland. Ich wurde Geschäftsführerin der Freundschaftsgesellschaft Äthiopien-DDR.

1. Klaus Willerding, „Grundlagen und Inhalt der Beziehungen der DDR zu den befreiten Staaten Asiens und Afrikas", in: *Deutsche Außenpolitik*, 21 (1976), Nr. 11, S. 1615–1628, hier S. 1615.

2. „Amerikaner" ist ein Gebäck mit Zitronenglasur. Warum es diesen Namen erhielt, ist nicht ganz klar. Angeblich erinnere die flache Oberfläche des Gebäcks an die Helme amerikanischer Soldaten.

3. Kenneth Kaunda was president of Zambia (1964–1991) and one of the most important politicians in the southern African liberation movement.

celebrate this too, and so a state delegation was scheduled to travel through Africa. The partner countries expected a member of the Central Committee to come. A decision was made in the end to send the former head of the Central Committee's Agriculture Department, who had responsibility at that time in the league for relations with African, Asian, and Latin American countries. I was to be one of the people to accompany him and was tasked with making contacts and acting as translator.

I felt that the decision was disrespectful to our partner countries. The East German representative was not a political figure of any significance within the leadership, as our partner countries expected. And I'm not an interpreter. On my own initiative, I went to the Ministry of Foreign Affairs and let off steam about it: "You have to stop this. It's going to be humiliating. When we meet Kaunda, we'll be received by heads of state … We need good people." But they just stopped me with a wave of the hand: "Oh come on, Ginga, don't get so worked up. In any case, you won't be meeting Kaunda."[3] That was the worst trip I ever went on. And of course we did meet Kaunda.

At the time, a lot of my colleagues were saying, "But Ginga, that's the trip of a lifetime." Sure, we also went to Zambia, Zimbabwe, Mauritius, La Réunion, and Madagascar. For me it was hell, though. Then we went on to Mozambique, where there was a very active East German Mozambique Friendship Society as well as an information office maintained by the league. That was in 1984, and there was a catastrophic famine in Mozambique that year.

The armed conflict between FRELIMO and RENAMO also intensified during this period.

Right, it was a difficult time for the country. And then the Friendship Society gave a dinner for us; we were hosted in a fancy hall, with a massive amount of food served in some kind of dream setting—exoticism to the nth degree, in other words. It really made me cringe. They needed us and wanted to make an impression, of course.

1984 stand der 35. Jahrestag der DDR an. Das wollten auch die Partnerländer und Organisationen feiern und so sollte eine Delegation aus der DDR durch Afrika reisen. Die Partnerländer erwarteten ein Mitglied aus dem Zentralkomitee. Am Ende wurde beschlossen, dass der ehemalige Leiter der Abteilung Landwirtschaft des ZK fahren sollte, der zu diesem Zeitpunkt in der Liga für die Beziehungen mit den Ländern in Afrika, Asien und Lateinamerika zuständig war. Ich sollte ihn mit anderen begleiten, Kontakte herstellen und übersetzen.

Ich empfand die Entscheidung als eine Missachtung unserer Partnerländer. Der Vertreter der DDR war keine bedeutende politische Führungspersönlichkeit, wie sie unsere Partnerländer erwarteten. Und ich selbst bin keine Dolmetscherin. Ich bin dann auf eigene Faust ins Außenministerium der DDR und habe gewettert: „Ihr müsst das verhindern. Das wird eine Schmach. Uns werden Staatschefs empfangen, wenn wir Kaunda treffen … Wir brauchen gute Leute." Aber die haben nur abgewunken: „Ach Ginga, reg dich nicht so auf. Ihr werdet doch nicht Kaunda treffen."[3] Das war die schlimmste Reise meines Lebens. Und natürlich haben wir Kaunda getroffen.

Damals haben viele meiner Kollegen gesagt: „Ginga, das ist doch eine Traumreise." Ja klar, wir waren ja auch noch in Sambia, Simbabwe, auf Mauritius, La Réunion und Madagaskar. Aber für mich war es die Hölle. Dann sind wir weiter nach Mosambik, wo es eine sehr engagierte Gesellschaft der Freundschaft Mosambik-DDR gab und durch die Liga ein Informationsbüro unterhalten wurde. Das war 1984 und es gab in diesem Jahr eine Hungerkatastrophe in Mosambik.

Auch die kriegerischen Auseinandersetzungen zwischen der FRELIMO und der RENAMO spitzten sich in dieser Zeit zu.

Klar, das war eine schwierige Zeit für das Land. Und dann gab die Gesellschaft für uns ein Essen, wir wurden in einem pompösen Saal empfangen, mit Unmengen von Essen in irgendeiner Traumumgebung – also Exotismus vom Feinsten. Ich habe mich geschämt. Die brauchten uns, die wollten uns natürlich imponieren.

3. Kenneth Kaunda war der Präsident Sambias (1964–1991) und einer der bedeutendsten Politiker für die Befreiungsbewegung des südlichen Afrika.

Did the banquet happen in the historic Polana Hotel?
Yes, probably, somewhere ostentatious like that—and the food they dished up was amazing! There were a huge number of Mozambicans there too, as well as Harald [Heinke], of course. A band was playing that evening, and although I don't speak Portuguese, or Spanish for that matter, I was struck by certain words. And then I asked someone—I don't remember who, Harald maybe—"Tell me, could it be that they're playing a song protesting against the famine?" "Erm, yes," came the rather sheepish answer. And we sat there and ate king prawns. I really didn't begrudge the Mozambicans their night out. It was probably one of the rare occasions when they could eat their fill for once. Because they were pulling out all the stops for the foreign guests from East Germany. It just made me cringe, though. I thought it was really decadent. Nor did I have the impression that Heinke was amused by it. I think it was difficult for him to stomach too.

Who laid on the dinner then?
FRELIMO organized it for the East German delegation, which was representing a friendly nation.

They probably wanted to ask the delegation for more financial support, would you say?
Absolutely. East Germany was very important for Mozambique. And at one time, Bruno Kiesler [who became the league's secretary in 1982] was also important, because he had previously been responsible for agriculture on the Central Committee, and we sent any number of experts down there, mining specialists in particular. So they felt they needed to offer us something extra.

What was actually spoken about at the meetings with the partner countries?
Basically, it was a lot of flowery words saying how important they were to us. "Vitally important! Our closest allies." And the other side always wanted a bit more money for the work they were doing or an extra university place.

Fand das Bankett im historischen Hotel Polana, statt?
Ja, wahrscheinlich, irgendwie so was Pompöses – und was sie an Essen aufgefahren haben! Natürlich waren unglaublich viele Mosambikaner dabei, und Harald [Heinke] natürlich auch. An dem Abend spielte eine Kapelle und ich kann kein Portugiesisch, ich kann auch kein Spanisch. Aber bestimmte Worte fielen mir dann doch auf. Und dann habe ich – ich weiß nicht mehr, wen, vielleicht Harald – gefragt: „Sag mal, kann das sein, dass die da ein Lied gegen den Hunger spielen?" „Mhm, ja", war die Antwort, verlegen. Und wir saßen da und aßen Gambas. Ich habe es den Mosambikanern wirklich gegönnt. Das war für sie wahrscheinlich eine der wenigen Gelegenheiten, wo sie sich mal sattessen konnten. Weil da für die ausländischen Gäste aus der DDR alles aufgeboten wurde. Aber ich fand's nur peinlich. Ich fand's wirklich dekadent. Ich hatte auch nicht den Eindruck, dass Heinke amused war. Ich glaube, ihm ist das auch aufgestoßen.

Von wem war das Essen denn organisiert worden?
Von der FRELIMO für die Delegation aus der DDR, aus dem Freundesland.

Die wollten die Delegation vermutlich um weitere finanzielle Unterstützung bitten?
Natürlich. Die DDR war sehr wichtig für Mosambik. Und Bruno Kiesler [ab 1982 Sekretär der Liga] war ja auch mal wichtig für Mosambik, weil er nämlich früher im ZK für die Landwirtschaft zuständig gewesen war, und wir haben ja jede Menge Fachleute da runter geschifft, vor allem für den Bergbau. Also, die hatten das Gefühl, sie müssten uns sonst was bieten.

Worüber wurde bei den Besprechungen mit den Partnerländern dann konkret gesprochen?
Das waren im Wesentlichen Floskeln: Wie wichtig sie uns sind. „Ganz wichtig! Unsere engsten Verbündeten." Und die andere Seite wollte immer noch ein bisschen Geld für ihre Arbeit haben oder noch einen Studienplatz mehr.

Did you feel free to express your opinion when you were on trips like this?
Or did you feel constrained or under strict control?

I never felt any lack of freedom. Really never. I did have my own sense of what was okay and what wasn't. It wasn't at odds with what my bosses thought. If it was, then at most I sometimes thought, based on my studies and other knowledge I had, that there might have been another way of saying something, or things should have been done differently! This trip to Mozambique, for example: it should have been done differently.

Hast du dich auf solchen Reisen frei gefühlt, deine Meinung zu äußern?
Oder hast du dich eingeschränkt oder stark kontrolliert gefühlt?

Ich habe nie Unfreiheit empfunden. Ich habe wirklich nie Unfreiheit empfunden. Ich hatte schon ein eigenes Gespür dafür, was geht und was nicht geht. Es stand nicht im Gegensatz zu dem, was meine Chefs dachten. Wenn, dann allenfalls, dass ich aufgrund des Studiums und auch sonstiger Kenntnisse manchmal dachte, das hätte man auch anders sagen können und anders machen müssen! Zum Beispiel diese Reise nach Mosambik: Das hätte man anders machen müssen.

There's always a political element to Eichler's words, and the party is a pervasive presence whenever she's speaking. She comes across as a fighter with a strong sense of justice and as a stout adherent to the socialist policy of peace. After we've taken our leave of one another, I listen to "Der Hugenottenfriedhof," a 1973 song by Wolf Biermann. The characters in the song wend their way to Brecht's grave, as they turn their minds to the November Revolution and Rosa Luxemburg. I walk along Friedrichstraße and think "East Berlin" sounds different now.

When I subsequently asked her whether she would consent to having the interview published, she said: "Yes, that's the way it was." That was how she remembered the trip to Mozambique. Yet she wondered too what other stories about the cooperation with Mozambique her words might be hiding. She asked a friend to read over the interview text. Her friend wrote back, asking Ginga why she was telling this particular story and not talking about what had been achieved in cooperation with the GDR's partner countries:

> The guy from the Central Committee, a splendid dinner during a famine, the cringeworthiness … Was THAT what stayed with you from your work in Africa? "Any number of experts" who were "sent down there" are relegated here to a negligible side note. Was all this work just flowery words and begging for money? Did you never experience anything that validated the good you were doing and the important projects you were supporting? The educational programs, the housing construction. Things like that. But perhaps I'm looking through rose-tinted glasses. Of course, people were trying to secure influence and "do" geopolitics. But do you see a difference there, say, between West Germany's activities/policies and the GDR's at the time?

This angle is important for us and reminds us of why we are writing this book. "Development aid" in both East and West targeted geopolitical influence, and not much has changed in that regard. We have absolutely no intention of belittling the GDR's "Africa work" in general. East Germany's policy of forging alliances with the countries of Africa, Asia, and Latin America was never exclusively geared to

---

Das Politische ist allgegenwärtig, wenn Ginga Eichler spricht, auch die Partei. In ihren Worten steckt ein kämpferischer Sinn für Gerechtigkeit und ein Festhalten an der sozialistischen Friedenspolitik. Nachdem wir uns verabschiedet haben, höre ich ein Lied von Wolf Biermann, „Der Hugenottenfriedhof" (1973). Er schlendert „zu Brecht seinem Grab", erinnert sich an die Novemberrevolution und an Rosa Luxemburg. Ich laufe die Friedrichstraße entlang und denke, „Ost-Berlin" hat gerade einen anderen Klang bekommen.

Als ich sie einige Zeit später fragte, ob sie der Veröffentlichung des Interviews zustimmen würde, sagte sie: „Ja, so ist es gewesen." Das seien ihre Erinnerungen an die Reise nach Mosambik. Zugleich frage sie sich, welche anderen Geschichten von der Kooperation mit Mosambik sie durch ihre Worte verdecke. Ginga Eichler bittet eine Freundin, den Interviewtext zu lesen. In ihrer Antwort fragt diese Ginga, warum sie gerade diese Geschichte erzähle und nicht über jene Dinge spreche, die in der Zusammenarbeit mit den Partnerländern erreicht wurden:

> „Der ZK-Mensch, ein pompöses Essen in Hungerszeiten, die Peinlichkeit … War es DAS, was für Dich hängengeblieben ist aus Deiner Afrikaarbeit? ‚Jede Menge Fachleute', die da ‚runter geschifft' wurden, werden hier zur nicht beachteten Randbemerkung. Bestand diese ganze Arbeit nur aus Floskeln und Geldbettelei? Hattest Du nie Erlebnisse, die Dir bestätigen, dass Du eine wichtige und gute Arbeit machst und unterstützt? Die Bildungsprogramme, der Wohnungsbau. So was. Aber vielleicht habe ich da eine rosarote Brille auf. Man wollte sich natürlich Einfluss sichern, Geopolitik machen. Aber: Siehst Du da einen Unterschied zum Beispiel zwischen den Aktivitäten / der Politik der Bundesrepublik und der DDR damals dort?"

Diese Perspektive ist uns wichtig, sie erinnert uns daran, warum wir dieses Buch schreiben. „Entwicklungshilfe" zielte sowohl im Westen als auch im Osten auf geopolitische Einflussnahme ab, und daran hat sich bis heute wenig geändert. Es ist keinesfalls unsere Absicht, die „Afrikaarbeit" der DDR pauschal abzuwerten. Die Bündnispolitik der DDR mit den Ländern Afrikas, Asiens und Lateinamerikas war nie ausschließlich wirtschaftlich orientiert. Die Zusammenarbeit führte auch dazu, dass der Fokus auf gemeinsame Ziele gerichtet wurde.

4. Ursula Püschel, *Der Schlangenbaum: Eine Reise nach Moçambique* (Mitteldeutscher Verlag, 1984), 208.

economics. The cooperation also meant that there was a focus on shared goals. This happened not only in the realm of the arts but also, more importantly, at the diplomatic level, in the UN committees and at the congresses of the World Peace Council (WPC). However, it is important for us to highlight why the relationship between Mozambique and the GDR was not, ultimately, one of equals.

The banquet for the East German delegation, which Eichler talks about, took place in 1984. That same year, a *Washington Post* journalist, Allister Sparks, took a photo of the hotel and noted: "Even with no hot water in the rooms and only chancy room service, the Polana Hotel in Maputo, Mozambique, offers a whiff of the faded glories of the Portuguese empire." The building is adorned with marble tiles, fountains, and chandeliers. Official events and prestigious occasions are still staged here in a setting that enshrines the aspirations and pretensions of empire. A memory of colonial luxury. The wind comes from the coast, blowing in off the Indian Ocean.

In the early 1980s, writer and journalist Ursula Püschel wrote a report documenting the variegated relationships between the two "friendly countries." Her East German colleagues invited her for a get-together at the Polana Hotel. As Püschel remarks, "I could bring a bathing suit if I wanted, as we might go for a swim. They talked in such a pointedly casual way that they revealed more than they concealed about how special it was. In the large hall, people kept appearing with briefcases. They'd sit down, with a serious expression. From time to time, they'd use a pocket calculator. I could hear Portuguese, English, Swedish … Outside, in the lovely garden … there wasn't much happening. It seems as if the ladies and sporty male types here are doing nothing more than working on an out-of-season tropical complexion. They move around idly and oil themselves. Or maybe they're East Germans taking a break on a business trip."[4]

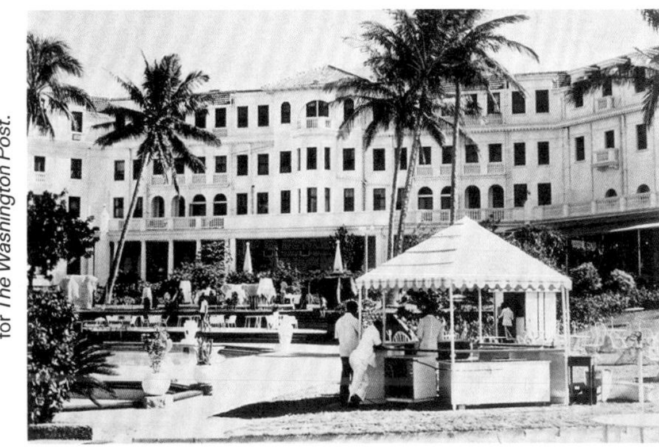

Fig. 40: The Polana Hotel in July 1984, photographed by Allister Sparks for *The Washington Post*.

Abb. 40: Das Polana Hotel im Juli 1984, fotografiert von Allister Sparks für die *Washington Post*

Das geschah nicht nur im Bereich der Künste, sondern insbesondere auch auf diplomatischer Ebene, in den Ausschüssen der Vereinten Nationen (UNO) und auf den Kongressen des Weltfriedensrates (WPC). Dennoch ist es uns wichtig aufzuzeigen, warum die Beziehung zwischen Mosambik und der DDR letztlich keinen gleichberechtigten Charakter hatte.

Das Bankett für die Delegation aus der DDR, von dem Ginga Eichler erzählt, fand 1984 statt. Im gleichen Jahr machte ein Journalist der *Washington Post*, Allister Sparks, ein Foto des Hotels, und notierte: „Auch wenn es kein heißes Wasser in den Zimmern gibt und der Zimmerservice nur spärlich ist, bietet das Polana Hotel in Maputo, Mozambique, einen Hauch des verblassten Glanzes des portugiesischen Reiches." Marmorfliesen, Springbrunnen und Kronleuchter schmücken das Gebäude. Bis heute finden hier offizielle und repräsentative Veranstaltungen statt. Ein Haus, das den imperialen Anspruch konserviert. Eine Erinnerung an den kolonialen Luxus. Von der Küste weht der Wind des Indischen Ozeans herein.

Die Schriftstellerin und Journalistin Ursula Püschel schrieb Anfang der 1980er Jahre eine Reportage, in der sie die vielfältigen Beziehungen zwischen den beiden „Freundesländern" dokumentierte. Ihre Kolleg·innen aus der DDR laden sie ein, sich im Hotel Polana zu treffen. „Ich könnte ja einen Badeanzug mitbringen, man würde vielleicht in den Swimmingpool steigen. Sie reden so betont beiläufig, daß sie das Besondere mehr enthüllen als verdecken",[4] kommentiert die Autorin. „In der großen Halle kommen immerzu Leute mit Managerkoffern an. Sie nehmen Platz, mit ernsten Mienen. Von Zeit zu Zeit werden Taschenrechner betätigt. Ich höre portugiesisch, englisch, schwedisch … Draußen in dem wunderschönen Garten … geht es überhaupt nicht geschäftig zu. Es scheint, als ob hier die Ladys und sportlichen Mannstypen an nichts anderem arbeiten als an einem tropischen Teint außerhalb der Saison. Sie bewegen sich träge und ölen sich. Vielleicht sind es auch DDR-Bürger in Dienstreisepausen."[5]

4. Ursula Püschel, *Der Schlangenbaum. Eine Reise nach Moçambique*, Halle und Leipzig: Mitteldeutscher Verlag 1984, S. 208.

5. Ebd.

5. Immanuel R. Harisch and Eric Burton, "Sozialistische Globalisierung: Tagebücher der DDR-Freundschaftsbrigaden in Afrika, Asien und Lateinamerika," *Zeithistorische Forschungen / Studies in Contemporary History* 17, no. 3 (2020): 578–91, here: 591.

Püschel and Eichler felt the contradiction between the declarations of "brotherhood" and the hierarchy that was clearly visible, perpetuated by ideas of superiority and economic dependency. Despite the ongoing civil war, FRELIMO tried hard to offer the best conditions to leading functionaries and technology experts from East Germany and other countries. They were furnished with privileges that did not exist in the GDR.

However, East Germans who traveled to the country with a Free German Youth (FDJ) brigade often lived in very simple conditions. The same went for those who had come to provide labor or operate machinery to help develop Mozambique's industrial, mining, and agriculture sectors. In many cases, it was a day-to-day challenge to obtain a supply of clean drinking water. The workers did not enjoy the same privileges as senior specialists or state delegations.

> The delegates had the opportunity to get to know countries and people on other continents and to play an active role in international settings. In some of the places they were deployed, they were able to lead a bourgeois life with domestic staff, which in East Germany would have been as impossible as it was illegal. However, the solidarity work that was sometimes carried out in conflict regions also presupposed a high degree of idealism, especially since brigade members often had to make do with worse food, more meager accommodation, and lower pay than East German expert cadres stationed abroad.[5]

What persisted, though, was the privilege of *being White*. It is a historical privilege that has accumulated over time, a self-image deriving from the colonial era that continued to shape ascriptions of importance and patterns of behavior even in the 1980s. And it still exerts an influence today. When I went to Mozambique in 2018, I met the Australian ambassador on the street, whereupon he invited me to a reception that was taking place that evening in the Polana Hotel. There was Prosecco and a buffet; and I had no reason for being there, apart from the fact that I was White.

Ursula Püschel und Ginga Eichler nahmen den Widerspruch zwischen der erklärten „Brüderlichkeit" und der sichtbaren Hierarchie wahr. Eine Hierarchie, die sich durch die Vorstellung von Überlegenheit und eine wirtschaftliche Abhängigkeit fortsetzte. Die FRELIMO war bemüht, trotz des anhaltenden Bürgerkriegs den leitenden Funktionären und Technologen aus der DDR und anderen Ländern die besten Bedingungen zu bieten. Sie waren mit Privilegien ausgestattet worden, die in der DDR nicht existierten.

DDR-Bürger·innen, die mit einer FDJ-Brigade ins Land reisten oder als Arbeiter·innen und Maschinenführer·innen in den mosambikanischen Betrieben den Aufbau von Industrie, Bergbau, und Landwirtschaft unterstützten, lebten jedoch oft in sehr einfachen Verhältnissen. Nicht selten war schon die Versorgung mit sauberem Trinkwasser in Mosambik eine alltägliche Herausforderung. Die genannten Privilegien existierten also nicht auf gleiche Weise für Arbeiter·innen wie für leitende Fachkräfte oder Staatsdelegationen.

> „Die Entsandten konnten Länder und Menschen auf anderen Kontinenten kennenlernen und in internationalen Kontexten agieren. An manchen Einsatzorten konnten sie ein geradezu bürgerliches Leben mit Hauspersonal führen, das in der DDR so unmöglich wie illegitim gewesen wäre. Die bisweilen in Konfliktregionen geleistete Solidaritätsarbeit setzte aber auch viel Idealismus voraus, zumal Brigademitglieder sich im Vergleich mit DDR-Auslandskadern von Expertenrang oft mit einer schlechteren Versorgungslage, dürftigeren Unterkünften und einer geringeren Vergütung zufriedengeben mussten."[6]

6. Immanuel R. Harisch und Eric Burton, „Sozialistische Globalisierung: Tagebücher der DDR-Freundschaftsbrigaden in Afrika, Asien und Lateinamerika", in: *Zeithistorische Forschungen / Studies in Contemporary History*, 17 (2020), Nr. 3, S. 578–591, hier S. 591.

Was jedoch blieb, war das Privileg des *Weißseins*. Es ist ein historisch akkumuliertes Privileg, ein Selbstverständnis aus der Kolonialzeit, das auch in den 1980er Jahren noch Bedeutungszuschreibungen und Handlungsmuster prägte. Und es wirkt bis heute. Auf meiner Reise nach Mosambik 2018 lernte ich auf der Straße den australischen Botschafter in Mosambik kennen. Daraufhin lud er mich zu einem Empfang ein, der noch am gleichen Abend im Hotel Polana stattfand. Es gab Prosecco und ein Buffet; und ich hatte keinen Grund, dort zu sein, abgesehen von meinem *Weißsein*.

AdK	Akademie der Künste (Academy of Arts)
AdK-O	Bestand im Archiv der Akademie der Künste (Group of records in the AdK archive)
ADN	Allgemeiner Deutscher Nachrichtendienst (General German News Service, *the GDR's state news agency*)
AMASP	Associação Moçambicana de Amizade e Solidariedade com os Povos (Mozambican Association of Friendship and Solidarity Between Peoples / Moçambikanische Gesellschaft für Freundschaft und Solidarität der Völker)
ANC	African National Congress (*national liberation movement and political party in South Africa*)
BArch	Bundesarchiv (German Federal Archives)
BE	Berliner Ensemble
CARBOMOC E.E.	Empresa Estatal Carbonífera de Moçambique (Mozambican National Mining Company)
CIA	Central Intelligence Agency (*US state agency for foreign intelligence*)
CNCD	Companhia Nacional de Canto e Dança (National Song and Dance Company of Mozambique)
CONCP	Conferência das Organizações Nacionalistas das Colónias Portuguesas (Conference of Nationalist Organizations in the Portuguese Colonies)
DEC	Departamento de Educação e Cultura (Department of Education and Culture of Mozambique)
DEFA	Deutsche Film Aktiengesellschaft (German Film Corporation, *the GDR's state-owned film studio*)
DNC	Direcção Nacional de Cultura (National Directorate of Culture)
FDJ	Freie Deutsche Jugend (Free German Youth)
FSLN	Frente Sandinista de Liberación Nacional (Sandinista National Liberation Front, *Marxist-Leninist movement in Nicaragua*)
GDR	German Democratic Republic (*East Germany*)
INC	Instituto Nacional de Cinema (National Cinema Institute of Mozambique)
ITI	International Theater Institute
League, Liga	Liga für Völkerfreundschaft (International Friendship League)
MfS	Ministerium für Staatssicherheit (Ministry for State Security)
MPLA	Movimento Popular de Libertação de Angola (Popular Movement for the Liberation of Angola)
OJM	Organização da Juventude Moçambicana (Mozambican Youth Organization)
PAIGC	Partido Africano para a Independência da Guiné e Cabo Verde (African Independence Party for Guinea and Cape Verde)
PRM	República Popular de Moçambique (People's Republic of Mozambique, *the name of the Republic of Mozambique from 1975 until 1990*)
SEC	Secretaria de Estado para Cultura (State Secretariat for Culture in Mozambique)
SED	Sozialistische Einheitspartei Deutschlands (Socialist Unity Party of Germany)
SKD	Staatliche Kunstsammlungen Dresden (Dresden State Art Collections, *public cultural institution of the State of Saxony*)
SODI	Solidaritätsdienst International e.V. (Solidarity Service International, *non-governmental organization*)
SWAPO	South West Africa People's Organisation (*Namibia's liberation movement and main political party*)
ZAPU	Zimbabwe African People's Union
ZfK	Zentrum für Kunstausstellungen (Center for Art Exhibitions)
ZK	Zentralkomitee (Central Committee, *the highest body within a socialist government*)

AdK	Akademie der Künste
AdK-O	Bestand im Archiv der Akademie der Künste
ADN	Allgemeiner Deutscher Nachrichtendienst (*staatliche Nachrichtenagentur der DDR*)
AMASP	Associação Moçambicana de Amizade e Solidariedade entre os Povos (Mosambikanische Gesellschaft für Freundschaft und Solidarität der Völker)
ANC	African National Congress (*nationale Befreiungsbewegung und politische Partei in Südafrika*)
BArch	Bundesarchiv
BE	Berliner Ensemble
CARBOMOC E. E.	Empresa Estatal Carbonífera de Moçambique (Staatliches mosambikanisches Bergbauunternehmen)
CIA	Central Intelligence Agency (*Auslandsnachrichtendienst der USA*)
CNCD	Companhia Nacional de Canto e Dança (Nationale Gesangs- und Tanzkompanie von Mosambik)
CONCP	Conferência das Organizações Nacionalistas das Colónias Portuguesas (Konferenz der nationalen Organisationen in den portugiesischen Kolonien)
DEC	Departamento de Educação e Cultura (Ministerium für Bildung und Kultur von Mosambik)
DEFA	Deutsche Film AG (*staatliches Filmstudio der DDR*)
DNC	Direcção Nacional de Cultura (Nationale Direktion für Kultur)
FDJ	Freie Deutsche Jugend
FSLN	Frente Sandinista de Liberación Nacional (Sandinistische Nationale Befreiungsfront, *marxistisch-leninistische Bewegung in Nicaragua*)
DDR	Deutsche Demokratische Republik
INC	Instituto Nacional de Cinema (Nationales Filminstitut von Mosambik)
ITI	Internationales Theaterinstitut
Liga	Liga für Völkerfreundschaft
MfS	Ministerium für Staatssicherheit
MPLA	Movimento Popular de Libertação de Angola (Volksbewegung zur Befreiung Angolas)
OJM	Organização da Juventude Moçambicana (Mosambikanische Jugendorganisation)
PAIGC	Partido Africano para a Independência da Guiné e Cabo Verde (Afrikanische Unabhängigkeitspartei von Guinea und Kap Verde)
PRM	República Popular de Moçambique (Volksrepublik Mosambik – *Name der Republik Mosambik von 1975 bis 1990*)
SEC	Secretaria de Estado para Cultura (Staatssekretariat für Kultur in Mosambik)
SED	Sozialistischen Einheitspartei Deutschlands
SKD	Staatliche Kunstsammlungen Dresden
SODI	Solidaritätsdienst International e. V. (*Nichtregierungsorganisation*)
SWAPO	South West Africa People's Organisation (*Namibias Befreiungsbewegung und wichtigste politische Partei*)
ZAPU	Zimbabwe African People's Union (Afrikanische Volksunion von Simbabwe)
ZfK	Zentrum für Kunstausstellungen
ZK	Zentralkomitee (*oberstes Entscheidungsgremium innerhalb einer sozialistischen Regierung*)

East German Academy of Arts	Founded in 1950, just six months after the formation of the GDR, it was the most important art institution in the country. Among its founding members were many artists and intellectuals who had gone into exile during the Nazi regime and decided to return and contribute to the building of the young East German state. As a state institution, the academy reflected the SED's political stance and promoted an art oriented towards "socialist realism." In 1993, the art academies of East and West Germany were merged into one institution, the Akademie der Künste (AdK).
Assimilado	Under Portuguese colonial rule, the "native" population was divided into an "uncivilized' majority, and a "civilized" minority, the *assimilados*, or "assimilated" citizens, who "had supposedly adopted an essentially Portuguese way of life" (Eduardo Mondlane, *The Struggle for Mozambique*, 1969).
Bantu Culture	The Bantu peoples are a group of around eighty-five million people who speak over five hundred distinct languages in Central and Southern Africa. The classification of Bantu is primarily linguistic, as cultural traditions within Bantu-speaking communities vary widely.
Berliner Ensemble	Renowned theater company established in 1949 by Helene Weigel and Bertolt Brecht upon their return from fifteen years of exile in Europe and the USA. Brecht's openly communist convictions, which shaped his theories and plays, made him and the Berliner Ensemble (BE) central to the GDR's theater and cultural policy abroad. The BE attracted theater makers from around the world, drawn to Brecht's work and theories, making it one of the most internationally recognized theater companies of the twentieth century. Today, the BE remains one of Berlin's most important theaters.
Casas da Cultura	Cultural centers established in urban residential areas as instruments to popularize and democratize access to culture and the arts. Guided by the slogans "culture for all" and "culture by all," designed these spaces promoted cultural activities and fostered a continuous exchange between artists and the general population ("the working masses"), as they were both considered "creators of the national cultural heritage."
FESTAC '77	Second World Black and African Festival of Arts and Culture—a festival featuring artists, performers, and intellectuals from fifty-five nations, which took place in Lagos, Nigeria in 1977. It is the largest pan-African festival in world history.
FRELIMO	*Frente de Libertação de Moçambique* (Mozambique Liberation Front) Mozambique's ruling party, founded in 1962 as a liberation movement that led the struggle for independence, which was achieved in 1975. FRELIMO became a political party and established a Marxist-Leninist single-party state until 1990, when it transitioned to a multiparty system. It has remained in power ever since.
Friendship Societies	*Deutsch-Mosambikanische Freundschaftsgesellschaft* (German-Mozambican Friendship Society) and *Associação Moçambicana de Amizade e Solidariedade com os Povos (AMASP)* Friendship societies, the former established in the GDR and the latter in Mozambique, which were responsible for fostering cultural relations and exchange between Mozambique and the GDR.
Homem Novo	The concept of the "New Man" was developed during the struggle for liberation as part of FRELIMO's national unity project, symbolizing a rupture with old ideas and colonial mentality. The New Man was envisioned as

Akademie der Künste der DDR	Die Akademie der Künste entstand 1950, nur sechs Monate nach der Gründung der DDR, und war eine der wichtigsten Kunstinstitution des Landes. Zu ihren Gründungsmitgliedern zählten viele Künstler·innen und Intellektuelle, die während der nationalsozialistischen Herrschaft ins Exil gegangen waren und in die DDR kamen, um zum Aufbau des jungen Staates beizutragen. Als staatliche Einrichtung spiegelte die Akademie die politische Haltung der SED wider und förderte eine am „sozialistischen Realismus" orientierte Kunst. 1993 wurden die Kunstakademien der DDR und der BRD zu einer Institution, der Akademie der Künste (AdK), zusammengeführt.
Assimilado	Unter der portugiesischen Kolonialherrschaft wurde innerhalb der „einheimischen" Bevölkerung zwischen einer „unzivilisierten" Mehrheit und einer „zivilisierten" Minderheit, den *Assimilados* oder „assimilierten" Bürger·innen, unterschieden, die „vermeintlich eine überwiegend portugiesische Lebensweise angenommen hatten" (Eduardo Mondlane, *The Struggle for Mozambique*, 1969).
Bantu-Kultur	Als zur Bantu-Kultur gehörig wird eine Gruppe von rund 85 Millionen Menschen bezeichnet, die im zentralen und südlichen Afrika leben und über 500 verschiedene Sprachen sprechen. Die Klassifizierung der Bantu ist in erster Linie linguistisch, da die kulturellen Traditionen innerhalb der bantusprachigen Gemeinschaften sehr unterschiedlich sind.
Berliner Ensemble	Ein renommiertes Theater, das 1949 von Helene Weigel und Bertolt Brecht nach ihrer Rückkehr aus dem 15-jährigen Exil in Europa und den USA gegründet wurde. Brechts offen kommunistische Überzeugungen, die seine Theorien und Stücke prägten, machten ihn und das BE zu einem zentralen Akteur der Theater- und Kulturpolitik der DDR, insbesondere im Ausland. Das Berliner Ensemble zog Regisseur·innen aus aller Welt an, die von Brechts Werk und Theorien begeistert waren, und machte es zu einem der international renommiertesten Theaterensembles des 20. Jahrhunderts. Auch heute noch ist das BE eines der wichtigsten Theater Berlins.
Casas da Cultura	Kulturzentren in städtischen Wohngebieten, die der Förderung und Demokratisierung des Zugangs zu Kultur und Kunst dienen. Unter dem Motto „Kultur für alle" förderten diese Orte kulturelle Aktivitäten und einen kontinuierlichen Austausch zwischen Künstler·innen und der allgemeinen Bevölkerung („den arbeitenden Massen"), da beide als „Schöpfer des nationalen Kulturerbes" angesehen wurden.
Dritte Welt	Der Begriff wurde in den frühen 1950er Jahren geprägt, um ehemals kolonialisierte und neuerdings unabhängige Nationen in Afrika, Asien und Lateinamerika zu beschreiben. Wenn man den Begriff heute liest, suggeriert er möglicherweise eine Hierarchie zwischen der „Ersten Welt" als dem erstrebenswerten Ideal der Moderne und der „Dritten Welt" als Nachzügler in der wirtschaftlichen und industriellen Entwicklung. In der Geschichte des Begriffs steht er jedoch für ein politisches Projekt, das die Länder der „Dritten Welt" einte, nämlich die Bewegung der Blockfreien Staaten: eigene Wege zu gehen, statt dem sozialistischen Osten, der sogenannten „Zweiten Welt", oder dem kapitalistischen Westen, der sogenannten „Ersten Welt", zu folgen. Der Kontext, in dem der Begriff entstanden ist, der Kalte Krieg, existiert so nicht mehr, und der Begriff wurde durch andere ersetzt wie „Globaler Süden", „Entwicklungs-" oder „Schwellenländer" oder „am wenigsten entwickelte" Staaten. In der Wissenschaft wird der Begriff „Dritte Welt" heute meist als historische Terminologie verwendet. Für manche dient der Begriff immer noch als Erinnerung an die Kämpfe der „Dritten Welt" um wirtschaftliche Unabhängigkeit und eine wirkliche Dekolonialisierung.
FESTAC '77	*Second World Black and African Festival of Arts and Culture* – ein Festival mit Künstler·innen, Performer·innen und Intellektuellen aus 55 Ländern, das 1977 in Lagos, Nigeria, stattfand. Es war das größte panafrikanische Festival der Weltgeschichte.

someone guided by revolutionary principles—righteous, hard-working, emancipated and free from vices, laziness, obscurantism, and tribalism. However, this homogeneous ideal became a tool for excluding and persecuting those who did not "fit" or those who thought "differently," often labeling them as "internal enemies" and sending them to re-education camps.

International Friendship League
Founded in 1961, it was the umbrella organization of all the GDR societies and committees focused on international friendship and cooperation. Its mission was to disseminate information about the GDR abroad, strengthen cultural relations with other countries, and consolidate the international reputation of the GDR.

Madgermanes (or Madjermanes)
Former contract workers from Mozambique, who lived and worked in the former GDR in the 1980s. Sent back to Mozambique after the reunification of Germany, they are fighting to this day for the payment of most of their salaries and social security contributions. Their withheld wages (40-60%) were used to pay off Mozambique's debts to the GDR.

Makonde Art
The Makonde are a Bantu matrilineal community living on both sides of Rovuma River, in northeastern Mozambique and southeastern Tanzania. They are renowned for their detailed wood carvings, particularly statues and masks.

Non-Aligned Movement
Formed in 1961 during the Cold War, the NAM is an organization of states that did not align with either the United States or the Soviet Union, instead seeking to create an independent path in global politics. The NAM still exists today, with 120 member states, mostly "developing" nations, and aims to represent their interests and aspirations.

Núcleo de Arte (Art Center)
Collaborative cultural center in Maputo, founded in 1921, and the oldest art association in Mozambique. With workshops and exhibition spaces, it serves as a hub for artists from various disciplines to create and showcase their work. After independence, the Núcleo de Arte was transformed into a "cooperative of cultural production and dissemination." As outlined in its founding document, the cooperative's mission was to "support and encourage artistic and cultural exchange and the ongoing training of its members, raising their artistic, technical, scientific and cultural knowledge, combating limiting and elitist manifestations and conceptions of artistic and cultural production, and contributing to the democratization of art and culture." (BArch N2841/27)

RENAMO
Resistência Nacional de Moçambique (Mozambican National Resistance)
Main opposition party in Mozambique, originally formed in 1976 as an insurgent movement against FRELIMO's Marxist-Leninist ideology. Backed by the Rhodesian and South African governments, which had no interest in having a Black communist government as a neighbor, it transitioned into a political party after the 1992 peace agreement with FRELIMO and has remained the primary opposition force in the country.

Samora Machel (1933–1986)
Mozambique's first president and an important national figure. Machel joined FRELIMO in 1962 and became its leader in 1970 after the assassination of Eduardo Mondlane, FRELIMO's first president. Machel died in a plane crash in South Africa in 1986, which many believe was the responsibility of the South African apartheid government.

Socialist Internationalism
International solidarity and unity of the working-class and socialist countries across national borders. The movement is based on the understanding that capitalism and imperialism operate as part of a global system, making the struggles of the proletariat interconnected and the fight for socialism inherently global.

FRELIMO
Frente de Libertação de Moçambique (Mosambikanische Befreiungsfront)
Mosambiks Regierungspartei, gegründet 1962 als Befreiungsbewegung im Kampf um die Unabhängigkeit, die 1975 erreicht wurde. Die FRELIMO wandelte sich zu einer politischen Partei und errichtete einen marxistisch-leninistischen Einparteienstaat bis 1990, als ein Mehrparteiensystem etabliert wurde. Seitdem ist sie an der Macht geblieben.

Freundschaftsgesellschaften
Deutsch-Mosambikanische Freundschaftsgesellschaft und *Associação Moçambicana de Amizade e Solidariedade entre os Povos (AMASP)*
Freundschaftsgesellschaften, von denen eine in der DDR und die andere in Mosambik gegründet wurde, hatten die Aufgabe, die kulturellen Beziehungen und den Austausch zwischen Mosambik und der DDR zu fördern.

Homem Novo
Das Konzept des „Neuen Menschen" wurde während des Befreiungskampfes als Teil des FRELIMO-Projekts einer nationalen Einheit entwickelt und symbolisierte den Bruch mit alten Ideen und kolonialer Mentalität. Der „Neue Mensch" wurde als jemand vorgestellt, der sich von revolutionären Prinzipien leiten lässt – rechtschaffen, fleißig, emanzipiert und frei von Lastern, Faulheit, Obskurantismus und Stammesdenken. Dieses homogenisierende Ideal wurde jedoch zu einem Instrument, um diejenigen auszugrenzen und zu verfolgen, die nicht „dazu passten" oder „anders" dachten, wobei sie oft als „innere Feinde" bezeichnet und in Umerziehungslager geschickt wurden.

Jugendorganisationen
FDJ – Freie Deutsche Jugend und *OJM – Organização da Juventude Moçambicana* (Organisation der mosambikanischen Jugend)
In vielen sozialistischen Ländern gab es Jugendorganisationen wie die FDJ in der DDR und die OJM in Mosambik. Diese Organisationen zielten darauf ab, sozialistische Werte (und parteipolitische Ansichten) zu vermitteln, die staatsbürgerliche Verantwortung zu fördern und den Gemeinschaftssinn der Jugendlichen zu stärken. Obwohl der Beitritt offiziell freiwillig war, konnte sich ein Nichtbeitritt negativ auf die Berufsaussichten auswirken, so dass sich viele junge Menschen gezwungen sahen beizutreten. Die OJM ist auch heute noch aktiv, allerdings nicht mehr als sozialistische Organisation, sondern als Jugendorganisation der FRELIMO-Partei – eine aktive Mitgliedschaft verbessert die Karrierechancen.

Liga für Völkerfreundschaft
Gegründet 1961 war die Liga die Dachorganisation aller auf internationale Freundschaft und Zusammenarbeit ausgerichteten Gesellschaften und Gremien der DDR. Ihre Aufgabe war es, Informationen über die DDR im Ausland zu verbreiten, die kulturellen Beziehungen mit anderen Ländern zu stärken und das internationale Ansehen der DDR zu festigen.

Madgermanes (oder Madjermanes)
Ehemalige Vertragsarbeiter·innen aus Mosambik, die in den 1980er Jahren in der ehemaligen DDR gelebt und gearbeitet haben. Nach der Wiedervereinigung Deutschlands nach Mosambik zurückgeschickt, kämpfen sie bis heute um die Auszahlung eines Großteils ihrer Löhne und Sozialversicherungsbeiträge. Ihre einbehaltenen Löhne (40–60 %) wurden verwendet, um die Schulden Mosambiks bei der DDR zu begleichen.

Makonde-Kunst
Die Makonde sind ein matrilineares Bantu-Volk, das auf beiden Seiten des Rovuma-Flusses im Nordosten Mosambiks und im Südosten Tansanias lebt. Sie sind bekannt für ihre detailreichen Holzschnitzereien, insbesondere Skulpturen und Masken.

Non-Aligned Movement
Die NAM wurde 1961 während des Kalten Krieges gegründet und ist eine Organisation von Staaten, die sich weder mit den Vereinigten Staaten noch mit der Sowjetunion verbündeten und stattdessen einen unabhängigen Weg in der Weltpolitik einschlagen wollten. Die NAM besteht auch heute noch und umfasst 120 Mitgliedsstaaten, zumeist „Entwicklungsländer", und hat sich zum Ziel gesetzt, deren Interessen und Bestrebungen zu vertreten.

Solidarity Committee	Organization in the GDR that coordinated development cooperation activities in "Third World" socialist countries and facilitated the implementation of GDR's foreign policy. It was funded by donations from trade unions and the general population. The Solidarity Committee was not directly bound by government directives and had relative freedom in determining the forms of support they provided. In 1990, the Solidarity Committee was transformed into the nongovernmental organization *Solidaritätsdienst International* (SODI).
Socialist Unity Party of Germany (SED)	Founded in 1946, the SED was the ruling party of the GDR from 1949 to 1990. With a Marxist-Leninist ideology, the SED had a strict hierarchical structure and effectively created a one-party state. Organized in state institutions and factories, the SED influenced every aspect of public—and often private—life.
Third World	The term was coined in the early 1950s to describe former colonized and newly independent nations in Africa, Asia, and Latin America. Read today, the term suggests a hierarchy from the "First World" as the most desirable ideal of modernity to the "Third World" as a latecomer in terms of economic and industrial development. Yet in the history of the term, it stands for a political project, the Non-Aligned Movement, shared by the countries of the "Third World": To pursue their own paths instead of following the socialist East, the so-called "Second World," or the capitalist West, the so-called "First World." The context in which the term was forged, the Cold War, has ended, and the term has been replaced by others, such as "global south," "developing," "emerging," or "least developed" countries. Today, the term "Third World" is often used by scholars as a piece of historical terminology. And for some, the term still serves as a reminder of the "Third World" struggles for economic independence and true decolonization.
Youth Organizations	*FDJ Freie Deutsche Jugend* (Free German Youth) and *OJM Organização da Juventude Moçambicana* (Mozambican Youth Organization)
Comité Central, Zentralkomitee (ZK)	Many socialist countries had youth organizations such as the FDJ in the GDR and the OJM in Mozambique. These organizations aimed to inculcate socialist values (and partisan views), promote civic responsibility and foster a sense of community among the youth. Although officially voluntary, not enrolling could impact career prospects, so many young people felt compelled to join. The OJM remains active today, no longer as a socialist organization but as the youth wing of the FRELIMO party—with active membership enhancing career opportunities.
Central Committee, (ZfK)	The Central Committee represented the party elite and, along with the Party Congress (which elected the CC), constituted the highest body of the party. The CC elected the members of its secretariat, which was responsible for ensuring the implementation and control of party policy. A central committee existed both in the GDR (Zentralkomittee, ZK) and in Mozambique (Comité Central, CC, which still exists today).
Center for Art Exhibitions	The Center for Art Exhibitions of the GDR, established in 1973, was a state institution aimed at promoting international cultural exchange. It organized interdisciplinary exhibitions, showcasing both art from other countries in the GDR and GDR art abroad.

Núcleo de Arte	Der 1921 in Maputo gegründete Kunstverein ist das älteste gemeinschaftliche Kulturzentrum in Mosambik. Mit Werkstätten und Ausstellungsräumen dient es Künstler·innen verschiedener Disziplinen als Treffpunkt, um ihre Arbeiten zu schaffen und auszustellen. Nach der Unabhängigkeit wurde der Núcleo de Arte in eine „Genossenschaft für kulturelle Produktion und Verbreitung" umgewandelt. Wie in ihrem Gründungsdokument dargelegt, bestand die Aufgabe der Genossenschaft darin, „den künstlerischen und kulturellen Austausch und die ständige Weiterbildung ihrer Mitglieder zu unterstützen und zu fördern, ihr künstlerisches, technisches, wissenschaftliches und kulturelles Wissen zu erweitern, einschränkende und elitäre Vorstellungen von künstlerischer und kultureller Produktion zu bekämpfen und zur Demokratisierung von Kunst und Kultur beizutragen." (BArch N2841/27)
RENAMO	*Resistência Nacional de Moçambique* (Nationaler Widerstand Mosambiks) Größte Oppositionspartei in Mosambik, ursprünglich 1976 als Aufstandsbewegung gegen die marxistisch-leninistische Ideologie der FRELIMO gegründet und unterstützt von den Regierungen Rhodesiens und Südafrikas, die Sorge vor einer Schwarzen kommunistischen Nachbarregierung hatten. Nach dem Friedensabkommen mit der FRELIMO 1992 wurde daraus eine politische Partei, die bis heute die wichtigste Oppositionskraft im Land ist.
Samora Machel (1933–1986)	Der erste Präsident von Mosambik und eine wichtige nationale Persönlichkeit. Machel trat 1962 der FRELIMO bei und wurde 1970 nach der Ermordung von Eduardo Mondlane, dem ersten Präsidenten der FRELIMO, ihr Vorsitzender. Machel kam 1986 bei einem Flugzeugabsturz in Südafrika ums Leben, für den nach weit verbreiteter Ansicht die südafrikanische Apartheidregierung verantwortlich ist.
Sozialistischer Internationalismus	Internationale Solidarität und die Einheit der Arbeiterklasse sowie der sozialistischen Länder über nationale Grenzen hinweg. Die Bewegung basiert auf dem Verständnis, dass Kapitalismus und Imperialismus als Teil eines globalen Systems funktionieren, wodurch die Kämpfe des Proletariats miteinander verbunden sind und der Kampf für den Sozialismus seinem Wesen nach global ist.
Solidaritätskomitee	Organisation in der DDR, die die Aktivitäten der Entwicklungszusammenarbeit in den sozialistischen Ländern der „Dritten Welt" koordinierte und die Umsetzung der Außenpolitik der DDR erleichterte. Das Solidaritätskomitee wurde durch Spenden der Gewerkschaften und der Bevölkerung finanziert. Es war nicht unmittelbar an die Weisungen der Regierung gebunden und konnte relativ frei über die Formen der Unterstützung entscheiden. Im Jahr 1990 wurde das Solidaritätskomitee in die Nichtregierungsorganisation Solidaritätsdienst International (SODI) umgewandelt.
Sozialistische Einheitspartei Deutschlands (SED)	Die 1946 gegründete SED war von 1949 bis 1990 die Regierungspartei der DDR. Mit ihrer marxistisch-leninistischen Ideologie hatte die SED eine strenge hierarchische Struktur und schuf faktisch einen Einparteienstaat. Organisiert in staatlichen Institutionen und Betrieben, beeinflusste die SED jeden Aspekt des öffentlichen – und oft auch privaten – Lebens.
Zentralkomitee (ZK), Comité Central	Das Zentralkomitee stellte die Führungskader der Partei und bildete zusammen mit dem Parteitag (der das ZK wählte) das höchste Gremium der Partei. Das ZK wählte die Mitglieder seines Sekretariats, das für die Umsetzung und Kontrolle der Parteipolitik verantwortlich war. Ein Zentralkomitee gab es sowohl in der DDR (Zentralkomitee – ZK) als auch in Mosambik (Comité Central – CC, das heute noch existiert).
Zentrum für Kunstausstellungen (ZfK)	Das 1973 gegründete Zentrum für Kunstausstellungen der DDR war eine staatliche Einrichtung zur Förderung des internationalen Kulturaustauschs. Es organisierte interdisziplinäre Ausstellungen, bei denen sowohl Kunst aus anderen Ländern in der DDR als auch DDR-Kunst im Ausland gezeigt wurde.

LEA MARIE NIENHOFF is an urban scholar, historian, and theater pedagogue. As part of the research project *Decolonizing Socialism: Entangled Internationalism*, she examines the GDR's global connections through personal memories, artworks, and archival traces. She creates exhibitions and other collaborative formats to engage audiences with her work. Her earlier research focused on Mozambican workers' housing conditions in the GDR, as well as the regulation and control of their lives. She is currently doing a PhD in urban studies at the University of Basel.

AMBRE ALFREDO is a Mozambican architect, urban planner, and researcher. She is doing a PhD in urban studies at the University of Basel as part of the project *Precarious Urbanisms in Coastal Africa*. Her research focuses on Cotonou, Benin, where she examines everyday experiences of flooding, and how residents navigate eviction threats. Her research analyzes national development plans, highlighting how they perpetuate historical social and spatial inequalities. Before joining the University of Basel, Ambre worked in international cooperation in Germany.

ALDA COSTA is an art historian, museologist, and cultural worker from Pemba, Mozambique. Her body of work, including numerous books, exhibition catalogs, and articles, provides a comprehensive study of modern and contemporary art in Mozambique. In addition to her teaching and research, she has led museum projects for the Ministry of Culture and served on art competition juries and on the editorial board of *Third Text Africa*. From 2010 to 2021, she was director of culture at Eduardo Mondlane University in Maputo.

LEA MARIE NIENHOFF ist Stadtforscherin, Historikerin und Theaterpädagogin. Im Rahmen des Forschungsprojekts *Decolonizing Socialism: Entangled Internationalism* untersucht sie die globalen Verbindungen der DDR anhand von Interviews, Kunstwerken und Archivspuren. Sie entwickelt Ausstellungen und andere kollaborative Formate, um das Publikum zu einer Auseinandersetzung mit ihrer Forschung einzuladen. In einem vorherigen Projekt dokumentierte sie die Wohnbedingungen mosambikanischer Arbeiter*innen in der DDR, sowie die Regulierung und Kontrolle ihres Alltagslebens. Sie ist Doktorandin im Fachbereich Urban Studies an der Universität Basel.

AMBRE ALFREDO ist eine mosambikanische Architektin, Stadtplanerin und Forscherin. Sie ist Doktorandin im Bereich Urban Studies an der Universität Basel und arbeitet im Forschungsprojekts *Precarious Urbanisms in Coastal Africa*. Ihre Forschungsarbeit beschäftigt sich mit der Stadt Cotonou in Benin, wo sie untersucht, welche alltäglichen Erfahrungen mit Überschwemmungen die dortigen Bewohner*innen machen und wie sie mit angedrohten Zwangsräumungen umgehen. Sie analysiert nationale Entwicklungspläne und beleuchtet, wie diese historische, soziale und räumliche Ungleichheiten fortschreiben. Bevor sie an die Universität Basel kam, war sie in Deutschland in der internationalen Zusammenarbeit tätig.

ALDA COSTA ist eine Kunsthistorikerin, Museumswissenschaftlerin und Kulturarbeiterin aus Pemba, Mosambik. Mit ihren zahlreichen Büchern, Ausstellungen, Katalogen und Artikeln liefert sie eine umfassende Analyse der modernen und zeitgenössischen Kunst in Mosambik. Neben ihren Lehr- und Forschungstätigkeiten hat sie im Auftrag des Kulturministeriums Museumsprojekte geleitet und war Mitglied zahlreicher Kunstpreisjurys sowie der Redaktionsleitung von *Third Text Africa*. Von 2010 bis 2021 war sie Direktorin für Kultur an der Eduardo Mondlane University in Maputo.

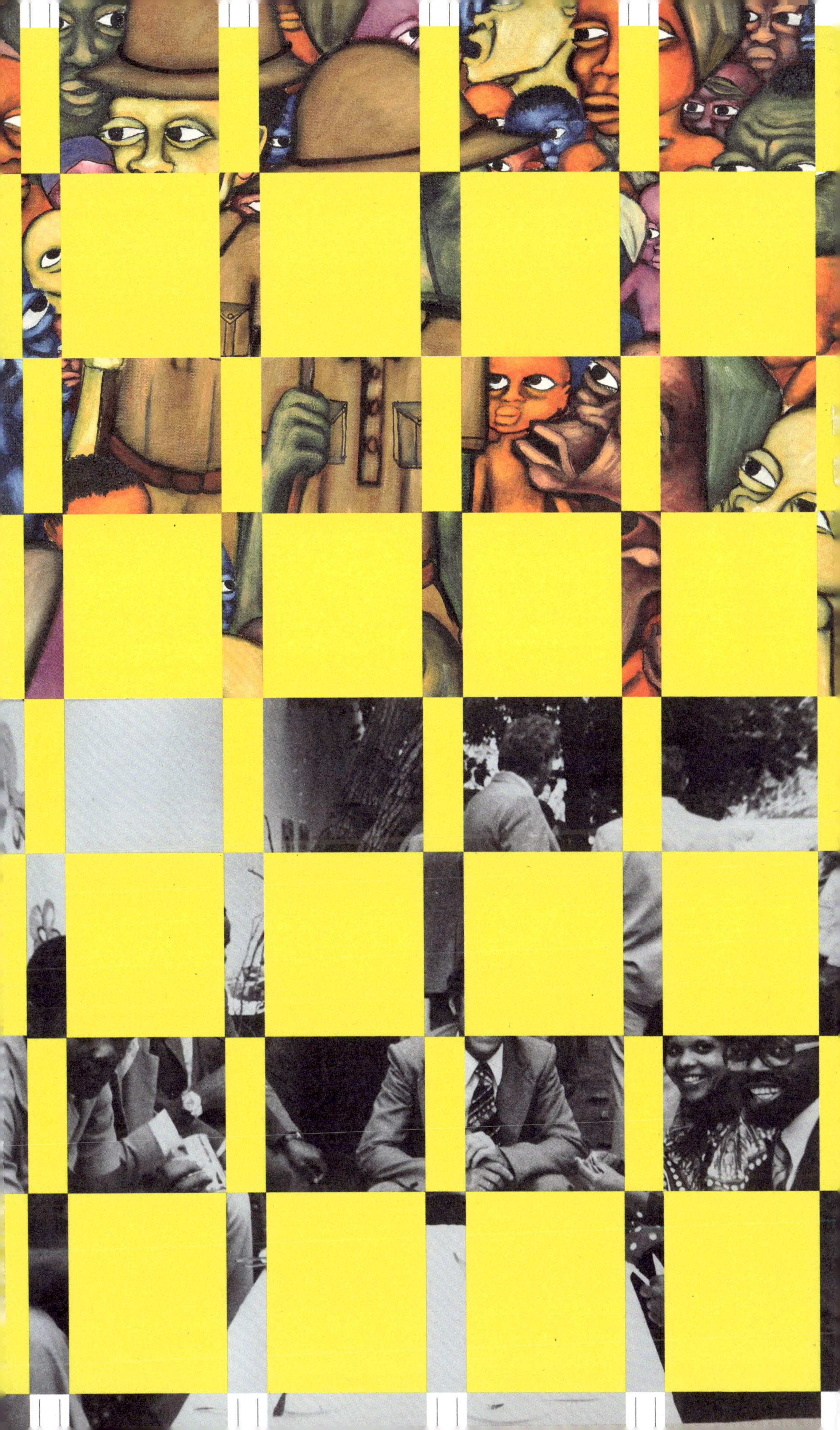

Entangled Internationalisms
Series editors: Staatliche Kunstsammlungen Dresden,
Doreen Mende,
with HEAD – Genève (HES-SO)

Till the Sun Rises, edited by vinit agarwal
Troubled Comradeship in the Arts, edited by Lea Marie
Nienhoff and Ambre Alfredo
The Missed Seminar, edited by Doreen Mende and
Avery F. Gordon
Reflexive Tema and Global Elsewheres …, edited by Kwasi
Ohene-Ayeh

*Troubled Comradeship in the Arts: On Mozambican Artists'
Experiences in the GDR, Their Work, and Political Imaginaries*
Edited by Lea Marie Nienhoff and Ambre Alfredo
Editorial coordination: Christin Krause, Jan Wenzel
Production: Oliver Baurhenn (October 2024–December
2024), Jesi Khadivi (October–December 2024), Elisabeth
Schmidt (January–September 2024)
Translations: Ambre Alfredo (PT–EN), Vinicio Altmann (PT–EN),
Simon Cowper (DE–EN), Birthe Mühlhoff (EN–DE)
Copyediting English: Jan Caspers
Copyediting German: Jan-Frederik Bandel
Research coordination: Océane Vé-Réveillac (until
September 2024)
Design and concept: Malin Gewinner and Lyosha Kritsouk
Lithography: Aleksey Novikov
Printing and binding: Druckhaus Sportflieger, Berlin

The academic research for the case studies was made
possible by the project funded by the Swiss National
Science Foundation (#184864) *Decolonizing Socialism:
Entangled Internationalism* (2019–2024) at HEAD – Genève,
part of the University of Applied Sciences and Arts
(HES-SO), Geneva.

The production of the artistic research edition was funded
by the Federal Government Commissioner for Culture
and the Media as part of the project *Museums as Active
Sites of Democracy* (MODemo).

Published by
Spector Books
Harkortstraße 10
04107 Leipzig
www.spectorbooks.com

Distribution:
Germany, Austria: GVA, Gemeinsame Verlagsauslieferung
Göttingen GmbH & Co. KG, www.gva-verlage.de
Switzerland: AVA Verlagsauslieferung AG, www.ava.ch
France, Belgium: Interart Paris, www.interart.fr
United Kingdom: Central Books Ltd, www.centralbooks.com
USA, Canada, Central and South America,
Africa: ARTBOOK / D.A.P., www.artbook.com
South Korea: The Book Society, www.thebooksociety.org
Japan: twelvebooks, https://twelve-books.com
Australia, New Zealand: Perimeter Distribution,
www.perimeterdistribution.com

© 2024, Staatliche Kunstsammlungen Dresden,
Spector Books OHG, Leipzig, authors, artists
1st edition: 2024
Printed in Germany
ISBN 978-3-95905-876-6

funded by

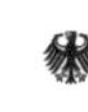

Staatliche
Kunstsammlungen
Dresden

Federal Government Commissioner
for Culture and the Media

Verflochtene Internationalismen
Herausgeber der Reihe: Staatliche Kunstsammlungen
Dresden, Doreen Mende
mit HEAD – Genève der HES-SO

Bis zum Sonnenaufgang, hg. von vinit agarwal
Kameradschaft in den Künsten,
hg. von Lea Marie Nienhoff und Ambre Alfredo
Das versäumte Seminar,
hg. von Doreen Mende und Avery F. Gordon
Tema und seine globalen Widerspiegelungen …,
hg. von Kwasi Ohene-Ayeh

*Kameradschaft in den Künsten. Die Erfahrungen
von Künstler•innen aus Mosambik in der DDR, ihr
künstlerisches Schaffen und ihre politischen Vorstellungen*
Herausgegeben von Lea Marie Nienhoff und Ambre Alfredo
Editorische Koordination: Christin Krause, Jan Wenzel
Produktion: Oliver Baurhenn (Oktober bis Dezember 2024),
Jesi Khadivi (Oktober bis Dezember 2024), Elisabeth
Schmidt (Januar bis September 2024)
Übersetzung: Ambre Alfredo (PT-EN),
Vinicio Altmann (PT-EN), Simon Cowper (DE-EN),
Birthe Mühlhoff (EN-DE)
Lektorat Englisch: Jan Caspers
Lektorat Deutsch: Jan-Frederik Bandel
Koordination der Forschung: Océane Vé-Réveillac
(bis September 2024)
Gestaltung und Konzept: Malin Gewinner und Lyosha Kritsouk
Bildbearbeitung: Aleksey Novikov
Druck und Bindung: Druckhaus Sportflieger, Berlin

Die akademische Forschung für die Fallstudien wurde im
Rahmen des durch den Schweizerischen Nationalfonds
(#184864) finanzierten Projektes *Decolonizing Socialism.
Entangled Internationalism* (2019–2024) an der
HEAD – Genève der HES-SO ermöglicht.

Die Produktion der künstlerischen Forschungsedition
wurde im Rahmen des Projektes „Museen als aktive Orte
der Demokratie" (MODemo) von der Beauftragten
der Bundesregierung für Kultur und Medien gefördert.

Erschienen im Verlag
Spector Books
Harkortstraße 10
04107 Leipzig
www.spectorbooks.com

Vertrieb:
Deutschland, Österreich: GVA, Gemeinsame
Verlagsauslieferung Göttingen GmbH & Co. KG,
www.gva-verlage.de
Schweiz: AVA Verlagsauslieferung AG, www.ava.ch
Frankreich, Belgien: Interart Paris, www.interart.fr
Vereinigtes Königreich: Central Books Ltd,
www.centralbooks.com
USA, Kanada, Mittel- und Südamerika,
Afrika: ARTBOOK / D.A.P., www.artbook.com
Südkorea: The Book Society, www.thebooksociety.org
Japan: twelvebooks, https://twelve-books.com
Australien, Neuseeland: Perimeter Distribution,
www.perimeterdistribution.com

© 2024, Staatliche Kunstsammlungen Dresden,
Spector Books OHG, Leipzig, Autor•innen, Künstler•innen
1. Auflage: 2024
Printed in Germany
ISBN 978-3-95905-876-6

gefördert von

Staatliche
Kunstsammlungen
Dresden

Die Beauftragte der Bundesregierung
für Kultur und Medien

TROUBLED COMRADESHIP IN THE ARTS ed.: Lea Marie Nienhoff, Ambre Alfredo

KAMERADSCHAFT IN DEN KÜNSTEN

ACKNOWLEDGEMENTS

Without the trust, input, and support of numerous people, the realization of the artistic research edition as a series would not have been possible. At the Dresden State Art Collections (Staatliche Kunstsammlungen Dresden, SKD), my very special thanks go to Hilke Wagner and her team at the Albertinum, to Stephanie Buck and her team at the Museum of Prints, Drawings and Photographs (Kupferstich-Kabinett), to Kathi Loch and her team at the Puppet Theatre Collection, to Marius Winzeler and his team at the Green Vault (Grünes Gewölbe) and Dresden Armory (Rüstkammer), to Sylvia Karges and her team at the Coin Collection (Münzkabinett), to Léontine Meijer van Mensch and her team of the State Ethnographic Collections of Saxony (Staatliche Ethnographische Sammlungen Sachsen) in Dresden and Leipzig, to Vera Wobad of the inhouse archive of SKD, to Tanja Schomaker and Christine Gerbich from Outreach und Gesellschaft for managing the project "Museums as Active Places of Democracy" (MODemo), to Nina C. Illgen for fundraising, to Cindy Mehliß for budget management, and to my wonderful core research team, Oliver Baurhenn, Romy Jeschke, Michael Mäder, Anna-Lisa Reith, Thomas Rudert, and Elisabeth Schmidt. Last but not least, my sincerest thanks for their foresight to the SKD's Director General Marion Ackermann and Commercial Director Cornelia Rabeneck with her team, specifically Romy Kraut.

I would also like to thank my colleagues in Switzerland: the directors of HEAD – Genève (HES-SO) Jean-Pierre Greff and Lada Umstätter, as head of the Institut de recherche en art et en design (IRAD) and, above all, Christelle Granite-Noble for budget management at HEAD – Genève (HES-SO). I thank Ute Holl and Kenny Cupers of the University of Basel for their kindness and collaboration and Susanne Grossniklaus from the Swiss National Science Foundation for their unwavering support of the process.

Without the scientific/artistic coordination of the academic project *Decolonizing Socialism: Entangled Internationalism* (2019–2024) by vinit agarwal, Rada Leu, and Océane Vé-Réveillac, the process would not have come to fruition. Thank you very much—your work has been invaluable! I would like to sincerely thank the PhD researcher of the project, the historian and theater pedagogue Lea Marie Nienhoff, for her thoughtful contributions to the overall project.

My sincere thanks go to Jan Wenzel and Christin Krause from Spector Books for developing the concept of the research edition. I would also like to express my deep appreciation for the work put in by Jesi Khadivi, who joined the editorial process in its final phase. Malin Gewinner and Lyosha Kritsouk are responsible for the stunning design concept of the research edition!

Doreen Mende, December 2024

DANK

Ohne das Vertrauen, die Gespräche und die Unterstützung zahlreicher Menschen wäre die Umsetzung der künstlerischen Forschungsedition als Reihe nicht möglich gewesen. Im Kontext der Staatlichen Kunstsammlungen Dresden (SKD) gehen meine ganz besonderen Dankesgrüße an Hilke Wagner und ihr Team im Albertinum, an Stephanie Buck und ihr Team des Kupferstich-Kabinetts, an Kathi Loch und ihr Team der Puppentheatersammlung, an Marius Winzeler und seine Teams des Grünen Gewölbes und der Rüstkammer, an Sylvia Karges und ihr Team des Münzkabinetts an Léontine Meijer van Mensch und ihr Team der Staatlichen Ethnografischen Sammlungen Sachsen, an Vera Wobad vom Hausarchiv der SKD, an Tanja Schomaker und Christine Gerbich von Outreach und Gesellschaft für die Projektleitung „Museen als aktive Orte der Demokratie", an Nina C. Illgen für das Fundraising, an Cindy Mehliß für das Budget-Controlling und an mein wunderbares Kernteam in der Abteilung Forschung: Oliver Baurhenn, Romy Jeschke, Michael Mäder, Anna-Lisa Reith, Thomas Rudert und Elisabeth Schmidt. Nicht zuletzt mein aufrichtigster Dank für ihre Weitsicht an die Generaldirektorin der SKD Marion Ackermann sowie an die Kaufmännische Direktorin Cornelia Rabeneck mit ihrem Team, insbesondere Romy Kraut.

Ebenso möchte ich meinen Kolleg·innen in der Schweiz sehr herzlich danken: Jean-Pierre Greff (bis Dezember 2022) und Lada Umstätter (seit Januar 2023) als Rektor beziehungsweise Rektorin sowie Anthony Masure als Leiter des Institut de recherche en art et en design (IRAD) und vor allem Christelle Granite-Noble für das Budget-Management an der HEAD – Genève der HES-SO; für die Freundschaft und Zusammenarbeit danke ich Ute Holl und Kenny Cupers an der Universität Basel; Susanne Grossniklaus gilt mein Dank für die immer prozessorientierte Betreuung durch den Schweizerischen Nationalfonds.

Ohne die wissenschaftliche/künstlerische Koordination des akademischen Projkts *Decolonizing Socialism. Entangled Internationalism* (2019–2024) von vinit agarwal, Rada Leu und Océane Vé-Réveillac wäre der Prozess nicht umsetzbar gewesen, vielen Dank! Der Doktorandin in diesem Projekt, der Historikerin und Theaterpädagogin Lea Marie Nienhoff, danke ich aufrichtig für ihr mitdenkendes Mitgestalten des Gesamtprojektes.

Für die überaus freundschaftliche Zusammenarbeit gilt mein aufrichtiger Dank Jan Wenzel und Christin Krause von Spector Books. Malin Gewinner und Lyosha Kritsouk zeichnen für das umwerfende Designkonzept der Forschungsedition verantwortlich!

Doreen Mende, Dezember 2024

9 783959 058766